essential guides

WH
SO

INVE   D1347619

3/14   INVE

14 MAR

3 APRIL 17

" Death is always a shock, even when it is expected. Knowing what to do can help – even if just a little. **"**

Anne Wadey

About the author
Anne Wadey is the Head of Bereavement Advice Centre. She originally trained as a nurse and midwife before spending 18 years providing acute bereavement support in large teaching hospitals in the NHS.

which? essential guides

WHAT TO DO WHEN
SOMEONE DIES

ANNE WADEY

With thanks to all the bereaved families who asked me questions and taught me what they needed to know.

Which? Books are commissioned and published by Which? Ltd,
2 Marylebone Road, London NW1 4DF
Email: books@which.co.uk

Distributed by Littlehampton Book Services Ltd,
Faraday Close, Durrington, Worthing, West Sussex BN13 3RB

British Library Cataloguing in Publication Data
A catalogue record for this book is available from the British Library

Based on the 2006 edition by Paul Harris.

The publishers would like to thank Gavin McEwan of Turcan Connell for advice on the law in Scotland, Tony Caher of Campbell and Caher for advice on the law in Northern Ireland and David Bunn of Blake Lapthorn for advice on probate.

Editor: Emma Callery
Designer: Bob Vickers
Indexer: Lynda Swindells
Printed and bound by Charterhouse, Hatfield

Arctic Volume White is an elemental chlorine-free paper produced at Arctic Paper Hafrestroms AB in Åsensbruk, Sweden, using timber from sustainably managed forests. The mill is ISO14001 and EMAS certified, and has FSC certified Chain of Custody.

For a full list of Which? Books, please call 01903 828557, access our website at www.which.co.uk, or write to Littlehampton Book Services. For other enquiries call 0800 252 100.

Contents

Introduction

The death of someone close is the most emotionally demanding situation most of us will face during our lifetime. For those closest to the person who has died there is also a very long list of tasks to be done, some immediately after the event and others that continue up to a year or more afterwards. This book will help you know what to do and the order in which to do them. We cannot diminish the pain of bereavement, but can provide a guide for what needs to be done.

The book is structured in chronological order. It begins with those things that need to be done most urgently and then moves on to the matters that are important but less immediate, and which can still cause concern because of their unfamiliarity.

IMMEDIATE TASKS

Although many of us experience bereavements when young, most of us have reached middle age before having to take responsibility for all the tasks that a death creates. We experience emotional turmoil and still have to get to grips with new terminology, forms and a variety of professional services. The first two chapters help you navigate the first few days, explaining who's who and which documents you need to obtain and for what purpose. The key elements are registering the death using a certificate from a doctor, or dealing with the coroner and then registering the death.

FUNERAL CHOICES

There are many decisions to take when making arrangements for a funeral. Although most people find a funeral director extremely helpful, the chapters about the funeral will help you to know what is available, how to make these choices and how much the funeral may cost. Many people will be guided by their own faith and cultural traditions, but others face an increasing number of options.

The same chapters deal with burial, cremation and memorials. This will help you decide what is most appropriate for the person who has died. Again, faith and culture may determine aspects of these choices for some, but these are significant decisions that cannot be changed once acted upon. For those who have no particular tradition or heritage it is important to take whatever time is necessary to reach a decision that will feel right and not be regretted later.

An overview of the contents of this book

This breakdown of what you need to be aware of assumes the most straightforward of scenarios. When there is a coroner involved, events become slightly more complicated (see pages 23–33).

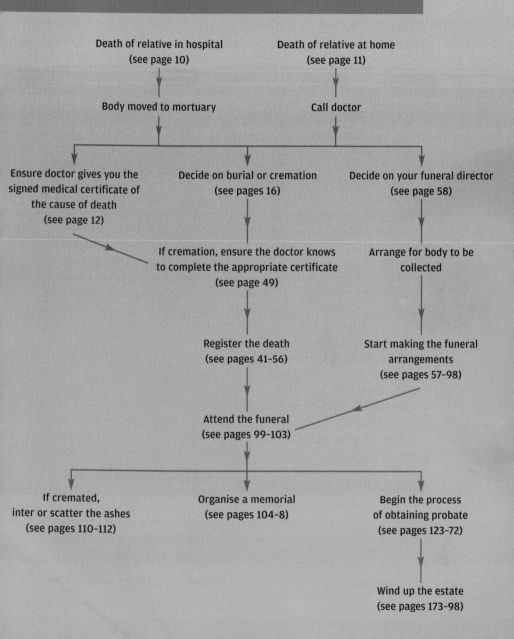

Death of relative in hospital
(see page 10)

Death of relative at home
(see page 11)

Body moved to mortuary

Call doctor

Ensure doctor gives you the signed medical certificate of the cause of death
(see page 12)

Decide on burial or cremation
(see pages 16)

Decide on your funeral director
(see page 58)

If cremation, ensure the doctor knows to complete the appropriate certificate
(see page 49)

Arrange for body to be collected

Register the death
(see pages 41–56)

Start making the funeral arrangements
(see pages 57–98)

Attend the funeral
(see pages 99–103)

If cremated, inter or scatter the ashes
(see pages 110–112)

Organise a memorial
(see pages 104–8)

Begin the process of obtaining probate
(see pages 123–72)

Wind up the estate
(see pages 173–98)

DEALING WITH THE ESTATE

The estate is all the belongings of the person who has died. These may be very few, in which case sorting everything out may take very little time and be straightforward. However, many estates are more complex, involve transfers or sale of property and have to be dealt with according to strict legal processes. This stage may take up to a year, or even longer, depending on the value of the estate, the number of institutions involved and prevailing market conditions if a property has to be sold. An estate is administered by the person(s) named as executor(s) according to the terms of a will, if one has been written, or by the administrator under the rules of intestacy if there is no will. Forms have to be completed for the Probate Registry and Her Majesty's Revenue & Customs. This book helps you decide if you want to do this work yourself or employ professional help, and describes the steps involved.

The last part of this section looks at which Department for Work and Pensions benefits are payable as a result of the death.

THE EXPERIENCE OF GRIEF

Although this book focuses on the practical aspects of coping after a death, there is a short chapter at the end describing how grief is commonly experienced and how to obtain support.

THE WAY THE BOOK IS WRITTEN

As well as the main text, flow charts show key processes, jargon-busting boxes help with interpreting technical terms and go-further boxes indicate where to access more detailed information. This helps to avoid repeating information in more than one section. At the end of the book there is a glossary of important technical terms, a useful contacts section and an index to you help with finding a topic quickly. Finally, a note on language: saying or writing 'the person who has died' when one cannot use his or her own name or relationship to you, is rather cumbersome. Therefore this book follows the custom of many professionals and uses the term 'the deceased'.

> **❝ Many estates are complex and must be dealt with according to strict legal processes. Some can take a year or more to deal with. ❞**

When someone dies

Grieving takes time and energy. The practicalities of certificates can seem like an unwelcome intrusion, but is an important formal acknowledgement of the ending of a life. Similarly, planning a funeral can give us an opportunity to celebrate and remember the life of the person who has died.

The first steps

All of us will, at some time, experience bereavement when a member of the family or a close friend dies. Depending on the circumstances, there are a few actions that need to be taken immediately.

DEATH IN HOSPITAL

During the twentieth century it became increasingly common to die in hospital or a nursing home. Over 50 per cent of people die in a hospital although government and local health care providers are now working to enable more of us to die in the place of our own choosing.

Whenever possible, the family of the dying person is called if they have indicated they want to be present at the end. Sometimes this is not possible because someone has collapsed unexpectedly or has been admitted to an accident and emergency department. The person named to the hospital as the person to be notified will then be called, or if the person who should be contacted is not known, police may be asked to assist.

Occasionally, a doctor may complete the documentation that is needed after the death on the ward, but most hospitals have a department that coordinates the paperwork, returns

Where to go in a hospital

Following the death of a relation or friend, you may have to go to the general office in the hospital. It may also be called the bereavement department or patient affairs. Many offices operate an appointment system to ensure everything is ready for you when you attend.

The deceased's property will usually have been listed and a signature required on collection. Sometimes valuable items, such as money or jewellery, have to be collected from a cashier's office and a letter of authorisation may be needed if collection is made on behalf of the named next of kin.

 A doctor's documentation is called the medical certificate of death and this is described on pages 16-17.

belongings and explains what you need to do next (see box, right). Ward staff will give you this information in person or on the telephone.

If family are present at the death, it will usually be possible to spend some time with the deceased before they have to be moved to the hospital mortuary. Most hospitals have a viewing room (religious symbols are usually optional) where you can make an appointment to see the deceased, but many people choose to wait until the body is at the funeral director's chapel of rest, where there is less pressure on time.

Reporting the death to the coroner

There are certain circumstances (such as death following an accident, during or after surgery, or where the cause is unknown) in which hospital staff must report the death to the coroner. Many coroners require notification of deaths in accident and emergency departments and deaths occurring within 24 hours of admission to hospital, to ensure there are no circumstances contributing to the death that may not be known to the medical staff (see page 13). Such discussions may lead to a short delay in issuing the certificates (see pages 16–17). Also the certificates can only be completed by doctors who were directly involved in the care of the patient, so medical staff shift patterns may lead to a delay of a day or so. This will be explained to you by the bereavement staff.

Bereavement staff

Each hospital has its own system for how communication with the bereaved is organised and how the paperwork is handled. An increasing number of hospitals have a person or department, often called the bereavement office, where staff are knowledgeable about what it means for a death to be referred to a coroner and how a death should be registered. They will also often have information about local support services for the bereaved. Scottish hospitals, with the exception of one or two children's hospitals, do not have bereavement staff and all formalities are dealt with on the ward where the patient dies.

❝In circumstances such as a death following an accident or during or after surgery, staff are obliged to report the death to the coroner.❞

11

DEATH IN A HOME OR CARE ENVIRONMENT

Provided the deceased has been seen and treated by a doctor regularly and the death is expected, it is not essential to call the doctor immediately. However, if the deceased has not been seen by their own doctor within the last 14 days (England, Scotland and Wales) or 28 days (Northern Ireland), a doctor will need to see the body to be able to certify the death (see page 16). This may be at the place of death or at the funeral director's premises. The doctor must be informed of the death and give permission for the funeral director to remove the body, even if it is not necessary to visit the home. Often the doctor will want to see the family to answer outstanding questions and offer condolences. This may be at home or in the surgery.

Very few people choose to keep a body at home until the funeral. If you would like to do this, keep the room cool, using fans if necessary, especially in warmer weather. Cloth-wrapped ice packs next to the body will also help delay deterioration. In hot weather, you may prefer to use a funeral director to carry out preservative treatment and then bring the deceased home before the funeral.

&& The doctor must be informed of the death and give permission for the removal of the body, even if they do not visit the home. 99

Verification and certification of death

In a hospital, care home or ambulance, depending on local policies, someone other than a doctor, who is appropriately qualified and trained, may confirm that someone has died. Even when this is done by a doctor, it is called verification of death. Certification of death is done by the doctor who writes the medical certificate of cause of death.

 Many people turn to a funeral director as a guide through the early days after a death because of their professional expertise in the procedures and decisions required during this period. See pages 60-2 for more on choosing a funeral director and how they can assist.

UNEXPECTED DEATH

If someone collapses unexpectedly or is found collapsed, immediately call the emergency services using 999 or 112. Describe the circumstances to the operator, who will give clear instructions as to what to do next. If it is possible to approach the person without risk, the operator will explain how to check if the person is still alive, or how to try and resuscitate him or her.

If someone is found collapsed, call both the ambulance service and the police. It is often not immediately obvious whether someone has become unwell or died due to natural causes or as a result of an accident or a criminal act. The surrounding area should be disturbed as little as possible, other than what is essential in trying to help the person. If it is clear that the person is dead, do not touch anything.

The ambulance paramedics may declare someone dead immediately or may attempt resuscitation and transfer the person to an accident and emergency department. If that person then dies in hospital without a diagnosis being made, either the emergency doctors or the police who attended the incident refer the death to the coroner (in some hospitals this is delegated to bereavement staff).

Police will be sympathetic to the distress of someone who discovered the body or who is a relative, but they will also need information quickly to be able to establish what has happened. A witness is not obliged to make a statement to the police, but if someone declines, this may give them reason for concern. If there is an inquest at a later date, a witness may be summoned by the coroner (see page 27).

❝If someone is found collapsed, call the ambulance service and the police. Disturb the surrounding area as little as possible.❞

Police evidence

Police will need to take away anything that may be helpful as evidence either for identifying the deceased or discovering what has happened, such as a note or a syringe and needle, and will also take into safe keeping any valuable items if the incident has not been in a home occupied by the family of the deceased. If items taken into safe keeping by the police are not needed for any continuing investigations, they will be placed in the police property store. Proof of identity and entitlement to retrieve the items will be needed to collect them and some police property stores have limited opening hours, so it is wise to enquire by telephone before attending in person.

13

IDENTIFICATION OF A BODY

If there is any possibility of the need for an inquest, a deceased person has to be formally identified. If someone has been present at the time of or shortly after death, this will normally be sufficient and the coroner's officer or a police officer acting for the coroner will ask for an identification statement. If a close relative has not seen the body, they will normally be asked to do so. This will usually be in a viewing suite at the mortuary, which will be at a local hospital or it may be a public mortuary managed by the local authority. In some mortuaries you are in the same room as the body, whereas in others the body is behind a window. It will be explained if the body has been damaged in any way and there will be someone present to give support. Occasionally, such as after a serious accident or house fire, identification has to be by other means such as fingerprints (if the deceased has ever been arrested) or dental records.

“Organ transplants save lives but less than a third of us are on the Organ Donor Register. ”

ORGAN AND TISSUE DONATION FOR TRANSPLANTATION

The coordination of organ and tissue transplantation in this country is organised by NHS Blood and Transplant (see box, below). Organ transplants save lives and in the year up to 31 March 2009, 3,513 organ transplants were performed from 1,854 donors, but at the same time 7,877 people were listed as being in need of a transplant. Despite the fact that the leadership of all major faith groups in this country support organ donation in principle, less than a third of the population has joined the Organ Donor Register (see also box, below). The majority of transplants are from patients who are ventilated in intensive care after an accident or brain haemorrhage, and it is much easier for the relatives to agree to a transplant if they know it is what the patient would have wanted.

Medical or nursing staff can find out whether someone had registered on the Organ Donor Register or someone may know that their family member had a donor card even if they were not carrying it at the time they became unwell or had an accident.

Organs usually have to be removed while the patient is still receiving

To find out more about organ donation, go to the NHS website www.organdonation.nhs.uk/ukt/default.jsp. You can also sign up to the Organ Donor Register by calling 0300 123 23 23 (the line is open 24 hours) or go to www.uktransplant.org.uk. There are downloadable leaflets in minority languages and explaining the specific stance of the major faiths.

artificial ventilation to get oxygen into their blood and drugs to make sure their heart keeps beating. Very careful tests are done twice by senior doctors to ensure that someone has died before donation can take place. Organs cannot usually be stored, so arrangements are put in place to transport them very quickly to wherever the patients are who need to receive them.

Tissues may be removed up to 48 hours after someone's heartbeat and breathing has stopped. This means many more people can donate tissues than organs. Most tissues can be stored until they are needed in specialist centres.

- Corneal transplants save the sight of thousands of people each year.
- Bones, tendons and cartilage can help reconstruction after an injury or prevent amputation in treatment for bone cancer.
- Skin grafts are used to treat burns victims.
- Heart valves can help children born with heart defects.

The list of possibilities grows each year, so if your relative is dying and you think they would want to donate please speak to medical or nursing staff to find out if this will be possible.

If organ donation is planned but the death has to be referred to the coroner, the coroner must be contacted to give permission for the procedure to go ahead. This will be organised by the medical staff or the hospital's transplant coordinator. A coroner will usually agree unless the organ may be essential for helping determine the cause of death at the later postmortem examination.

Whole body donation

People who wish to donate their whole body to medical research and the training of medical students and surgeons must give witnessed signed consent for this during their lifetime. Further information is available from the anatomy office at the local medical school and a complete list is available on the website of the Human Tissue Authority - www.hta.gov.uk - or by calling them on 020 7211 3400. Contact the medical school as soon as possible after the person died as it is not always possible to accept a donation, depending on the circumstances and cause of death. A medical certificate of cause of death must be issued before a body donation can be considered. The medical school will need to carry out preservative treatment within five days of the death, so registration of the death (see pages 42-56) and the issue of the 'green form' must take place within this period.

MEDICAL CERTIFICATE OF CAUSE OF DEATH

When the cause of a death is known and is from natural causes, such as heart disease, a doctor who was caring for the deceased during the final illness should issue a medical certificate of cause of death. This gives the name of the deceased, the age, place of death and what is believed to be the cause of death. The cause of death is divided into the main cause, which may be a sequence of conditions, and other conditions that have contributed to the death.

The doctor also has to state when they last saw the patient and whether the deceased has been seen after death. The doctor has to sign and give qualifications. It is helpful if the doctor prints their name to make it easier for the registrar to read.

In a hospital it is usually administrative staff who give the family the certificate, and they may allow the family to see it before placing it in the envelope that gives further information about registering. For deaths out of hospital, the general practitioner (GP) may give the certificate personally or it may be collected from a receptionist.

Do not be embarrassed to ask for an explanation of the certificate as they are usually written in formal medical terminology, which may seem different from what you have been told. You need the certificate to register the death (unless the coroner is involved – see pages 23–33) and the information about why people have died is used to create national statistics in order to help central and local government plan services.

If a person dies very soon after admission to hospital and the hospital refers the death to the coroner, the coroner's officer will often ask the GP if it is possible to issue a medical certificate. If the GP does not know the reason for the death, the coroner will order a postmortem examination (see pages 19–21).

❝ Don't be embarrassed to ask for the certificate to be explained to you. They are written in medical terminology that may seem different from what you were told. ❞

Burial or cremation

The choice of burial or cremation is discussed in more detail on pages 63-72, but if it is known which will be chosen, it is important to inform the doctor completing the medical certificate or the coroner's officer. Additional forms are needed for a cremation to take place, and it is much easier for the professional staff if they are aware of this requirement at an early stage (see page 49).

Improving death certification

The Coroners and Justice Act 2009 has introduced a new role of medical examiner. In future, all medical certificates will be scrutinised by a specially trained senior doctor to ensure that the cause of death given is consistent with the medical history of the deceased. Medical examiners will be assisted by medical examiners' officers, who will also ensure that the cause of death is understood by the family. When the medical examiner is satisfied, the medical certificate will be released to the family to enable the death to be registered.

This is a major change of procedure and more new laws need to be passed before it can be fully implemented. A number of pilot projects have been initiated to work out how best to implement the changes: there will be different issues and concerns in rural areas and inner cities, for example. The changes will be fully implemented during 2012. Meanwhile, the detail of how the medical certificate will be issued may vary slightly from what is written here. The professionals involved will steer the family through the necessary processes. Scotland is also reviewing its death certification system, but new laws are not yet planned.

WHAT HAPPENS TO THE BODY?

If someone dies in hospital, the body is transferred to the mortuary until a funeral director has been authorised to remove it. If the death was expected, in a hospice or care home, the staff will usually ask the family to arrange for a funeral director to remove the body. Some may have an arrangement with a local funeral director to store bodies if there is to be a delay before collection by the funeral director acting for the family; for example, if the family are abroad at the time of death.

In hospital, nursing staff ensure the body is clean and dress it in the patient's own nightwear, if requested, or a shroud. It helps the nursing staff if they are told of particular requirements related to the faith of the deceased, such as the way the hands are positioned or if a rosary is to be kept with the body.

❝ It helps if the nursing staff are told of requirements relating to the faith of the deceased, such as the way the hands are positioned. ❞

For more information about the new medical certificate go to the Department of Health website at www.dh.gov.uk/deathcertification, where there is a section detailing changes in death certification and progress.

Hospital mortuaries

Hospital mortuaries keep bodies extremely cold, but do not freeze them unless it is known that storage needs to be for an extended period of several weeks. They do not usually carry out any preservative treatment and this should be discussed with the funeral director (see pages 60-1).

If the death is subject to investigation by the coroner, the funeral director acting for the coroner will remove the body; usually to the nearest hospital mortuary where postmortems are carried out for the coroner (some major cities have a public mortuary). If a death has to be investigated by a coroner, it is usual for any intravenous lines or other tubes from resuscitation or treatment to be left in place to assist with finding the cause of death. Although this can be upsetting, they will be removed during the postmortem and the appearance restored.

❝If a coroner is to investigate a death, tubes are left in place to assist their inquiry. These will be removed and the appearance restored.❞

Postmortem examinations

A postmortem examination is a careful visual examination of the exterior of the body followed by a detailed internal examination of all the major organs of the body in the chest and abdomen, together with the brain.

These examinations are carried out by pathologists who are fully qualified doctors with additional specialist training. Pathologists are assisted by anatomical pathology technologists (the correct term for mortuary technicians with specialist training). There are two types of postmortem: a coroner's postmortem and a hospital or medical interest postmortem.

❝ In a postmortem, the nature of the injuries often gives essential information about the sequence of events. ❞

A coroner's postmortem

A coroner can order a postmortem examination for any death that has been referred to them. The purpose is to establish the cause of death where this is not known, or to give additional information to confirm the cause of death. For example, after a death in a road traffic collision, the nature of the injuries often gives essential information about the sequence of events. The consent of the family is not required, but they will be informed of the postmortem, if at all possible, and they can have a medical representative present, although very few families choose to do this.

Tissue samples can only be retained if they are needed to help establish the cause of death – in which case they

---

Objecting to a postmortem examination

If a family has a strong objection to a postmortem for reasons of faith, they may make this known. Research shows that in some cases, non-invasive scans may be an alternative, but this is not always appropriate or available.

must be retained for as long as the coroner needs them. Often the pathologist is able to give the cause of death to the coroner immediately after the examination, although it may be longer before the full written report is available.

Sometimes further tests are also required: histology (examining tissue samples under a microscope) to determine the exact nature of an illness if it is not immediately obvious during the initial examination or to confirm the pathologist's initial findings, and toxicology (examining tissue and body fluid samples for abnormal levels of, for example, paracetamol) after a suspected overdose.

66 Sometimes microbiologists are called in to help identify a suspected infection. These tests can take up to several weeks. **99**

A HOSPITAL OR MEDICAL INTEREST POSTMORTEM

This is a postmortem carried out with the full written consent of the next of kin. Medical staff may ask for permission to carry out a postmortem if the cause of death is known but there are aspects of the disease that are not fully understood or perhaps the patient did not respond to treatment in the way that had been expected. Some conditions are quite rare and it is important to take every opportunity to learn more about them in the hope that improved treatment can be offered in the future. These examinations also give the opportunity for teaching students and doctors.

The actual process of the examination is the same as for a coroner's postmortem and the possible retention of either organs and tissue is discussed during the conversations requesting consent. The Human Tissue Act 2004 laid down a strict hierarchy of who can give consent, starting with a person who has been nominated by the deceased to have this authority – called a nominated representative. If there is no nominated representative, consent may be given by a surviving spouse or partner. This does not have to be a formal civil partnership but someone of the same or opposite gender who had lived with the deceased in an enduring family relationship. If there is no partner, a parent or child can give consent and so on until, if there is no other person available, a friend of long standing can give consent.

Hospital postmortems can be either:

- **Full.** This involves a detailed examination of all the internal organs, including the brain, heart, lungs, liver, kidneys, intestines, blood vessels and small glands. These are removed from the body, examined in detail and then returned to the body; or

- **Limited.** For those who are uncomfortable about agreeing to a full postmortem, a limited postmortem may be carried out. This involves examination only of those organs directly connected with the patient's last illness and the pathologist will examine only the organs about which agreement has been reached, such as the use in the chest cavity if it is known that the heart and lungs are the main area of interest. Some families find this more acceptable, but it may limit the usefulness of the examination, and mean that no information will be available about possible abnormalities present in other organs that may have contributed to the patient's death.

RETENTION AND DISPOSAL OF TISSUE AFTER A POSTMORTEM

Most pathologists believe that the microscopic examination of very small samples of tissue after the main visual examination of the body is an integral part of the postmortem examination. This is the only way to see inside cells and these samples can confirm what

has already been seen, or give new information about disease in a particular body and help determine the cause of death. Usually, only very small samples are needed, but occasionally it may be necessary to retain a whole organ for a period of time.

To be able to examine tissue samples, they must first be treated with a preservative (formaldehyde) and then encased in paraffin wax to make them hard. These can be cut more finely than a human hair and placed on glass microscope slides. Using different chemicals, pathologists can examine different parts of each structure.

Families may choose to have material reunited with the body. If a whole organ is required for a short period, it is common to delay the funeral so the organ can be replaced in the body before it is collected by the funeral

Sample donation

After both coroners' and hospital postmortems, families can choose to donate any samples permanently to form part of the medical record of the patient. These samples can then be re-examined in the future (especially if more than one family member is affected by a condition) in the light of new discoveries, be used in the education of medical professionals and in checking the quality of work of an individual pathologist or pathology department.

director. More careful thought needs to be given to the return of blocks (small squares of chemically treated tissue) and slides as not all crematoria will allow the cremation of glass slides. It should also be noted that since it became mandatory to give families a choice about what happens to retained material, any return and disposal after the funeral will have to take place at the family's expense.

If a family discovers that tissue has been retained following a postmortem prior to around 2001, hospitals will have procedures in place for return and reuniting. Address any enquiries to the bereavement service or the head of pathology services.

Reuniting of retained tissue after a postmortem examination

If a family have been made aware that tissue has been retained during a postmortem examination, and expresses a wish to have the samples reunited with the body, there is a choice of whether to delay the funeral or reunite at a later date. If you choose the second option, this will be at your expense and some hospitals only release samples to a funeral director. Others will return directly to the family. Because samples will have been chemically treated with formaldehyde, and microscopic tissue mounted on to glass slides, there may be restrictions on how the tissue can be disposed. Some crematoria will not allow cremation of glass, and natural burial grounds will not accept glass or chemically treated tissue.

❝ Tissue that was retained during a postmortem can be reunited with the body if the family chooses, but there may be restrictions on how it is disposed. ❞

 For more information about postmortems, go to the Department of Health website at www.dh.gov.uk.

The coroner

The role of the coroner is to investigate deaths from unknown and unnatural causes and deaths in custody. The full title of a coroner is Her Majesty's Coroner for *the area for which they have responsibility.* Coroners are usually solicitors, although a few are doctors.

The law governing the work of coroners is the responsibility of the Ministry of Justice but coroners themselves are appointed and funded by local government. This may sound confusing, but in practice they are fully independent judicial officers responsible to the Crown in the person of the Lord Chancellor. The Coroners and Justice Act 2009 has, for the first time, created the possibility of a national system with a chief coroner. This means that, in the future, families will have rights of appeal if they do not agree with the decision of a local coroner. The Act will not be fully implemented until 2012 as secondary legislation and regulations need to be written, so it is not yet possible to describe the new procedures.

In most areas, the council also employs the coroners' officers, but in few they are employed by the police force. Traditionally, coroners' officers were seconded police officers, but increasingly they are civilians from a variety of professional backgrounds in the police, health services and elsewhere. They carry out the day-to-day investigations required by the coroner to reach a decision as to whether an inquest will be necessary.

❝ The 2009 Act creates the possibility of a national system of coroners plus rights of appeal against coroners' decisions. ❞

Explanation of death in law

Not every country requires the cause of death of all its residents to be known, but in the countries of the United Kingdom every individual is so valued in law that an explanation for their death is required. Not only is an explanation of the death important to most families, but it is essential for society as a whole that measures are taken to prevent avoidable deaths in the future.

Procedure following a death

Use this chart to establish the order of events when a coroner becomes involved in the proceedings.

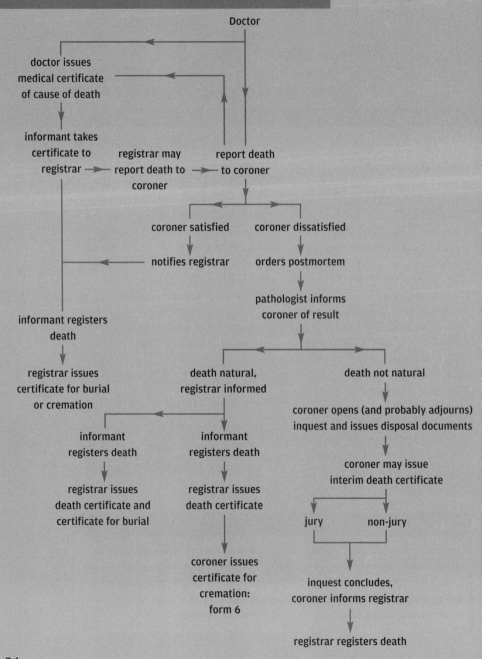

Doctor

doctor issues
medical certificate
of cause of death

informant takes
certificate to
registrar

registrar may
report death to
coroner

report death
to coroner

coroner satisfied

coroner dissatisfied

notifies registrar

orders postmortem

informant registers
death

pathologist informs
coroner of result

registrar issues
certificate for burial
or cremation

death natural,
registrar informed

death not natural

informant
registers death

informant
registers death

coroner opens (and probably adjourns)
inquest and issues disposal documents

registrar issues
death certificate and
certificate for burial

registrar issues
death certificate

coroner may issue
interim death certificate

jury

non-jury

coroner issues
certificate for
cremation:
form 6

inquest concludes,
coroner informs registrar

registrar registers death

DEATHS REPORTED TO THE CORONER

Most deaths are reported to the coroner by doctors or police officers, but anyone who is concerned that a death may not be natural has the right to inform the coroner. The **registrar of deaths** is obliged to notify the coroner of a death if they are dissatisfied with a medical certificate of cause of death given to them, or if the family mentions other circumstances that cause concern.

Deaths that have to be reported to the coroner are those that are unexplained (even if thought to be of natural causes) and all deaths that might not be natural due to an accident, suicide or homicide. They also investigate deaths that may be caused by medical error, and deaths in police custody or prison. Deaths that may be caused by an industrial disease and as a consequence of military service are also investigated by the coroner. In 2008, 46.7 per cent of all deaths in England and Wales were notified to the coroner.

HOW THE CORONER INVESTIGATES DEATHS

Not all deaths reported to the coroner result in a full investigation. For example, a person may have been admitted to hospital with a major medical emergency; if immediate surgery is attempted, but the patient does not survive, the coroner may allow a doctor to issue a medical certificate, provided:

- The family is entirely satisfied that everything possible was done.
- It was a natural disease process that caused the emergency.
- There were no procedural problems with the treatment.

The coroner might also permit a doctor to issue a certificate for someone who has been terminally ill at home and attended daily by a nurse, even if the doctor has not visited within the previous two weeks. The doctor can

Jargon buster

Registrar of deaths The person employed by a local authority (council) to register deaths. This is a statutory role and anyone who knowingly gives false information to a registrar can be charged with perjury

The system for investigating deaths in Scotland varies from that in England and Wales and is described on page 31.

mark the medical certificate to show the registrar of deaths that a discussion with the coroner's office has taken place, and the coroner will issue an additional certificate (called 100A) to the registrar confirming that he is aware of the death, but does not require further investigation.

If the death does have to be investigated, the first steps will be to gather background information, such as the deceased's medical history and the circumstances of the death, as well as speaking with the immediate family if at all possible.

Less than half the deaths notified to the coroner lead to a postmortem examination (see pages 19–20). The background information is given to the pathologist who will carry out the postmortem examination, who will report his findings back to the coroner. Provided the pathologist confirms that the death is the result of natural causes, the coroner will then issue a document to the registrar (called 100B), which allows the death to be registered (unless the death was in custody). This replaces the medical certificate of cause of death.

If a cremation is planned, the coroner will also issue an authorisation for the cremation (burial order or cremation form 6 – see page 82), which is usually collected by the funeral director. The family will be informed of the cause of death and told that they may now make an appointment to register. In the majority of cases, the involvement of the coroner does not delay the funeral, although it is unwise to book a definite date until advised that you can do so by the coroner's staff.

❝ Less than half the deaths notified to the coroners result in a postmortem examination. ❞

Religious considerations

The legal requirement for a postmortem overrides any objections to a postmortem based on religious grounds. However, if the coroner is aware that an urgent funeral is required for this reason, they will usually try to make the arrangements for the postmortem as quickly as possible to minimise any delay.

INQUESTS

If the cause of death is not natural, or the person was in custody at the time of death, the coroner is obliged by law to hold an inquest. An inquest is a formal court of law, but differs from all other courts in that there are no parties in opposition to each other. An inquest is an inquiry to establish who has died and how that person died, together with the additional information, such as occupation, that is needed to register the death. Although inquests are formal to respect the seriousness of the subject, and all evidence is given on oath, there is much less ceremony than in other courts. Coroners do not wear robes and in most inquests no lawyers are required to represent witnesses or other parties.

Opening an inquest

Most coroners open an inquest as soon as possible after the postmortem examination. The family may choose to attend but the proceedings are usually brief and it may not be necessary. The purpose at this time is to ensure that the deceased has been properly identified and that the body can be released without causing any difficulty for ongoing investigations. Therefore, if specimens have been kept for histology and toxicology (see box, page 21) the pathologist can inform the coroner that the body itself is not needed. The coroner can then allow the funeral to take place and will issue the appropriate documents. Sometimes a coroner will set the date for the main inquest, but often this is left open until the coroner has been advised by his or her staff that all the evidence needed has been obtained.

In court

Having seen and evaluated all the evidence and statements, a coroner will decide who should be asked to give evidence at the inquest. Although the coroner has the power to issue a formal summons to potential witnesses, this will normally be done by informal telephone calls. However, a **subpoena** can be issued and a failure to attend the inquest is contempt of court and the person can be fined or imprisoned as a consequence.

❝An inquest is a formal court of law and must be held if the cause of death is not natural or the deceased was in custody.**❞**

Witnesses

If you are called as a witness, you will need to bring evidence to be able to claim your travel expenses from the coroner's officer and you can discuss with the officer or the court administrator whether you are entitled to submit a claim for loss of earnings.

Jargon buster

Crown Prosecution Service (CPS) The CPS is responsible for prosecuting criminal cases investigated by the police in England and Wales

Grant of Probate The document issued by the Probate Registry to the executors of a will to authorise them to administer the estate

Subpoena Issued by a court to require a witness to attend or face punishment

An inquest is open to the public and journalists may be present (see box, right). The coroner calls the witnesses from the court – they do not have to wait outside. Once the coroner has asked any questions, other interested persons are invited to put any questions to the witness, if they wish to do so. The coroner decides who is an interested person in a particular case, but unless the death is at all contentious (such as if a mistake has been made during an operation), the main people with an interest are family members.

Although a coroner will try to put the family at ease, an inquest can be quite a daunting experience. If the family informs the coroner of any concerns beforehand, these areas are usually in the coroner's questions. One or more members of the family may be asked to give evidence concerning the identity and the lifestyle of the deceased and the circumstances of the death, if family are present. The coroner and coroner's staff understand how difficult this may be for the family, whether the inquest is quite soon after the death or some months have passed. The coroner may give the family the opportunity to leave the court while the pathologist gives a report if it is deemed that the details of the postmortem might be distressing.

It is essential to remember that an inquest can only establish the facts of the death. In law an inquest cannot blame any individual for the death. A coroner will not permit any questions that seem to be trying to attribute blame.

Deaths that are suspicious are dealt with in a different way by the coronial system. See page 34 for a description of how this works.

Expenses

There should be no expense to the family arising out of an inquest. Representation by a lawyer is not necessary in the majority of inquests, and in cases where there is no controversy, the family should not need to incur such expense.

A jury

A few inquests, such as those following an industrial accident or a death in custody, have to be held in front of a jury. As in other courts, a jury is summoned from individuals on the electoral register who are eligible for jury service, and there may be between 7 and 11 people who can return a majority verdict.

After all the evidence has been heard, the coroner will sum up. If there is a jury, the coroner will explain the law to them and suggest what conclusions are available. The conclusion is the legal term for what is commonly called the verdict at the end of the inquest. Otherwise the coroner will deliver the verdict.

There are simple phrase verdicts, such as accidental death, unlawful killing, suicide and natural causes. Only 13 per cent of the deaths referred to the coroner in 2008 required an inquest and, of these, 26 per cent returned a verdict of natural causes. Many coroners use what is called a narrative verdict, using a sentence to describe what happened, such as: 'Mr X died as a result of head injuries sustained from colliding with a tree after he suffered a non-fatal heart attack while driving.' If there is insufficient evidence to show how someone died, such as if the body was discovered too long after the death for a postmortem examination to be helpful, there will be an open verdict.

At the close of the inquest, the coroner sends a copy of the conclusion to the registrar of deaths and the death is formally registered. The family can then purchase certified copies (see page 48), but do not need to attend in person unless they so choose to do so.

The conclusion

The conclusion cannot indicate any suggestion of criminal or civil liability for a death. However, a coroner can decide to forward papers from an inquest to the **Crown Prosecution Service**. A coroner's investigation may also be ongoing at the same time as an investigation by the Health and Safety Executive, which has the power to bring prosecutions.

❝Inquests following industrial accidents or a death in custody must be held in front of a jury. ❞

INTERIM CERTIFICATE

As the death cannot be registered until the conclusion of the inquest, the family may feel anxious about not being able to deal with the estate of the deceased. To avoid this, the coroner will issue a coroner's interim certificate. This enables a personal representative (see page 128) to begin the administration of the estate. Most of the work of administration can usually be done using the interim certificate, including obtaining a **Grant of Probate**. However, if an insurance policy will be invalidated by the deceased having committed suicide, payment may be withheld until the close of the inquest and no estate can be distributed to any beneficiaries before the completion of the inquest.

" If the deceased has committed suicide their insurance policy may be invalidated and payment withheld until the close of the inquest. "

The press and inquests

Inevitably some deaths are widely reported either because the deceased or their family is well known or the circumstances of the death are unusual. Since inquests are held in public, journalists can and often do attend. There are restrictions on the publication of the names of minors (those people under the age of 18 years), but in other matters there are no reporting restrictions. The purpose of an inquest is to discover the facts of a death and in some cases these may be distressing or even embarrassing for a family and close friends. However, the public reporting of reality can also help end inaccurate speculation and rumour mongering. If a bereaved family feels harassed in any way by a journalist, they can contact a 24-hour helpline operated by the Press Complaints Commission and Ofcom (which deals with TV and radio) on 07659 152656. A message is forwarded to the relevant editors although a journalist cannot be forced to withdraw.

Cancellation of pension and benefits

It is also possible to attend the register office with the coroner's interim certificate to obtain the free notification or registration of death certificate (also called a BDS). This notifies the Department for Work and Pensions to cancel state pensions and benefits of the deceased. This is particularly important as you are then able to claim death-related benefits and avoid over-payments that would need to be refunded (see page 49).

IMPROVING THE CORONIAL SYSTEM

The Coroners and Justice Act 2009 has introduced a number of changes to the coronial system, for the first time bringing them into a national network under a chief coroner. It will take time for all of the proposed changes to be implemented, as new regulations need to be created. There will be:

- **A new charter** for bereaved families who come into contact with the coroner's system.
- **A system whereby families can make an appeal** against decisions made by a coroner.
- **A limit to the length of time** a funeral can be delayed.

However, it is unlikely that most of the changes will be implemented before 2012.

❝ Changes to the coronial system will include a charter for bereaved families and a limit to the length of time a funeral can be delayed. **❞**

THE CORONIAL SYSTEM IN SCOTLAND

There are no coroners in Scotland. The equivalent role of investigating deaths in Scotland is carried out by a procurator fiscal, a full-time law officer, who comes under the authority of the Lord Advocate.

The procurator fiscal has many functions, including responsibility for investigating all sudden, unexpected and violent deaths and also any deaths that occurred under suspicious circumstances. If satisfied with the doctor's medical certificate and any evidence received from the police, the procurator fiscal need take no further action. If the cause of death appears to be natural, a medical practitioner may be approached with a view to issuing a death certificate.

Postmortem

If a medical practitioner is unable to give the cause of death, the procurator fiscal may ask a pathologist to carry out an external examination of the body. Provided this examination and information received from the police confirm that there are no suspicious circumstances, the pathologist is permitted to issue a certificate enabling the family to register the death.

The coronial system in Northern Ireland

Northern Ireland also has a coroner's service based in Belfast, which serves the whole province. The system is very similar to that in England and Wales.

Most postmortem examinations are carried out by one pathologist, but if there is any possibility of suspicious or untoward circumstances, such as medical neglect or a death in custody, two pathologists with forensic accreditation are required.

Due to the geographical distances in some parts of Scotland, this may lead to a delay, although the procurator's office will do everything possible to minimise this.

The most important distinction in Scotland from the systems in England, Wales and Northern Ireland is that the procurator fiscal does not issue an interim death certificate. Instead, a death certificate is issued after the postmortem examination, thereby allowing the death to be registered by the pathologist.

Public inquiry

The specific name for a public inquiry into the circumstances of a death is a fatal accident inquiry. Only if it is mandatory, such as a death in custody or due to an industrial accident, will a fatal accident inquiry definitely be held. In other cases, the procurator fiscal may consider it in the public interest to hold a fatal accident inquiry, and this will be discussed with the family, who must consent.

If there is any question of a 'systemic failure' contributing to a death, such as in a hospital or care home, an

❝ If the circumstances of the death are suspicious, two pathologists must carry out the post-mortem examination. ❞

Crown Office cases

Cases that are reported to the Crown Office because they may result in a public inquiry are essentially those involving a matter of the public interest – for instance, to prevent a recurrence of similar circumstances. Deaths that are directly or indirectly connected with the action of a third party, such as road traffic deaths, may be reported to the Crown Office for consideration either of criminal proceedings or of a public inquiry.

 The information that is given on these pages only concerns subjects that are treated differently in Scotland to England and Wales. For all other information, please read the main sections in the book.

independent medical report is commissioned by the procurator fiscal. This can mean there is a considerable delay of months or even a year or more before the fatal accident inquiry takes place.

In Scotland, the family of the deceased may be entitled to apply for legal aid to be represented at the fatal accident inquiry.

A public inquiry is heard before the sheriff in the local sheriff court. The procurator fiscal and representatives of any other interested parties examine the witnesses, but it is the sheriff who determines the circumstances of the death.

The procurator fiscal has to report certain cases to the Crown Office (see box left) and it is the Lord Advocate who makes the final decision about whether to apply to a sheriff for an inquiry to be held. In all other cases, investigations made into sudden deaths are carried out by the procurator fiscal confidentially. Before reporting a case to the Crown Office, the procurator fiscal may interview witnesses and take statements from them. The technical term for this is precognition.

❝ The differences between Scottish and English law mean a far smaller proportion of deaths are examined in a fatal accident enquiry in Scotland. ❞

Special case deaths

This section explains the first steps that need to be taken when a death has occurred in more unusual circumstances, such as when someone is abroad either working or on holiday. In addition, this section tells you what happens in the early stages if a baby is stillborn or dies very early in their lives.

DEATHS THAT ARE SUSPICIOUS

If a death is thought to be suspicious, the police will carry out an investigation. The postmortem will be carried out by a forensic pathologist, who is qualified to interpret evidence of unnatural death and is accredited by the Home Office for this work. Unfortunately, in these cases there may be a delay before the funeral can be held. If someone is charged with causing the death, they can request that a second and independent postmortem is performed. It is still the coroner's decision as to when the body can be released, but the coroner will want to be certain that the process of law and obtaining justice will be not be prejudiced by doing this too soon. Contact with the family will usually be the responsibility of a police family liaison officer, so there may be less direct contact with the coroner or the coroner's officers.

If someone has been charged with causing the death, the coroner will usually forward documents to the registrar so that the death can be registered without further delay and there will be no inquest at a later date to avoid two courts examining the same evidence.

> **❝ Once someone has been charged with causing the death, it can be registered without further delay. ❞**

To find a local solicitor in England and Wales, go to www.lawsociety.org.uk; in Northern Ireland, go to www.lawsoc-ni-org; in Scotland go to www.lawscot.org.uk. The Law Society is especially helpful if you are searching for specialist practitioners.

DEATHS WHERE THERE MAY BE A CIVIL LIABILITY

There are circumstances in which a family may wish to pursue a complaint or a claim for compensation against an individual or organisation, even if no one will be charged. This may be after an accident, or if the family believe that medical care was inadequate or negligent. Most people instruct a solicitor for this purpose, and in these circumstances it can be helpful if the family is also represented by the solicitor at the inquest.

The charity **INQUEST** provides information and support to people facing the inquest system after a death in custody: go to www.inquest.org.uk. The organisation produces a useful pack entitled *Inquests – An Information Pack for Families, Friends and Advisors.* Deaths in custody are also investigated by the Prisons and Probation Ombudsman. Go to www.ppo.gov.uk.

Not all solicitors are experienced in this type of work, so a firm with specialist practitioners should be used (see, below left). There is no legal aid available for this type of work, but it may be possible to arrange a free or low-charge initial interview with a solicitor to assess whether this will be a worthwhile course of action, or what sort of costs may be involved.

DEATHS ABROAD

Deaths abroad have to be investigated and registered according to the laws of the country where the death occurred. If the person was working overseas, their employer may offer assistance to the family and deal with formalities on their behalf. There will usually be tour company representatives to assist if someone was on a package holiday. The nearest British consulate will be able to offer advice but may be at a considerable physical distance and cannot offer any financial assistance.

❝ If death resulted from inadequate medical care, a complaint or claim for compensation may subsequently follow. ❞

To find an embassy, go to the 'Find an Embassy' page on the Foreign & Commonwealth Office (FCO) website: www.fco.gov.uk/en/travel-and-living-abroad/find-an-embassy/.

Note that normal holiday insurance does not usually cover dangerous sports such as paragliding or scuba diving; additional cover must be taken out to cover such activities.

The Foreign & Commonwealth Office will appoint a caseworker to give information and advice to the family.

Anyone travelling overseas should have comprehensive insurance that covers the cost of repatriation after death, as well as medical expenses and evacuation in the case of illness. Insurance companies often have contracts with specialist funeral directors with repatriation departments.

Repatriation arrangements

If the individual was not insured, or the insurance company does not recommend a company, it is best to contact a UK funeral director who will obtain specialist advice. It is not normally possible for private individuals to make repatriation arrangements because of their complexity. Specialist repatriation firms have staff who speak a variety of languages and who are aware of the unique requirements of each country, including clearing customs on arrival in the UK.

The funeral director will work with the local authorities to arrange any documentation needed for the release of the body. They will organise the embalming required (see page 74) and place the body in a metal-lined coffin, which is a requirement of air transport. The coffin is then covered in a protective layer of card or fabric and will be conveyed in the hold of the aircraft. For requirements after arrival in the UK, see page 52 for registration.

Special arrangements may be made if the death has been in a major incident involving many casualties, and teams from both funeral directors and support agencies may fly out from the UK to support bereaved families who wish to visit the scene or who need to identify a body.

The military authorities take responsibility for the repatriation of all servicemen and women who die while on active service and liaise closely with their families.

"Overseas travellers should have insurance for repatriation on death."

 For more information about international repatriation and specific coffin requirements see pages 84–5.

Repatriation of ashes

If requested to do so, the crematorium will issue documentation confirming that the ashes are the cremated remains of the deceased. As with repatriation of bodies, the regulations vary from country to country and some countries do not differentiate between bodies and ashes. Many countries insist on a funeral director to funeral director transfer, with or without a consular seal on the casket. Advice can be obtained by the funeral director, or the consulate of the country concerned can be contacted for advice.

 It may be possible for an individual to carry the ashes as part of hand luggage as a private passenger but this cannot be assumed. The person carrying the ashes must be prepared for customs or security personnel to want to inspect the contents of the container if a consular seal has not been attached.

Death at sea and on an aircraft

Deaths on UK-registered aircrafts have to be dealt with under UK law, but may also be subject to the law of the country where the body is removed from the aircraft or ship. Deaths at sea are generally registered through the Maritime and Coastguard Agency (MCA). Deaths on aircrafts are notified to the Civil Aviation Authority (CAA), who will forward the information to a local register office for certificates to be issued.

When a death occurs on a foreign ship, it counts as a death abroad; the death must be recorded in the ship's log, and the port superintendent where the ship's crew are discharged must make enquiries into the cause of death. However, if the ship docks at a British port, the Martime and Coastguard Agency have a form (RBD3), which requests the captain to complete as a 'return of death'.

When death occurs on a British-registered ship, the death is recorded in the captain's log, and all facts and particulars relating to the death must be recorded and delivered to the Registry of Shipping and Seamen (part of the Maritime and Coastguard Agency) on arrival at any port within or outside the UK. The master of any ship

 The website for the Maritime and Coastguard Agency is www.mcga.gov.uk and that for the Civil Aviation Authority is www.caa.co.uk

has the authority to decide whether, for health reasons, a body should be immediately disposed of at sea, or kept for disposal later. As in most of these cases the death is unexpected, the body is usually kept in order to assist with a coroner's enquiry. Most cruise ships have mortuary facilities for cold storage of those who have died on board.

When a body is brought into a British port on a UK-registered vessel, the captain completes an RBD1 for the Maritime and Coastguard Agency, which then ensures that the necessary liaison takes place with the coroner, police, shipping company and anyone else who has to be involved, such as a funeral director. If the coroner decides to order an enquiry, in which case the body cannot be moved without his consent. The registrar of the district in which the funeral is to take place must also issue a certificate of no liability to register, for which either a copy of the entry in the captain's log or certified extract may be obtained from the shipping company that owns the ship concerned, or the port superintendent where the body was brought ashore. Copies of the certified extract may be obtained from the Registry of Shipping and Seamen. This will normally all be dealt with by the funeral director.

If the ship docks overseas, advice should be sought from the Foreign & Commonwealth Office or a local British consulate and a funeral director with detailed knowledge of repatriation issues.

CHILDREN

Every death is unique in its impact on those affected, however many people find the death of a young person particularly difficult. Sadly, almost one in every 200 babies born is stillborn (2007 figures). Together with those babies who die very early in their lives, about one in every 100 families expecting to celebrate finds themselves grieving instead.

As far as the involvement of the coroner and registration are concerned, the deaths of children over 28 days old are treated the same as adults. However, recent tragic cases of the deaths of children, which might have been prevented, have brought about increased scrutiny of the deaths of children, especially if they are unexpected. This can be extremely difficult for families who may be interviewed by the police and feel that they are under suspicion if, for example, a child has suffered an accident. Families should be treated with sensitivity, discretion and respect, and be kept informed of the progress of any investigations.

Neonatal deaths

A neonatal death is one that occurs between birth and up to and including 28 days of life. The only procedural difference from other deaths is that there is space on the medical certificate for any medical conditions suffered by the mother that may have contributed to the death of the baby.

Miscarriages and stillbirths

A miscarriage is any baby (fetus) who is delivered dead before the 24th week of pregnancy. There is no formal documentation required, but many hospitals and some register offices will issue a commemorative certificate to help acknowledge the value of this brief life to the family.

If the mother was in hospital at the time, the hospital may offer to arrange for the disposal of the remains. But if the parents would like their child to be buried or cremated in the usual way, it is possible to arrange this with a local cemetery or crematorium, provided the hospital completes a certificate authorising this.

A stillbirth is a baby who is born dead after the 24th week of pregnancy. There is a specific medicial certificate called a stillbirth certificate, which may be issued by a doctor or a midwife and it is the only time the cause of the death may be given as unknown. A stillbirth can only be referred to a coroner if it is uncertain whether the baby was alive when born but died very shortly afterwards.

Professionals who care for expectant families understand that whatever the legal definition – fetus, stillbirth or baby – for the bereaved family the child that

Finding the graves of babies who died in the past

The need of parents to grieve following the death of a baby during pregnancy or at birth has only been fully recognised in the last 30 years or so. Many women whose babies died before that time were not told what had happened to the bodies. It has been possible to find where some babies have been buried, but this depends on how long ago the death happened and whether records have been kept, especially if it was a hospital that has since closed. Anyone wanting to start a search should contact the bereavement office or chaplain at the hospital or the manager of the nearest cemetery to where the birth occurred. Even if a grave cannot be traced, it is possible to ask a hospital chaplain or other minister or celebrant to create a memorial ceremony if this would be helpful.

Information on registering a stillbirth is given on pages 56-7. For further information on stillbirths and support, contact the Stillbirth and Neonatal Death Society (SANDS) at www.uk-sands.org. The Foundation for the Study of Infant Deaths (FSID) (website: www.fsid.org.uk) publishes a booklet *When a Baby Dies Suddenly and Unexpectedly*, which contains lots of helpful advice.

has died is a unique individual to be mourned. Many hospitals offer parents a burial or cremation (which will depend on local circumstances), frequently free of charge. Often these services are at regular intervals, conducted by a hospital chaplain in a manner that makes them acceptable to both those with a religious belief and those who have no adherence to any faith. Family members have the choice to be present or not and some find it of comfort to realise they are not alone in their experience and distress.

Parents may choose to make arrangements themselves with a funeral director of their choice, in which case they will be responsible for any charges that may be incurred. Bereaved parents considering a cremation funeral for their baby need to be aware that there will very seldom be any cremated remains available for later scattering or interment. Babies who are stillborn or who die very soon after death must be registered before a funeral can take place, which is explained in the following chapter.

❝ Hospitals may offer a burial or cremation service for stillborn or miscarried babies, or parents can make their own arrangements. ❞

Registering a death

After the doctor has given you the medical certificate of cause of death you need to register the death of the deceased. This chapter looks at who has to carry out this legal requirement and how to do so. You may start planning a funeral before registering but you will not be able to confirm the arrangements until the death has been registered (unless the coroner is involved and you have the authority of the coroner to proceed).

2

Registering the death

Registration is the formal legal recording of the fact that a person has died. All deaths must be registered by law and not to do so is an offence. The documents issued allow the family to arrange a funeral and administer the estate. The information below applies to England and Wales. The process is similar in Scotland and Northern Ireland but the specific variations are on pages 54-6.

WHERE TO REGISTER

Once you have been given the medical certificate of cause of death, or the coroner has confirmed that the authorisation for registration has been supplied to the registrar, you must register the death. This is usually done at the register office where births, marriages and deaths are all registered, often in the same suite of offices. Some hospitals now have registrars working within them to reduce the travelling and waiting time for the family. The hospital will advise if this service is available. Often the envelope in which the medical certificate is placed will give the contact details for the appropriate register office (but see also the box, below).

The majority of register offices have appointment systems so it is best to make a telephone call before attending. This will also allow you to check that the office contacted is the appropriate one for the place of death. It used to be that all deaths had to be registered in the registration district where the death occurred. However, some areas have adopted a countywide system so that any of the offices in that area can be attended if this is more convenient for you.

Finding your local registrar

The council website or a local telephone directory will have a contact number for the registration service if it is not given with the medical certificate. Many offices are only open on a part-time basis so in the larger registration districts it may be necessary to travel if there is a need to register urgently.

❝Call a register office before attending to check on the appointment system and if you are attending the correct register office.❞

WHO CAN REGISTER A DEATH?

There are only certain people who are qualified by law to inform the registrar of the details of the death which has occurred.

If the death has occurred in a home or building of any kind, such as a hospital or care home, a number of people are permitted to register the death. The Government's wording of who can do this has recently been considerably simplified to:

- A relative.
- Someone present at the death.
- An occupant of the home.
- An official from the hospital (or care home).
- The person making the funeral arrangements.

There may be circumstances in which someone lower down the list may register instead of someone higher up, such as a flatmate registering instead of a sole elderly frail relative living overseas. In general, however, it is best that a close relative registers if possible.

If the person has been found dead elsewhere, the following are qualified to register the death:

- Any relative of the deceased able to provide the registrar with the required details.
- Any person present at the time of death.
- The person who found the body.

- The person in charge of the body.
- The person accepting responsibility for arranging the funeral.

The person who registers the death is known as the **informant**. The responsibility cannot be delegated to a person who is not qualified to act as informant: should such a person attend the register office, the registrar will refuse to register the death and will require a qualified informant to attend.

In cases where a coroner's inquest has been held (see pages 27–9), the coroner will act as the informant and provide the registrar with all the necessary details. In this case, there is no need for the family and relatives to register the death, but they will need to attend the register office if copies of the death certificate are needed, or arrange for them to be sent by post.

Although the person acting as the informant does not have to swear an oath, notices are displayed stating that

Jargon buster

Attesting registrar An interim register office, which passes all relevant information to the receiving registrar
Informant The person who registers a death
Receiving registrar The register office where the death must be registered. It must be in the sub-district in which the death took place or where the body was found

What if there is no one available to register a death?

If someone dies and there are no relatives known or they cannot be traced, or even if they are traced but decline to be involved, responsibility for registering the death and making arrangements will depend on where the person died. In England and Wales, the NHS hospital has to take responsibility if the deceased was in hospital at the time of their death. Otherwise responsibility passes to the local authority, which also deals with all such cases in Scotland. A funeral will be arranged which is simple and dignified and appropriate to the faith of the deceased, if this is known.

if incorrect information is knowingly given to the registrar, a prosecution for perjury could follow and the informant has to sign the register as a true record.

WHEN TO REGISTER A DEATH

In England and Wales, deaths should normally be registered within five days and within the appropriate district. If getting to the appropriate district is impossible, a death can be declared at a different register office. In this case, the registrar who sees the informant is termed the **attesting registrar** and the one who carries out the registration is called the **receiving registrar**.

This process depends on the transfer of documents by post, so there is the possibility that it may be subject to significant delays.

It is therefore unwise to book a funeral until the full exchange of documents has taken place and the certificates has been collected from the attesting registrar.

> **❝** It is best not to book the funeral until you know that the death has been properly registered. This can occasionally take some time to sort out. **❞**

Out-of-hours service

Many register offices offer an out-of-hours service at weekends and bank holidays for those communities for whom a burial as soon as possible after death is a tenet of their faith. A full registration service is not always available, but a limited service to issue a certificate for burial is often in place. The medical certificate of cause of death must have been issued to allow this to take place.

WHAT TO TAKE WITH YOU

Although the only document required to register the death is the medical certificate or coroner's form (see table, below), it is often helpful to have the birth and marriage certificates of the deceased, and the death certificate for the spouse or civil partner if the deceased was already widowed.

In the early stages of bereavement, many people find that they cannot recall even basic information such as their own phone number, so the former occupation of a pre-deceased father-in-law can easily be forgotten. Some people find it helpful to write down all the information that will be needed:

- Full name.
- Maiden name and any other previous surnames (other surnames are not absolutely essential but this will be helpful if, for example, an old insurance policy is discovered that was taken out during an earlier marriage).

Documents for registration

Document	Source	Function	Recipient
notice to informant	doctor	gives details of who must register death and what particulars will be required	via relative to registrar
medical certificate of cause of death	doctor	states cause of death	to registrar (direct or via relative)
If coroner involved: coroner's notification	coroner	confirms or gives details of cause of death	to registrar (direct or via relative)
or coroner's certificate after inquest	coroner	gives all the particulars required for death to be registered	direct to registrar

 The medical certificate of the cause of death is the most essential item to obtain before going to the registrar - if you don't yet have it, see pages 13-15.

- Date and place of birth of the deceased (town and county in the UK or, if overseas, this is the country of birth as it exists today, such as Bangladesh rather than East Pakistan or India).
- Date and place of death.
- The occupation or former occupation of the deceased.
- The last usual address of the deceased.
- The date of birth, name and occupation of a surviving spouse or civil partner (name and occupation only if spouse or civil partner has already died).
- Whether the deceased received a state pension or other pension or benefits from public funds, such as a local authority retirement pension or Department of Work and Pension benefits and their National Insurance number, if known.
- If the person who died was a child, the details of the parents will be required.

The registrar will also take the deceased's NHS Medical Card if available. However, if you don't have it, registering should not be delayed as the card is not absolutely essential.

❝ It is worth writing down information such as the date and place of death, occupation, date of birth and last address of the deceased so that you have them to hand. ❞

The process of registering

The actual process of registering is quite informal, involving a face-to-face interview with the registrar. Most offices only have space for two or three people to be present during the interview.

The medical certificate is handed over, often at reception, to allow it to be checked by the registrar before the interview. If the registrar detects a problem, then he or she is duty bound to inform the coroner, who will carry out checks before allowing the registrar to proceed.

The registrar invites the informant into her office and the information given is usually entered on a web-based computer system. A draft entry is printed and the informant should check this very carefully. It is possible to make changes (called corrections) to a death certificate, but the process is not straightforward, sometimes requiring the authorisation of the Registrar General. Also a reissued certificate will still have the original information with the correction noted in small print near the bottom of the page.

Provided the informant believes the draft entry to be correct, he will be invited to sign the entry. This must be done with the pen provided by the registrar, which is filled with an ink that has been specifically manufactured for this purpose.

Some of the information requested by the registrar, such as the NHS number, is used to notify other government departments or for statistical purposes, but does not appear on the actual death certificate.

❝ The death is usually registered on a web-based computer system, and the informant should check the entry very carefully. ❞

The registration process varies slightly depending on the circumstances. If you are registering a stillborn or very young baby, see page 50; for registering a death that occurs overseas, see pages 52–4. For Northern Ireland, see page 54, and for Scotland see page 55.

THE DOCUMENTS ISSUED BY THE REGISTRAR

Depending on the circumstances of the death, you will be handed several different documents.

The death certificate

The terminology of death certificates can seem confusing. The actual death certificate is the entry in the death register, which is retained by the registrar. What the registrar will issue are certified copies of the entry. These are individually signed by the registrar but not by the informant whose name is printed on the form.

This document is the one required by banks and other institutions to confirm the death so it is wise to have a number of copies. Although registration is free, the certified copies have to be purchased. The usual fee at August 2009 in £3.50 per copy, but local authorities can vary this. If someone asks for 'an original certificate' this is the document referred to. The number of copies required will depend on the complexity of the estate, but one per major asset holder is reasonable. These certificates should not be photocopied as they are quite distinctive and a photocopy will not be accepted as proof of the death. It is also a breach of crown copyright. An organisation such as a bank can take a copy for its own use as evidence of having seen the original and then return the original to you. At the time of going to print, a review of fees is underway, and they may rise significantly in 2010.

Each individual certificate has a unique reference number in the top right-hand corner. This is in addition to the unique number given to each entry in the register of deaths. Make a note of this number, which the registrar will give you, the date of registration and the registration district. This will be invaluable for the purchase of additional certificates at a later date if needed. The simplest way to do this is on the internet from the website of the General Register Office (see below). Alternatively, contact the register office where the death was registered. The cost of additional certificates will depend on whether the current volume of the register is still open and this varies, depending on how busy the office is.

❝ Buy a number of copies of the original certificate to help in dealing with banks and other institutions. ❞

 The website for the General Register Office for obtaining additional certificates is www.gro.gov.uk/gro/content/certificates.

A certificate of notification or registration of death

This certificate, which is also called BD8, is free and has a form to be completed on the reverse to notify the Department for Work and Pensions (DWP) of the death from where information is forwarded to Her Majesty's Revenue & Customs (HMRC). This form should be completed as soon as possible or there may be a substantial accidental over-payment of benefits, which would have to be reimbursed, and also the time frame for claiming for bereavement benefits (see pages 190–1) may expire.

Jargon buster

Certificate for cremation 6
Certificate issued by a coroner if a postmortem has been ordered

Certificate of no liability to register
A registrar's certificate, issued under certain circumstances such as a death overseas, confirming that a death does not need to be registered

Form BD8 A free form supplied by the registrar for notifying the Department of Work & Pensions of the death

Green certificate The official certificate provided by the registrar authorising a burial or cremation to take place

Order for burial Certificate issued by a coroner if a postmortem has been ordered

A certificate for burial or cremation

This is commonly known as the green form, but is also rather insensitively sometimes called the disposal form. It is also free and most funeral directors will not collect a body from a hospital or confirm funeral arrangements until they have received it. If there has been a coroner's postmortem and there is to be a cremation, the green form is replaced by an authorisation from the coroner, which is usually collected by the funeral director on behalf of the family.

The green form has two sections and it is important not to separate these. The funeral director needs the green form for the cemetery (including churchyards) or crematorium to be able to confirm a booking. Once cremation or burial has taken place, the cemetery or crematorium office returns part of the form to the registrar. If the form is not returned within a certain period of time, officially 14 days, the registrar may contact the informant to find out why the funeral has been delayed.

❝ Complete the BD8 certificate as soon as possible to avoid over-payment of benefits, which will then have to be paid back. ❞

REGISTRATION OF A STILLBORN OR VERY YOUNG BABY

If a baby has been born alive but dies soon afterwards, it is possible that the death has occurred before the parents have been able to register the birth. As registrars register both births and deaths it is usually possible to register both at the same appointment. This should be explained when making the appointment as the registrar will book a longer appointment time. No documents are needed to register a birth as the information is automatically notified from the midwife to the registrar. Many large maternity units have a registrar on site to make registration easier.

The midwife will explain what information is needed to register a birth and how this is affected by whether or not the parents are formally married. Seek advice from the midwife and registrar if the mother is very unwell and unable to participate in the registration.

The documents provided by the registrar following the death of a baby are the same as for any other death registration.

Registration of a stillborn baby should take place within 42 days of the event. However, many families find that it feels more difficult the longer it is delayed. The medical certificate of stillbirth can be issued by either a doctor or midwife. If the parents are married, either parent can carry out the stillbirth registration and supply the information required which is:

- The name of the child if a name is to be given.
- The names, dates of birth and occupations of both parents.
- The usual address.
- The date of the parents' marriage.

The registrar will also record the numbers of any previous children, including any stillborn babies, for statistical purposes, although this will not appear on the certificate.

If the parents are not married, it is easiest if they register together, otherwise statutory declarations are required (a document signed in front of a commissioner for oaths, usually a local solicitor, for which there will be a fee) from the absent parent to confirm the paternity of the father. Without this, only the mother's details will appear on the certificate.

After registration of a stillbirth, the registrar will issue a certified copy of the certificate of stillbirth for which there will be a charge, and the certificate for burial or cremation, which is free. For a stillborn baby this form is white rather than green.

"Many families find registering a stillborn baby more difficult the longer it is delayed."

IMPROVING DEATH REGISTRATION

The Coroners and Justice Act 2009 has introduced the beginning of legislation to change the procedures for registration of deaths in England and Wales. Other secondary legislation and regulations need to be passed before the changes can be fully implemented, but some areas are already running pilot projects so that the finer details of how to make the changes work in practice can be determined.

• **Medical certificates of death will be issued** as now, but before being released to families, they will be checked by a medical examiner, who is an experienced doctor with specific training for this role. The medical examiner will have to be assured that the cause of death is consistent with the medical history, be satisfied that the family are aware of the cause of death and satisfied that this is accurate and that there is no reason to refer the death to the coroner. The medical examiner will then authorise the medical certificate to be issued and the registration can proceed. All deaths will be scrutinised regardless of whether there is to be a burial or cremation and separate cremation medical forms (see pages 80–1) will eventually be abolished.

• **When a death has been referred to the coroner** and there is a postmortem examination that gives results not requiring an inquest, the cause of death will be forwarded to the medical examiner, who will authorise the death to be registered and burial or cremation to proceed. Only those cases needing inquests will need documentation for burial or cremation from the coroner.

Although the new system may delay registration slightly, studies so far indicate it will not delay the funeral. It should reduce the number of inappropriate referrals to the coroner and increase the accuracy of causes of deaths given on medical certificates. Together with changes to the coronial system, these changes will bring about some of the improvements identified as necessary in the Shipman Enquiry reports and other recent reviews commissioned by government.

Full implementation will not be until 2012, so be guided by the professionals who give the medical certificate as to exactly what procedures are in place where the death occurred. The changes will be implemented gradually, and there may be transitional arrangements in place, with both systems running in parallel for a time.

More information is available about changes to death certificates at the Department of Health: www.dh.gov.uk

REGISTERING A DEATH THAT OCCURS OVERSEAS

If someone dies overseas, all the usual processes of that country with regard to investigation of a death and its registration must be observed. The extent to which deaths are investigated varies greatly across the world and in some countries the majority faith may mean postmortem examination is regarded with abhorrence and is not available. Many countries do not record the cause of death on a death certificate, even in Europe.

In some English speaking countries – Australia, Canada, New Zealand, Republic of Ireland, South Africa, UK Overseas Territories – the death certificate issued is valid for all purposes in the UK and no additional procedure is required. In other countries, registration with the British authorities can take place at the consulate in the country of death if this is convenient, or it can be done after returning to the UK. Doing this means that eventually British-style death certificates will be available from the General Register Office. However, the process can take some months and the certificates are expensive. Not many people will want, or be able, to wait this long before beginning the practical processes that need to be done after a

Families have a choice when they have registered a death in a foreign country. They may also register with the British authorities to obtain a British-style death certificate.

death, and you may choose to get formal translations of the foreign death certificate into English.

If repatriation of the body or cremated remains is planned, a funeral director must be used, preferably one with expertise in international matters. They will be able to source a professional translation service at a reasonable cost. Also take the advice of the funeral director for the number of certificates required, as they will be needed to arrange transport of the body and also to help get a flight home for family members at the same time if this is required.

Contact with the registrar and the coroner may be needed if the body is to be brought back to the UK for the funeral. If the death overseas was from circumstances that would lead to investigations by a coroner, the death

To get in touch with the Foreign and Commonwealth Office, go to www.fco.gov.uk and key in 'death abroad? into the Quick Search box. There is lots of advice and links to other helpful agencies.

Death certificates in a foreign language

These processes are not an either/or situation. You may decide to use a translated death certificate initially but also register with the UK authorities.

must be notified and the coroner will decide if a postmortem examination is needed. After the coroner has completed initial investigations, he will issue a burial order or form 6 for cremation. If appropriate, the coroner will then hold an inquest in the usual way, although gathering evidence is usually more difficult as the coroner cannot summon witnesses from overseas. Procurators do not have a legal interest in deaths overseas (although this is due to change in 2012 when the death is of military personnel).

Unfortunately, postmortem practice in non-UK countries does not always include the return of major organs to the body. This fact, together with any embalming that has been carried out, may limit the information that can be obtained from the postmortem examination.

If the cause of death is known and a burial is planned, the registrar of deaths must be notified and they will issue a no liability to register form allowing the burial to take place. However, if a cremation is wanted, it is the coroner who has to issue a form 6 for cremation and the registrar is not involved.

There is no documentation required from the registrar or coroner if cremated remains are brought back to the UK.

" No documentation is required if cremated remains are brought back to the UK. "

Fees payable

A consular fee is payable for the registration of the death in the UK, and a further fee is payable for each certificate issued at the time of registration; these fees vary periodically, and applicants should ask the FCO what fees are needed to accompany their application. This is a lengthy process, and considerable delay should be expected. Current fees are shown on the FCO website: www.fco.gov.uk.

REGISTRATION OF DEATH ON BOARD AN AIRCRAFT

When death occurs in an aircraft, the death must be registered in the country to which that aircraft belongs. At the next landing following the death, the captain must notify the local police authorities and the appropriate registration authority, which may not be in the same country as the one where the aircraft has landed. Subsequent action concerning arrangements for the body varies according to local regulations, but as far as relatives are concerned, the procedure is the same as that for a death that occurs abroad. These arrangements can be extremely complicated, and will normally be dealt with by the funeral director in conjunction with a specialist repatriation service.

❝ If the death occurs in an aircraft it must be registered in the country to which the aircraft belongs, and notified in the country where the plane lands next. ❞

REGISTERING IN NORTHERN IRELAND

Registering a death in Northern Ireland is very similar to England and Wales, except there is a 28-day period for a doctor to have seen the deceased prior to death.

Registration should take place within five days, either in the district where the death occurred or where the deceased lived. The forms issued are as follows:

- A certified copy of the death certificate, which cost £6 each (at August 2009).
- Form GRO 21, which is the authority for burial or cremation.
- Form 36 to deal with Social Security benefits.

Additional certificates may be ordered by post, phone or online and will be supplied within seven to ten working days. There is an express service, which costs £29. If attending at the GRO in person before 3pm, certificates can then be obtained within an hour. Express applications made by phone or online before 2.30pm will be processed and certificates sent out to be received on the next working day.

 Useful websites for obtaining death certificates at a later date are: www.gro.gov.uk (the General Register Office), www.groni.gov.uk (Registrar General, Northern Ireland) and www.gro-scotland.gov.uk (General Register Office, Scotland). If a death occurs on an overseas registered aircraft, contact the Civil Aviation Authority on www.caa.co.uk.

REGISTERING IN SCOTLAND

In Scotland, the law requires that every death must be registered within eight days from the date of death. The person qualified to act as informant for registering a death is:

- Any relative of the deceased.
- Any person present at the death.
- The deceased's executor or other legal representative.
- The occupier of the premises where the death took place.
- Any person having knowledge of the particulars to be registered.

The death may be registered in any Scottish registration office and a visitor to Scotland must be registered at a Scottish registration office.

As in England and Wales, the procedure for registering a death is a simple question-and-answer interview between registrar and informant. The registrar will request the production of a medical certificate of cause of death or, failing that, the name and address of a doctor who can be asked to give the certificate. The information required by a Scottish registrar to register a death is much the same as in England and Wales (see page 45–6), except that he also needs to know:

- The time of death.
- If the deceased had ever been married and, if so, the name, surname and occupation of each spouse and date of birth of the surviving spouse.

- The name and occupation of the deceased's father.
- The name, occupation and maiden name of the mother.
- If the parents are alive or dead.

If one or two of these additional items of information are not known, then registration of the death can usually proceed without the information, but it is always better to produce this information for the registrar, where possible, in order not to delay the process.

❝ Scottish law says that every death must be registered within eight days. ❞

The documents issued by the registrar

These are similar to those issued in England and Wales, but with minor differences.

- **Full extract of the death entry,** for which a fee must be paid of £9 for each copy (at August 2009). This is the equivalent of a certified copy in England and Wales. It is usually needed to deal with the estate of the deceased.
- **Registration or notification of death certificate (form 334/SI).** This is used for notifying the Department for Work and Pensions of the death and is free.

- Certificate of registration of death (form 14). There is no direct equivalent in Scotland of a green certificate. After registration, the registrar issues to the informant the certificate of registration of death, which should be given to the funeral director to give to the keeper of the burial ground or to the crematorium authorities. There is no charge for this certificate.

An additional free form is available, which is an abbreviated extract of the death entry. This cannot normally be used for any legal or financial purposes.

Registering a stillbirth

A stillbirth in Scotland must be registered within 21 days and can be registered in any registration district in Scotland. As in England, if no doctor or midwife can issue a certificate of stillbirth, an informant must make a declaration on a special form. In Scotland this is form 7, obtainable from the registrar. All such cases, and any case where there is doubt as to whether the child was alive or not, are reported to the procurator fiscal, who notifies the **Registrar General** of the results of their investigations.

If the body is to be cremated, an additional certificate of stillbirth must be given by the doctor who was in attendance at the delivery (or who conducted the postmortem). The stillbirth must be registered before cremation can take place.

The informant must produce for the registrar a doctor's or midwife's certificate, or the completed form 7, and is required to give the same information as in England and, in addition, the time of the stillbirth and, where applicable, the place of the parents' marriage.

❝ A stillbirth in Scotland must be registered within 21 days. This can be done in any registration district in Scotland. ❞

Arranging a funeral

Arranging a funeral will usually be the family's main focus in the period immediately after the death. This chapter covers the practical aspects of making arrangements, and the following chapter with the content of the ceremony itself.

First decisions

The first decision to make with regard to the funeral is whether or not to use a funeral director. The alternative is to make your own arrangements.

Provided the deceased is not to be moved out of the UK country where he or she has died, it is quite possible to organise a funeral yourself. If you are considering this course of action, read through these next two chapters to understand what is involved and to work out if you have the time and energy to cope.

The next step is to discover if the deceased has left any specific instructions about the funeral. These may be in a will, in an advance funeral wishes form or other written format, or have been told to a close family member or friend.

Choosing not to have a ceremony

There is no law requiring any ceremony, and a very few people will choose to have the body buried or cremated with no ceremony and no mourners present.

PRE-PAID FUNERAL PLANS/POLICIES

It is possible that the deceased had purchased a pre-paid funeral plan/policy. There are a number of these available, which differ in how they work, but the deceased will have a policy folder, which gives instructions for what should be done after death.

Some policies are centrally registered and, on notifying the company, the family will be told whether they need to contact a specific local funeral director, or whether there is a choice of who is to be used. Other policies will have been arranged through a particular funeral director. This is important to check because if arrangements are started through a different funeral director, there will be a charge for any work already done and probably no refund from the funeral director nominated in the policy.

Usually the plan will include the cost of the burial or cremation, as well as

 When a spouse or close relative dies you may become eligible for certain state benefits. See pages 189–92 for an outline of what state benefits are available and how to claim for them.

5

...s is
...s are
kin,
. It is
legally
...ow
may
...e

...ed, and
...y to
implement everyth...... been
requested; or the deceased may not
have left space within a ceremony for
a eulogy or tribute to be given, and the
family may feel this is essential.

❝ Most people will want
to follow the deceased's
wishes, but this might not
be possible and it is the
only part of the will that
is not legally binding. **❞**

Using a funeral director

The overwhelming majority of bereaved families choose to use a funeral director to make the practical arrangements on their behalf.

There is no statutory regulation of funeral directors, so to ensure you receive a professional service, choose one who belongs to one of the two trade associations, which have codes of practice to which members have to adhere. These are the National Association of Funeral Directors (NAFD) and the National Society of Allied and Independent Funeral Directors (SAIF). Both have logos that members usually display in the windows of their premises and on their stationery – you can see these on their websites (see below).

A good funeral director will comply with the Office of Fair Trading consumer code, which includes making it clear who controls the business (there are still more independent funeral directors than branches of major businesses), having price lists clearly displayed and available for people to take away, and providing clear written estimates before potential clients decide to go ahead with the arrangements. Most funeral directors provide a simple funeral if asked (a requirement of membership of the NAFD). In 2009, the cost of this was usually between £1,000 and £1,800 for the funeral director's fees. The costs associated with the burial or cremation must be added to this.

It can be very difficult to think of a funeral as a business transaction, but the funeral director's services are being purchased to help with a highly significant event. The

 Both NAFD and SAIF have complaints procedures. In the unusual event that you do experience a problem that cannot be resolved by discussing it with the funeral director, there is someone independent to turn to.

 The website for the National Association of Funeral Directors is www.nafd.org.uk, and that for the Independent Funeral Directors is www.saif.org.uk. The Office of Fair Trading website is www.oft.gov.uk.

recommendation of trusted family or friends is very helpful but it is not unreasonable to approach more than one company before deciding who will be entrusted with the care of the person who has died.

WHAT A FUNERAL DIRECTOR DOES

The funeral director can make all the practical arrangements, such as looking after the deceased up to and on the day of the funeral, and also any later requirements such as placing a head stone. Some families are content to allow the funeral director to take care of everything, but many others want a much greater involvement. This can include precise planning of the content of a ceremony, helping with the dressing of the deceased and wanting family and friends to act as bearers at the funeral. If there is no specific format dictated by the religious tradition of the deceased and the family, there are many decisions to make in arranging a funeral. It is important, therefore to take all the time required to feel you are doing the right thing.

The key elements of the funeral director's role are:

- Taking care of the body of the deceased (including being available 24 hours a day for removing the deceased from a home if requested).
- Ensuring all the necessary documentation is completed to legally allow the burial or cremation to go ahead.

- Making sure everything happens at the right time, in the right place, with the right people present, on the day of the funeral itself.

Who's who at the funeral directors

There are a number of roles within the service provided by the funeral director, and in a small company everyone may multitask.

- The funeral conductor is the person with overall responsibility on the day of the funeral and will be a senior member of staff. Ask to meet this person before the funeral itself.
- Many funeral directors also have funeral arrangers who meet the people who come into the premises, explain the choices available to families and then deal with the behind-the-scenes paperwork and telephone calls.
- On the day of the funeral you will meet the drivers and bearers – they will be a discreet background presence.
- There are also staff such as an embalmer (they have their own professional qualifications and association) and employees for premises and vehicle maintenance.

❝ There are many decisions to take and it is important to take your time and feel you are doing the right thing. ❞

61

Funeral directing is very labour intensive and also requires quite large and specialised premises. As well as the reception area there needs to be space for private interviewing of clients, at least one chapel of rest for a family to spend time with the deceased, cold storage for the deceased, an area for preservative treatment, garaging for the vehicles and storage/workshops for coffins as well as general office space, changing rooms and toilet facilities.

The premises need to be aesthetically acceptable for the bereaved and there are also health and safety requirements specific to this type of business. Much of the funeral director's work is done behind the scenes, but this quick overview will help with understanding why the funeral director's fees will not be as inflated as many people seem to assume.

“ Funeral directing is very labour intensive and requires large and specialised premises. Fees are not as inflated as some people assume. ”

Burial

Whether or not to bury (also known as interment) the deceased may be determined by faith and cultural tradition, but cost may also be a factor as cremation is usually less expensive.

Where there is space in a churchyard, parishioners (those people living in the parish), will usually have the right of burial there, but most churchyards in towns and cities are full and it is mainly in rural areas that spaces are available. Churchyards that are closed for burials may still have space for the interment of ashes, especially if other family members are buried there.

> **" Most churchyards in towns and cities are full, so they are closed for burials. However, they may have space for the interment of ashes. "**

CEMETERIES

Cemeteries may be run by local authorities or by private companies. Each has its own character in terms of the surroundings, but they are usually peaceful places, even when surrounded by city buildings. Local wildlife is increasingly encouraged to find sanctuary in cemeteries. Likewise, access for disabled visitors is taken into account, and there are sometimes dedicated areas for the burial of children and babies. Some have areas dedicated to the use of particular faith groups or traditionally used by people of certain ethnic backgrounds.

Another factor to consider is whether the cemetery has a chapel for ceremonies, or whether the entire committal has to be at the graveside.

Most cemeteries will welcome direct enquiries and visits from the public although it is always wise to make an appointment to ensure staff are available to help and are not away

 For a full description of burial ceremonies, both in a church and crematorium, see pages 100–3.

If a family is settled in a particular location, a grave can provide a place to specifically remember the deceased. However, if regular moves are required because of work commitments, it may be difficult to move away from the area where a loved one is buried.

TYPES OF GRAVE

Each cemetery has its own regulations about what is available in terms of graves, and also the style of memorial that is permitted. Unfortunately, increasing pressure on space has led to upward pressure on costs, but there are a number of other factors that influence the price. Grave plots near to main access points, for example, are likely to be more expensive.

Many cemeteries permit the purchase of exclusive rights of burial in a plot, in which case the grave is purchased, but with a lease limited to a certain number of years (often 50). If the grave has space for more than one coffin, the person who purchases the deeds to the plot has the right to determine who else is buried there.

from the office supervising a funeral. Your funeral director will also be aware of all the choices available, such as a council-run cemetery or natural burial ground, and will be able to advise on costs and other issues, such as whether a grave surround – a specific demarcation of the plot rather than grass that is continuous with the surrounding lawn – is allowed.

&& Each cemetery has its own regulations about what is available and the style of memorial. ??

 Check the cemetery's rules on flowers. Some cemeteries do not allow flowers to be planted on graves; many forbid artificial flowers or other decorations, such as balloons or toys.

 There are some rules and stipulations for memorials in cemeteries and graveyards – see pages 104–8 for an explanation of what these might be.

Jargon buster

Common grave When the burial authority has the right to bury another person in the same plot

Deed of grant Confirms the existence of a private grave (see exclusive right of burial) and names who can make this decision

Exclusive right of burial When a plot is leased for x number of years

Lawn grave When a grave consists of a headstone with mown grass around it

Mausoleum A large, brick-built construction

Some cemeteries allow burial in a plot without the exclusive right of burial, although this can sometimes be purchased at a later date. Some cemeteries also provide common graves. This is the least expensive option, but such a grave will have several burials in it of unrelated individuals.

Most cemeteries will charge considerably more for a burial of someone who lives outside the boundaries of the area that is served by the cemetery – sometimes as much as three times the price for a local resident.

This can be difficult if someone wants to be buried in the area in which they were brought up but where they no longer live.

ECO-FRIENDLY CEMETERIES

People arranging funerals are increasingly taking account of environmental concerns when planning, as are cemetery authorities, as already mentioned.

For people arranging the funeral, the choice of coffin (see pages 73–4) and whether to have flowers (see pages 76–7) will be the main decisions if a traditional cemetery or churchyard are to be used.

Many cemeteries are being managed in a more environmentally friendly way, perhaps leaving areas of longer grass or even deliberate wilderness in very old cemeteries where subsidence has made areas unsafe for public access. Flowers and other green waste are composted. Some neglected cemeteries are being restored as green open spaces, sometimes using people serving community service orders.

Some cemeteries include areas for woodland burials or offer the chance to place a bench as an alternative to a grave stone. Some offer the opportunity to contribute to planting drifts of spring bulbs or other enhancement of the environment.

❝Some old and neglected cemeteries are being restored to reflect today's environmental concerns. ❞

An increasing number of people are asking for charitable donations in place of flowers at funerals. Some feel that a funeral with no flowers is very sad, but many others feel that the money spent on providing floral tributes, only to be left withering outside the crematorium, could be put to better use. The environmental damage caused by extensive production of cut flowers is also a cause for concern.

❝ The owners of natural burial grounds are usually very helpful and many funerals held in them are not traditional. ❞

GREEN BURIAL GROUNDS

There are also natural or green burial grounds. These are usually designed to be natural woodland and meadows in perpetuity, and although they are carefully mapped so the location of a particular grave is known, often no markers or above ground memorials are permitted. Often there is little to distinguish the burial ground from the surrounding countryside. In some cases, an older, traditional landscape is being restored following deforestation or agricultural use. Some sites mark the burial plots with trees – a choice may be given, but these will be native species appropriate to the local area. A few sites will allow small marker plaques, but many do not.

There are an increasing number of these throughout the country and many also take cremated remains. The owners of natural burial grounds are usually extremely helpful and many funerals are not traditional. Families create their own words and may use 'alternative' vehicles such as a tractor-pulled trailer or even a horse and cart. The only very strict rule is that everything being placed in the ground must be biodegradable. This includes the coffin and any clothing the deceased is dressed in – and there can be no preservative treatment of the body.

 To find out more about green burial grounds, contact the Natural Death Centre (www.naturaldeath.org.uk), which is an excellent source of information.

An increasing number of local authorities, as well as private landowners, are providing natural burial grounds.

BURIAL AT SEA

This is rare and needs to be discussed with a funeral director who will take specialist advice. A licence is required from the Marine Concerns and Environment Unit, Department for Food and Rural Affairs or National Environment Assembly for Wales. Burial is only permitted at two places, both off the south of England, and the expense is considerable.

BURIAL ON PRIVATE LAND

No law prevents a burial taking place on private land, provided all the normal procedures of registration of the death have been completed, and the coroner, if involved, is satisfied that the investigations have also been completed. The registrar of deaths will issue the normal green certificate, or the coroner will provide a coroner's certificate for burial; the detachable section (part C) must be completed by the person arranging the burial and returned to the registrar within 14 days of the funeral taking place.

If you are considering this option, a number of serious considerations must be taken into account.

- You must obtain permission from the owner of the land where the burial is to take place if it is not your own.
- You must consult the local environmental health officer regarding the burial procedure and any possible effect it may have on nearby watercourses, and the local water table.
- You must ensure that you are a safe distance from any utility pipes or cables. Seek advice from suppliers if in doubt.
- You must inform any individual or mortgage company with an interest in the property of your intentions.
- Notification that a burial has taken place, together with an accurate map of the location, should be attached to the deeds of the property.
- The presence of a grave on the property may reduce its value and make any future resale difficult.
- If you decide to move and want to remove the grave to a new location, a licence for exhumation must be obtained from the Ministry of Justice; professional assistance may be needed to deal with the exhumation.

Burial on farmland is an option that may be considered by some landowners; this may involve setting

To contact the Marine and Fisheries Agency, go to www.mfa.gov.uk and on the site map go to Burial at Sea. The DEFRA website is www.defra.gov.uk and for the National Assembly for Wales, go to www.wales.gov.uk.

up a formal burial ground and require a long-term commitment to the project. Statutory requirements regarding the maintenance of burial records must be observed, and local planning authorities must be consulted as this would constitute a change of use of the land. Several such burial grounds have been established, and provide a valuable service to the local community.

Unless a small part of private grounds can be set aside in perpetuity as a private cemetery, which may well be possible on an estate, farm or family house with a large garden, arrangements for burial at home are likely to present difficulties.

A possible solution to this problem is to arrange for a cremation, and then to scatter or bury the ashes in the garden or field. An ashes casket buried in private ground is subject to the same laws of exhumation as a coffin; it can, however, legally be moved from one part of the private grounds to another. If ashes caskets are 'buried' above ground in, say, a purpose-built rockery or mausoleum, the casket can be moved elsewhere without difficulty.

The Natural Death Centre (see box at the bottom of page 66) is the best authority to consult if you are planning on arranging a funeral yourself – and see also pages 92–3.

“One solution if you wish to bury the deceased at home is to arrange a cremation and scatter or bury the ashes in a garden or field. ”

Cremation

In 2008-9 just over 72 per cent of the population of England and Wales was cremated, the highest proportion ever. Not only is cremation usually significantly less expensive than burial, many people prefer the flexibility offered by being able to choose where to bury or scatter the cremated remains - generally called ashes.

When cremation was first introduced in Victorian times it was promoted as being a more hygienic way of dealing with bodies, but it is now recognised that cremation is not as environmentally friendly as first thought. Crematoria use significant amounts of fossil fuel and contribute to atmospheric pollution, especially from the vapour emitted from mercury fillings in teeth. This is one of the reasons why many crematoria will not permit a body to be dressed in clothing that is made from man-made fibres, and there are restrictions on what other items may be placed inside a coffin. To comply with new legislation, crematoria have to install new equipment to trap mercury and other possible pollutants. The equipment is so large that, in some cases, crematoria have had to extend their buildings to accommodate it, and the costs involved are very high.

THE PROCESS OF CREMATION

A common anxiety around cremation is whether the ashes returned are really those of their own relative. Great care is taken in mortuaries and by funeral directors to ensure that a body and the coffin it is in are clearly identified at all times. Once a coffin has arrived in the crematorium chapel it cannot be opened and an identification marker is kept with the coffin and the remains from the moment they leave the chapel. The coffin is always cremated with the body inside. Therefore any nameplates and handles have to be combustible.

❝ Cremation is not as environmentally friendly as first thought, and requires large and expensive equipment. ❞

Pacemakers and other implants

Families are always asked, often more than once, whether the deceased had a pacemaker or any other medical implants. A number of these have to be deactivated or removed before someone can be cremated as they can pose a serious risk of explosion within the cremator. The removal or deactivation can be done by the hospital or the funeral director, and there may be a charge. If the deceased had an implanted defibrillator it is especially important to tell hospital staff or the funeral director. These must be deactivated by a cardiac technician before being removed or there is a risk of an electrical shock to staff. At the moment, the only implant that may completely prevent cremation is radioactive implant treatment for cancer of the prostate.

Recycling metal

Metal hips and other orthopaedic implants are collected by crematorium staff after cremation. An orthopaedic surgeon from Holland has started a recycling scheme with a colleague and so these metals are recycled from the majority of British crematoria and money is raised for charity through the scheme.

Open pyre cremations

There has been recent interest in having open pyre cremations, as would be the usual practice in India. So far, the legal right to this has not been established in the UK. However, most crematoria allow two representatives of the family to switch on the cremator, to allow them to comply as closely as possible with cultural tradition about the lighting of the pyre. If you want to find out more about this, talk to the funeral director or crematorium management as it will need to be booked in advance.

Cost of cremation

In an urban area there will probably be a choice of crematoria, but in rural areas it may be quite some distance to the nearest. For example, there are seven crematoria in Tyne and Wear, but only one in largely rural Northumbria. Some crematoria have a standard fee, while others differentiate between a standard fee and one that includes items such as music, use of the waiting area and display of floral tributes – but the extra is only a small proportion of the cost. The range of prices for cremation at 1 April 2009 was between £400 and £600. Remember that this is just the cost associated with the crematorium, to which the funeral director's costs and other disbursements (see page 88) must be added.

Are there alternatives to burial and cremation?

The simple answer is, not yet. Scientists in Scandinavia have been trying to develop a technique called promession, which involves freeze drying the body and then vibrating it so that it crumbles to a very fine powder. So far there are no signs that this will be available in the near future.

Another possibility is called water resomation. This claims to be much more environmentally friendly as it uses less fuel than cremation and does not give off harmful emissions. The technique involves heating the body in water to which an alkali has been added. The result is a fluid in which there is no organic material (that is, nothing from the body except water) and a powder, which is finer than cremated remains. The first of these resomators may be built in the USA within a couple of years, and there would be no new legislation needed for it to be introduced into the UK.

SCATTERING THE ASHES

It is possible to ask the crematorium or the funeral director to keep the ashes until a further decision has been made about what to do with them. Many people choose to scatter them at a location that was special to the deceased. It is essential to seek permission of the landowner – many people are surprised by the quantity of ashes; the usual amount from an adult varies between 2.5 and 3.5kg. Take care, too, in areas of particular ecological sensitivity as cremated remains contain a different balance of elements to soil and water, and in some areas a damaging effect on local plant life has been observed.

Football grounds and other sporting venues are also popular places for scattering ashes – some are able to accommodate this, but not all. It is possible for ashes to be placed in fireworks, turned into glass or even into diamonds, and there is a location in the USA where they can be used as the foundation for a new coral reef. Some of these choices are very expensive. Either ask the funeral director to research this or contact a specific venue.

❝ If you wish to scatter ashes at a special location it is essential to seek the permission of the landowner. ❞

There are companies that will deliver and scatter ashes almost anywhere in the world, but be aware that not all courier companies will agree to transport cremated remains. For ashes to be scattered at sea, there is a tradition of asking the Royal National Lifeboat Institution to carry this out. If this is wanted, the funeral director or family can approach the coxswain of the lifeboat station of choice. This is completely at the discretion of the coxswain of a particular crew, but many will assist. A donation to the RNLI would be expected. If a family is scattering ashes, they should note the direction of the wind and make sure everyone present stands upwind of the direction in which they are to be strewn.

“It is possible for ashes to be placed in fireworks, turned into glass or diamonds, and even used as the foundation for a new coral reef.”

Further choices

There are many practical decisions to be made for a funeral, in addition to the detail of the actual ceremony. It is part of the role of the funeral director to help a family make these choices.

If you have something particular in mind that the funeral director has not done before, they should be willing to discuss what you want and how they can make it happen for you. If a funeral director appears reluctant to make arrangements as the family wants them, it may be time to consider using a different company.

However, the funeral director can help a family think through all the implications of their choices. An experienced funeral director can be a source of wisdom and expertise.

CONDUCTING THE FUNERAL

The choices that are available for who can conduct the funeral is discussed in detail on pages 101–2. If this is not known, the funeral director will discuss the options with you and contact the appropriate person. Availability of that person may affect the date and timing of the funeral.

TYPE OF COFFIN

There is an extraordinary choice of coffins available: coffins can be manufactured from cardboard, recycled wood, solid wood and other materials, such as bamboo, wicker, rattan and banana leaf, among others. There is a very wide range of price, too. Some can be decorated with images such as football colours, flowers or a favourite vehicle, or the woven type can have flowers threaded into them. Caskets tend to be more expensive as the lid is hinged rather than separate. There is also a choice of fittings, such as the style of handle and lining. It is worth remembering that the coffin for someone who is to be cremated will be completely destroyed. All the fittings, including the handles, have to be combustible.

Woven coffins of willow, bamboo and other natural materials are popular for natural burial grounds. It is even possible to have a cardboard coffin covered in woollen fabric. Some critics

❝ There is a very wide choice of coffins, including cardboard, recycled or solid wood or materials such as bamboo or banana leaf. ❞

of cardboard coffins have suggested that they are not very robust, but unless the person who died was unusually heavy, this does not appear to be a problem.

The funeral director can act as a guide through the maze of choices and prices, and also what is suitable for cremation or burial.

WHAT THE DECEASED WILL WEAR

Such decisions are a personal choice; will it be her favourite outfit or his fishing clothes? In some communities it is traditional for a woman to be made a wedding-style dress. Remember that natural fibres will be preferred for cremation, and many cemeteries now prefer fabrics that are biodegradable.

EMBALMING OF THE DECEASED

Some funeral directors consider embalming to be a standard procedure and include it within their basic offer. Indeed, most funeral directors will not want to allow an open coffin in their chapel of rest if embalming has not been performed. It will also be recommended by the funeral director if the deceased is to be viewed at home. However, natural burial grounds will not accept bodies that have been embalmed because of the chemicals involved.

There are alternatives on the market that claim to be both environmentally friendly and effective at embalming, but they have yet to be generally accepted by the funeral industry.

Embalming

Embalming is a process intended to delay the process of decomposition and involves replacing the blood in the blood vessels with a preservative, normally a solution of formalin. The process is sometimes called 'preservative' or 'hygienic' treatment. It has no long-term preservative value.

Embalming is advisable if the body is to be returned to a private house before the funeral, or if the funeral is to be held more than four or five days from the date of death and the body cannot be kept in cold storage. Permission for embalming should always be obtained from the next of kin or executor after a full discussion.

Before a body can be embalmed, the doctor must have completed the medical certificate of the cause of death, and the death must have been registered. Where cremation is involved, cremation forms 4 and 5 must also have been completed (see page 80). If the coroner is involved, embalming must not take place until his or her authority has been obtained. An embalmer should be qualified by examination, and abide by the code of practice laid down by the British Institute of Embalmers: www.bioe.co.uk.

VIEWING THE DECEASED

In some cultures it is traditional to view the deceased, even as part of the actual funeral ceremony. For others it is a very personal choice. For many it does help to confirm that the death has happened. This may be especially true if the death was sudden and unexpected and there has been no previous opportunity to see the person since the death.

Traditionally, funeral directors were protective of families if the deceased had been damaged in an accident, but often what we imagine is far worse than reality, however difficult that may be. If uncertain, ask the funeral director to describe exactly how the person looks.

Occasionally there may be a problem with odour and, in these instances, a Polaroid or digital photograph may help with making a decision. It is normal to feel very protective of children, but often they are very matter of fact about things that adults do not cope well with.

❝ Don't publish the address of the deceased in an obituary: many houses have been burgled during funerals. ❞

PLACING AN ANNOUNCEMENT IN LOCAL PAPERS

This is a good way of making details of the funeral known to friends and acquaintances of the deceased who may not be known to the immediate family. The address of the deceased should never be included.

Announcements of deaths can be placed in local papers, and sometimes the national dailies; the cost for an average announcement in a local paper is likely to be about £80, and in a national paper about £150–£300. Newspapers will not normally accept text for death announcements by telephone, unless placed by a funeral director; even then there is a rigorous callback and checking system because of many distressing hoaxes. The papers do not usually ask for evidence that the death has occurred, unless the notice is submitted by someone who is not a relative, executor or funeral director.

National daily newspapers prefer a standard form of announcement, and are likely to restrict the format and words that can be used. Most funeral directors are well aware of the system, and will advise accordingly. The address of the deceased should not be inserted into the announcement: too many houses have been burgled while the funeral is taking place.

Further advice on helping children coping with bereavement can be obtained from Winston's Wish at www.winstonswish.org.uk and the Child Bereavement Charity (CBC) at www.childbereavement.org.uk.

Donations

Many funerals give people the opportunity of making donations to a nominated charity in memory of the deceased, as well as, or in place of, flowers (see box, below). This information is usually contained in the death accouncement, and the funeral director's name and address are given so that information can be given and donations made.

Funeral details

Details of the date, time and place of the funeral can be included in the death announcement. Anyone who has not been specifically invited but wishes to attend is expected to arrive independently at the time and place announced in the press. If the family wants to restrict attendance at the funeral, the death announcement should state 'private funeral service'; in this case, only those invited by the family should attend. If the family think that a great many people may wish to attend, arrangements may be made for a funeral service in a large church or auditorium followed by cremation or burial which is attended only by the family and close friends; alternatively, a private funeral for the family only may be followed some time later by a memorial service (see pages 104–8) and all who wish to pay their last respects to the deceased may attend. If no details of the time or place are published, it should be assumed that the funeral is to be private.

" If the family wants to restrict attendance at the funeral, the death announcement should state 'private funeral service'. "

Flowers

The press notice should make clear whether there are to be no flowers, family flowers only, or the option of a memorial donation. A 'no flowers' request should be strictly observed. Flowers are normally sent to the funeral director's premises; most florists are aware of this, and will contact the funeral director to ask what time flowers should be delivered. It is not normal for press notices nowadays to say where flowers should be sent: the funeral director will collect any that are sent to the family home when calling at the house for the funeral service, and will normally supply the

---

Charitable donations

An increasing number of people ask family and friends to make donations to a nominated charity in memory of the deceased, and regard this as a fitting memorial for the person concerned. Usually, the funeral director will collect and forward donations to the appropriate charity, sending receipts to each donor and providing the charity and family with a list of donations received.

Flower cards may be collected and returned to the family if the funeral director is asked to do so.

family with a list of those who sent flowers when submitting the account.

When a body is buried, flowers are normally left on the grave after it has been filled in. At the crematorium, it is likely that there will be restrictions as to where flowers can be placed, and the length of time they will be displayed: some are on display for only 24 hours after the funeral and others for a week or more. Traditional wreaths are rare nowadays; it is common for the family to request flowers in the form of bouquets or arrangements.

Unfortunately, problems with infection control mean that often it is no longer possible to donate flowers to a hospital or care home. Some funeral directors offer the opportunity to have some of the flowers preserved in a pressed flower picture or dried flower arrangement.

❝ It may not be possible to donate flowers to a hospital or care home because of problems with infection control. ❞

PRINTED ORDER OF SERVICE

A number of printers now offer web-based printing services to funeral directors, so one or two photos of the deceased can be included. This will be particularly valued by mourners who may have been fond of the deceased, but do not have their own photograph of him or her.

HOSPITALITY AFTER THE SERVICE

Depending on the number expected, it may be possible to provide a buffet meal at home or use an appropriate local venue. There is then a choice whether to call on friends and family to assist with catering or to use a professional service. You might choose to provide food at a local pub or wine bar, but mourners would purchase their own drinks at the bar.

OTHER DECISIONS

- **Transport to the funeral.** You might want to use limousines provided by the funeral director for immediate family and close friends or ask everyone to make their own way to the funeral. Using a funeral director's vehicle for the immediate family can relieve the anxiety around timekeeping, as they will be familiar with all the possible routes and local traffic conditions.
- **Whether the funeral will start from the home of the deceased** and follow a particular route, or will everyone meet at the funeral venue?

The paperwork for a funeral

Arranging a funeral requires yet more forms, but it is part of the role of the funeral director to support families in their completion, and make sure everything is done in the necessary timeframe.

Until the changes to death registration described on page 51 come into force, the process for cremation is more rigorous than for burial. Exhumation is rare, and a last resort in the investigation of a suspicious death, but in the Shipman case it was the bodies that had been buried that allowed him to be convicted of so many murders. Only an estimate could be made of his possible victims who had been cremated.

Jargon buster

Deeds Legal document showing who has the right to decide who is buried in a grave not in a churchyard
Diocese Geographical area under a bishop in the Roman Catholic and Church of England churches
Faculty Authority given by church authorities for burial in a churchyard

Why so much paperwork?

The purpose of the paperwork is to ensure that no one is buried or cremated inappropriately. The death has been registered or investigated to the point where there is no further need of the body itself as evidence.

FOR BURIAL AND CREMATION

Both burial and cremation require the green form from the registrar (or authority from the coroner) to be given to the funeral director to be forwarded to the burial or cremation authority.

FOR BURIAL

Burial also requires an application form for the cemetery in which the type of grave and other details will be specified. The funeral director assists with the completion of this. In response, the burial authority will issue a copy of the entry in the burial register as evidence of the burial and describing the location of the grave.

❝ The funeral director will assist with the application form for the cemetery where the type of grave is specified. ❞

Documents for burial

Document	Source	Function	Recipient
registrar's green certificate for burial *or* if inquest is to be held: coroner's order for burial	registrar coroner	required before burial can take place authorises burial	via relative and funeral director to burial authorities; part C returned to registrar
application for burial in cemetery	cemetery via funeral director, usually signed by executor or next of kin	applies for burial and confirms arrangements	cemetery authorities
grave deeds *or* faculty (see page 80)	cemetery *or* diocese	proves right to grave	executor or next of kin
copy of entry in burial register (see page 113)	burial authorities	proves burial and locates grave	executor or next of kin
registrar's white form for a stillborn baby	registrar	required before burial can take place	via next of kin and funeral director to burial authorities

❝The date and time of a funeral cannot be set until the death has been registered or the coroner has given permission. You can then ensure you have all the appropriate papers ready, as shown above.❞

The deeds or faculty will have to be produced if there is to be a further burial in that grave in the future and a grant of probate or statutory declaration will be needed to transfer the deeds or faculty if the person named as the deeds holder then dies. A statutory declaration is a statement sworn in front of a commissioner for oaths – usually a local solicitor.

If exclusive rights of burial have been purchased, there will also be **deeds** to the grave issued. However, in a churchyard the deeds will be replaced by a **faculty** issued by the **diocese**.

66 It is important to be aware that the ashes can only be released to the applicant unless they are authorised to be given to another person. 99

FOR CREMATION IN ENGLAND AND WALES

There are a few statutory forms that need to be filled in before cremation can take place.

Cremation form 1

Cremation requires that form 1 applying to the crematorium authority is filled in by the person arranging the funeral. This person is then called the applicant. The applicant must also complete a form instructing what to do with the ashes, which may be on the reverse of form 1. It is important to be aware that the ashes can only be released to the applicant, unless they are authorised to be released to another person or company. All the forms needed for cremation can be seen in full on the Ministry of Justice website (see below).

Cremation forms 4 and 5

Cremation requires two doctors to complete certificates confirming the cause of death. The first form is usually completed by the doctor who filled in the medical certificate of cause of death. This is why it is helpful to let the hospital or doctor know as soon as possible if cremation is planned, as they will often complete both forms at the same time.

The website of the Ministry of Justice is www.justice.gov.uk

Completing the cremation form (form 4) requires a doctor to have seen the body after death, so if the death was at home and the doctor did not visit to verify death, they will arrange to visit the funeral director. A second doctor who does not work with the first doctor must also complete a form (form 5), having spoken with the first doctor and someone else who was involved in the care of the deceased

" The person arranging the funeral should fill in form 1 and is then known as the applicant. Forms 4 and 5 are filled in by doctors. "

Documents most commonly required for cremation

When death is due to natural causes and the coroner is not involved, the death must be registered before a cremation can take place. The forms specific to cremation are usually produced by the crematorium and supplied to doctors and funeral directors. The funeral director will assist the family and coordinate completion of all forms. If you are arranging the funeral yourself, seek advice at an early stage from the crematorium. The forms can also be downloaded from the Ministry of Justice: www.justice.gov.uk/. The forms required are:

- Registrar's certificate for burial or cremation (a green form or white form for a stillborn baby) OR crematorium form 6 from the coroner
- Cremation 1 (application for cremation completed by next of kin or representative)

OR Cremation 3 (application for cremation of a stillborn baby)

- Form giving instructions for the disposal of the cremated remains (ashes): usually completed by the next of kin or personal representative
- Service details form (completed by the funeral director for the crematorium)
- Cremation 4 medical certificate (completed by the doctor who was treating the deceased and usually the one who signed the medical certificate)
- Cremation 5 confirmatory medical certificate (completed by an independent doctor)

OR Cremation 9 certificate of stillbirth (completed by a doctor or midwife)

- Cremation 10 authorisation of cremation of deceased person by medical referee (the doctor employed by the crematorium) OR Cremation 13 authorisation of cremation of stillborn baby by medical referee.

Documents for cremation

Document	Source	Function	Recipient
registrar's certificate for burial or cremation (green form) *or*	registrar	proves registrar is satisfied that medical certificate issued or death registered	via relative and funeral director to crematorium
Cremation 1 application for cremation	crematorium via funeral director: to be completed by next of kin or personal rep	applies for cremation and tells crematorium who is responsible for the arrangements	crematorium
Cremation 3 application for cremation of a stillborn child	crematorium via funeral director: to be completed by next of kin or personal rep	applies for cremation of a stillborn baby	crematorium
Cremation 4 medical certificate * †	doctor or hospital	gives cause of death	medical referee at crematorium
Cremation 5 * † confirmatory medical certificate	doctor or hospital, to be completed by second doctor	confirms cause of death	medical referee at crematorium
Cremation 6 certificate of coroner	coroner after postmortem or inquest	allows cremation when coroner involved	
ashes disposal form	funeral director or crematorium	gives instructions for storage, return to family or funeral director and disposal of ashes	crematorium authorities
Cremation 9 certificate of stillbirth	doctor or midwife	gives cause of death	medical referee at crematorium
Cremation 10 authorisation of cremation of deceased person by medical referee	completed by medical referee	confirms information given by doctors/coroner	crematorium authorities
certificate for disposal of cremated remains	crematorium	confirms date and place of cremation	next of kin or personal representative to give to burial authorities if ashes to be buried
certificate of cremation	crematorium	copy of entry in crematorium register	next of kin or personal representative

* Not required if coroner involved

† Not required if a hospital postmortem carried out by a doctor qualified for more than 5 years – replaced by cremation 11 certificate after postmortem examination

Forms with other numbers are specialist forms used following anatomical examination or for cremation of body parts

such as a nurse, care home manager or even a member of the family. This doctor must also see the body. Most hospitals have a panel of doctors who make themselves available for this duty, and a GP or a funeral director will ask a GP from a different practice to do this. There is a fee for these forms, which will be paid by the funeral director on behalf of the applicant. This fee may vary.

Processing the forms

These forms are usually delivered to the crematorium by the funeral director, and often have to be there a minimum of 48 hours before the ceremony. At the crematorium, they are checked by a doctor employed by the crematorium, known as the medical referee. Only when the medical referee is satisfied can a cremation proceed. The medical referee has the authority to order a postmortem examination, although in practice they would usually refer the death to the coroner.

A recent change in regulations means that the family of the deceased have the right to inspect the cremation medical forms once they have been

❝ Forms often need to be delivered to the crematorium by the funeral director a minimum of 48 hours before the ceremony. ❞

delivered to the crematorium. The funeral director will explain this in more detail, but few families exercise this right as it can create a delay before the funeral can go ahead.

Other forms

Other forms that may be required at the crematorium, such as after a consented postmortem examination are summarised in the table in the box, left.

CREMATION IN SCOTLAND AND NORTHERN IRELAND

The new cremation regulations introduced in England and Wales in 2009 do not apply to Scotland and Northern Ireland. The application for cremation is called form A. The medical certificates are certificates B and C.

In addition, if a postmortem examination has been ordered instead of the B and C forms, an E form is issued by the procurator fiscal (Scotland) or coroner (Northern Ireland).

Form F is issued by the medical referee at the crematorium.

Specialist forms are available for special circumstances, such as the cremation of a stillborn baby or for cremation of body parts.

Crematoria in Scotland and Northern Ireland will usually accept cremation medical certificates completed in England and Wales as these contain more detail than their Scottish and Northern Irish equivalents. However, if a body is to be moved to England and

Wales from other parts of the United Kingdom, it is preferable for doctors in Scotland and Northern Ireland to download forms from the Ministry of Justice website (or the funeral director will supply them).

FUNERALS AWAY FROM HOME IN THE UK

As people move from place to place more often nowadays, they often express a wish to be buried or cremated in a district other than the one in which they died. In such cases, funeral arrangements have to link the two places: where the death occurred, and where the funeral is to take place. Most funeral directors are accustomed to this. However if the distance involved is considerable, the arrangements are usually made with a funeral director where the funeral is to take place as this requires the greatest degree of

❝ There is some time-consuming paperwork required for funerals at home for those who die abroad, so take advice on the timing. ❞

local knowledge and contacts. They may subcontract collection of the deceased to a company who specialise in long distance removals.

Bodies were traditionally conveyed by hearse within the UK but air transport is increasingly used for longer distances as this reduces the cost for families. Any coffin that is conveyed by public transport, air or ferry, must be prepared as for international transfers, including the fact that the body should be embalmed.

FUNERALS AT HOME FOR THOSE WHO DIED ABROAD

If the funeral is to involve burial, all the documents received with the coffin must be taken to the registrar in the district where the funeral will take place, with the relevant papers suitably translated. The funeral director will normally attend to this. The registrar will issue a 'certificate of no liability to register', which takes the place of the green certificate and is the only document required by the burial authorities, whether a church or local authority.

If the funeral is to involve cremation, the registrar of deaths is not involved. The funeral director will deal with most of the documentation, which must be presented to the coroner, usually in the

The Ministry of Justice website for downloading appropriate cremation forms is www.justice.gov.uk.

district in which the body is lying or where the funeral is to take place. The coroner will issue a form 6 for cremation.

If the coroner is investigating the death for any reason, he will issue the burial order or cremation form 6, depending on the wishes of the family.

- If originals or certified copies of the relevant documents do not accompany the returned coffin, contact the funeral directors who assisted with the deceased in the country where death occurred. Alternatively, contact the person who issued the original documents requesting a certified copy. In certain circumstances, the Consular Division of the Foreign and Commonwealth Office (FCO) may be able to help.
- If documents are in a foreign language, you must have them officially translated. However, some European countries now use a multi-lingual death certificate, with each relevant section in five languages. In most cases, the coroner will be able to accept documents in most Western European languages.

SENDING A BODY ABROAD

When someone who has died in England or Wales is going to be buried or cremated in another country (including Scotland, Northern Ireland and the Channel Islands), permission

must first be obtained from the local coroner. Form 104 gives notice to a coroner of the intention to remove a body from England, which will be supplied by the registrar or funeral director: usually the funeral director deals with this.

&&If a coroner is investigating the death, the body will not be released for removal from England until it is certain the body won't need further examination.&&

If the registrar knows before registration that the body is to be taken out of England, he will not issue a certificate for burial or cremation; if, however, such a certificate has already been issued, it must be sent to the coroner together with the 'out of England' form. Four clear working days must normally elapse before the coroner gives permission on form 103. However, in cases of urgency, please telephone the coroner's office. A personal visit with all necessary documentation and information concerning the death may, provided the coroner is satisfied, enable the form to be signed and the body removed immediately. If the coroner is investigating the death, he will not release the body for removal from England until satisfied that it will not be required for further examination.

There are no legal restrictions on taking cremated remains out of the UK, but other countries may impose their own restrictions. For example:

- **Italy is one of the most difficult:** the ashes are treated exactly the same as a body, with all the same documents required, together with permission to import from the local prefect of police in the area of intended disposal. A hermetically sealed container is required, the sealing of which must have been witnessed by a representative of the consul.
- **Greece treats ashes in the same way as an exhumed body,** which may not be imported into the country until one year after death.
- **France requires consular sealing** of a hermetically sealed container bearing an engraved plate that gives the name of the deceased, date of death and death certificate number.
- **India requires** a High Commission permit.

❝Arranging to take a body into another country for burial or cremation is a complex matter and you will need expert help. ❞

Always check with the relevant embassy or consulate for the regulations for the destination country.

Making the arrangements

Making the arrangements to take a body into another country for burial or cremation is usually an extremely complex matter and should not be attempted without expert help and advice. Generally, the body must be embalmed and contained in a metal-lined coffin, which must be suitably packaged. All necessary freight documents must be completed, and a death certificate provided for UK customs clearance. Consular requirements of the destination country must be met, and all documents required must be translated and authenticated at the relevant consulate for a fee.

Consular regulations

Consular regulations change frequently, so in every case enquiries should be made at the local consulate of the country concerned. The requirements usually include:

- Consular permission to take the body into the relevant country.
- At least one copy of the death certificate supplied by the registrar, suitably translated.

 The British Foreign and Commonwealth Office is always a good place to start to find out information for overseas administration. Go to www.fco.gov.uk.

- A certificate of embalming.
- A declaration from the funeral director that the coffin contains only the body of the deceased and accompanying clothing and packing.
- Details of the route, flight number and date of departure.
- A freedom from infection (FFI) certificate.
- A certificate of exhumation and a copy of the Ministry of Justice licence to exhume, in the case of exhumed bodies.
- A passport wherever it is necessary for the body to pass through another country on the way to its destination – this does not apply to air transport.
- A consul representative's presence at the sealing of the coffin/crate.

In addition, the consulate will also provide information about formalities that will be required on arrival of the body, and what arrangements must be made beforehand.

❝ In every case, make enquiries at the consulate of the county concerned. ❞

Paying for the funeral

It is important to be aware that whoever signs the papers at the funeral directors has entered into a formal contract with them, and has become responsible for paying for the funeral. Therefore it is wise to be confident how the funeral will be paid for prior to signing.

FUNERAL DIRECTORS' FEES

Funeral directors' fees are made up of the fees they charge for the services they have provided (such as the coffin and vehicles), and what are called the disbursements. These are the fees they pay to third parties, such as a minister, doctors' forms when it is a cremation, and the cemetery or crematorium. Most of these disbursements have to be paid in advance of the funeral, and this is why many funeral directors now ask for a deposit when the funeral booking is confirmed. Unfortunately, in the past, many families have booked funerals and then not paid. This has caused financial difficulties for funeral directors, so inevitably they have had to take steps to protect themselves.

Home visits

If the funeral director makes a home visit they will ask the family to sign a disclaimer waiving the right to the statutory seven-day cooling off period that applies to home-based sales or there will be a delay to the funeral.

VAT

The services of the funeral director, minister and cemetery or crematorium are exempt from VAT. If, however, the funeral director supplies flowers, catering or any form of memorial, the VAT must be paid on these items.

HELP WITH FUNERAL COSTS

Payment for the funeral takes priority over all other claims on the estate, including any money owed to the Government. Often a bank will be prepared to release funds to a funeral director even if the account has been frozen. If there is not enough money in the estate, the cost will need to be met by family members.

Some people find the expenses of a funeral very difficult to meet, and are embarrassed about telling the funeral director. In fact, one of the first things a funeral director should do is to find out whether or not there is a problem about money and, if there is, advise the client of ways in which help may be provided. All members of NAFD and SAIF are pledged to provide a basic funeral. This may be given a different title by different funeral directors, but it will provide:

- **The removal and care** of the deceased during normal office hours within a limited locality.
- **The arrangement** of a basic funeral.
- **The provision of a hearse** only and staff to the nearest crematorium or cemetery.
- **The provision of a basic coffin**.
- **No chapel visits** (although such visits are generally permitted during office hours).
- **The conducting of the funeral** at a time suitable to the funeral directors.

This will be provided at an inclusive package price, which is significantly lower than standard charges, and many funeral directors will go well beyond the minimum requirements when supplying a basic funeral.

Normally, the cost of the funeral is paid for from the estate of the deceased – the money and property that has been left. Banks will normally release funds to pay for the funeral from the bank account of the deceased, if they are presented with an itemised account from the funeral director and a copy of the death certificate.

Social Fund Funeral Payment

If you do not have enough money to pay for the funeral, and you or your partner are getting Income Support, income-based Jobseeker's Allowance, Pension Credit, Housing Benefit, Child Tax Credit (at a rate higher than the family element), Working Tax Credit (where a disabled element is included) or Council Tax Benefit, you may be able to get a Funeral Payment from the Social Fund to help with the cost. The decision is based on your financial circumstances, not those of the person who died, and your savings are not taken into consideration. For more information, see leaflet SF200 *Help with Funeral Expenses from the Social Fund*, available from your local Jobcentre Plus office.

> **"** Many funeral directors will go well beyond the minimum requirements when they are supplying a basic funeral. **"**

For further information on bereavement and other State-funded benefits, see pages 190–1.

Some funeral directors will not arrange funerals where a claim to the Social Fund is to be made, but others offer more flexible arrangements and may offer payment by instalments. The Social Fund Funeral Payment will not cover the entire cost of the funeral, so consider how the balance is to be paid.

Local Authority funerals

If you do not qualify for the Social Fund and really cannot afford even a simple funeral, contact the hospital where the person died, or the local authority of the area in which they died if it was outside hospital. They have a duty to arrange simple funerals in these circumstances, but are within their rights to ask about the financial situation of the deceased and the family. The procedure varies from area to area and, in Scotland, all of these arrangements are made by the local authority. There is not normally a

 Always remember that the person who takes responsibility for arranging the funeral also becomes responsible for ensuring that the funeral account is paid.

choice of coffin, and any mourners may have to make their way to the cemetery or crematorium themselves, but will usually be able to attend. The ceremony will respect the faith of the deceased. Most benevolent funds and charities do not make grants to help with funeral costs.

PAYING FOR A FUNERAL IN ADVANCE

While in terms of purchasing power, the cost of a funeral is less than half what it was 70 years ago, a funeral still costs a considerable amount of money. Some people who have had to pay for the funerals of relatives and friends have found it difficult to find the money to pay the bill, and have decided that they want to pay for their own funeral in advance. For some, this is not only to spare relatives from facing the cost of their funeral, but because they want to specify how things are to be done, and what they would like to take place at their own funeral. To find out more, contact the following (see pages 203–9 for contact details):

Age Concern
Cruse Bereavement Care
Dignity Funeral Plans
Golden Charter Funeral Plans
Golden Leaves Funeral Plan

 The Funeral Planning Authority (FPA) is an independent organisation that works to protect consumers' interests relating to funeral planning. Their website is www.funeralplanningauthority.com.

Help the Aged
Perfect Choice.

These are among many plans that are available. Ensure any plan purchased is registered with the Funeral Planning Authority.

DEATH WHILE IN THE ARMED FORCES

The overwhelming majority of families choose to have a military arranged funeral, which will be planned in consultation with them. If the family prefer a private funeral, a substantial grant is made towards the cost (the exact amount will be advised by the visiting officer from the Joint Casualty Compassionate Centre, which is part of the Ministry of Defence).

Relatives of someone who was in receipt of a war disablement pension who has died as a result of the condition causing the disability or were receiving a constant attendance allowance for it, should contact the Service Personnel and Veterans Agency to check for entitlements before making funeral arrangements.

INTERNATIONAL REPATRIATION

In many cases the cost will be considerably reduced by having a cremation in the country where the deceased died and then repatriating the ashes, but this is not acceptable to some ethnic and faith groups, and countries where the predominant community does not accept cremation may not have cremation facilities.

For more information about the Service Personnel and Veterans Agency and the Joint Casualty Compassionate Centre, see below and also on page 95.

❝Following a death while in the armed forces, most families choose to have a military arranged funeral.❞

 If you need to contact the Service Personnel and Veterans Agency, go through www.royalmarinesassociation.org.uk/veteransagency.asp.

Arranging a funeral without a funeral director

If you are thinking of arranging the funeral yourself, you will now have some idea of the practical aspects that need to be considered. It will be easier to decide whether to take responsibility for all the arrangements, or whether to give more attention just to the content of the ceremony.

PARTICULAR ISSUES TO CONSIDER

In addition to the decisions outlined earlier in this chapter, there are other arrangements that you will have to make for yourself.

Storage of the body prior to the funeral

If the death was in hospital, the mortuary will probably be able to store the body until it is collected en route to the funeral. You will need a photocopy of the green form or the coroner's authorisation, as the original will already have been given to the cemetery or crematorium authorities. If no other suitable premises are available, you will need the services of a funeral director to provide cold storage for the body. An air conditioning unit can be hired if the body is to be kept at home, especially in warmer weather. Unfortunately, bodies begin to deteriorate immediately after death and, with some diseases, deterioration can be much more rapid.

Seek advice from the crematorium or cemetery authorities early on

Some crematoria and cemeteries do not permit funerals that are not arranged by funeral directors. Book the date and time and they will advise on the documentation they need, and any other regulations to be complied with. They will supply the forms that need to be completed.

 Helpful advice on organising a funeral yourself can be obtained from the Natural Death Centre (www.naturaldeath.org.uk).

Purchasing a coffin

Unfortunately, many coffin manufacturers do not supply directly to the public, so it may be necessary to purchase a coffin from a funeral director. If family members decide to make the coffin, ensure it is lined with a moisture-resistant lining.

Moving and transporting the body requires care

The loss of muscle tone that occurs after death makes bodies more difficult to move, and health and safety regulations may prevent mortuary staff from helping you place the body in the coffin. Each mortuary has its own opening times, so do make an appointment. Bodies should not be moved in such a way that they are visible to the public, and most funeral directors do not use hearses to remove bodies from the mortuary. An estate car rather than a van can be used, but it is recommended that a blanket be used to drape over the coffin, to deter morbid curiosity.

It is also essential to think about how the coffin will be moved at the cemetery or crematorium – there may be a trolley available, or a funeral director may have one that can be borrowed or hired. However, if there is rough ground at the cemetery, the coffin must be robust enough to be carried some distance, and probably six people will be needed to carry it safely without risk of injury.

For health and safety reasons, it is usually appropriate to employ a professional grave digger if this is not included within the services of a cemetery. The cemetery management can help you with this. Seek advice from a professional about the lowering of the coffin into the grave so that this can be done at the funeral in a dignified way.

❝ When transporting a body it must not be visible to the public. If you are not using a hearse, drape the coffin with a blanket to deter morbid curiosity. ❞

 The Natural Death Centre (see opposite) also publishes *The Natural Death Handbook*, which gives advice and information on all aspects of arranging and conducting funerals yourself.

Special case funerals

Funerals for babies and small children and those of military personnel, or their families, need special care and planning. This section explains what your options are.

FUNERALS FOR BABIES AND SMALL CHILDREN

Some funeral directors will not charge for their professional services for arranging funerals for babies and young children. This is at their discretion, and each will have their own policy regarding the age at which they may charge.

Most hospitals will offer a free funeral for stillborn babies or those who die very soon after death. Every hospital has its own policy and sometimes what they can offer is constrained by the policies of local crematoria and cemeteries. In many hospitals the chaplain is closely involved in providing this service, but it will be available to people of every faith and none. Stillbirths and babies who have lived have individual funerals, but if the baby was very small there may be no ashes available after a cremation.

❝ Funerals for stillborn babies are often provided for free by the hospital. The chaplain is usually closely involved. ❞

Funerals for babies delivered before 24 weeks gestation who have never lived

Most hospitals provide a regular, usually monthly, ceremony for babies (fetuses) who have been miscarried, or where the pregnancy has had to be ended deliberately. Each hospital has its own policy, but the service may not be available before 12 or 16 weeks gestation. Parents will have the choice

 The SPVA operates a helpline on all finance issues on 0800 169 2277 and its website is www.veterans-uk.info.

as to whether they wish to attend and may have the opportunity for their baby to be named during the ceremony. If the service offered is burial, the babies may be placed in a shared grave dedicated to this purpose. If cremation is offered, it is often not possible for ashes to be recovered because the babies are so very small.

DEATHS OF MILITARY PERSONNEL OR IN THEIR FAMILIES

Although each service and regiment has retained some of its own traditions, there is now a single organisation that oversees the procedure for informing families of military personnel. The Joint Casualty and Compassionate Centre (JCCC) – which is part of the Ministry of Defence (see below) – coordinates support afterwards, including repatriation and liaison with authorities

"A great deal of support is provided by various agencies should military personnel die while in service. "

investigating the death, if required. They ensure families are aware of and supported in their choices regarding funeral arrangements.

As well as being involved after the death of a soldier, sailor or mariner, the JCCC can be contacted in the event of a death in the family or serious illness to request the return home of someone in the armed forces. These decisions are ultimately the responsibility of a commanding officer, but JCCC can assist with the request and make arrangements if appropriate.

The Service Personnel & Veterans Agency operates a freephone helpline for bereaved families (see below) for advice and guidance on all pension pay, allowances and compensation issues. This can include entitlements for funeral support with funeral arrangements.

SSAFA Forces Help (Soldiers, Sailors, Airmen and Families Association) exists to give support to both serving and former service personnel and their families, as does the British Legion. Even if direct financial assistance is not necessarily available, these organisations understand the culture and particular issues faces by armed forces personnel and their families and their particular rights to welfare and other assistance.

For more information, you can contact JCCC via the Ministry of Defence website at www.mod.uk/DefenceInternet/AboutDefence/WhatWeDo/Personnel/SPVA/Jccc.htm or call their 24-hour helpline on 01452 519951.

Funerals in Scotland

In Scotland, following registration (see pages 55-6), the certificate of registration of death is given to the informant by the registrar. The certificate must then be given to the person in charge of the place of interment or cremation. No part of the certificate is returned to the registrar.

BURIAL

In Scotland, a grave is referred to as a lair. As in England, it is possible to purchase the exclusive right of burial in a cemetery plot, usually in perpetuity, which is 99 years. Cemeteries are often administered by the local council on behalf of a church, even if the graves are on kirk land. In Scotland, cemetery chapels are rare.

At burials in urban cemeteries, silk tasselled cords, called courtesy cords, may be attached to the coffin. Specific mourners are sent a card beforehand

 Anyone who dies in Scotland has the right to a Church of Scotland funeral, which will normally be conducted by the Minister of the Parish in which the person lived (or the Minister of the Parish where the deceased was a member of the congregation, if different). There is usually no charge although a donation to church funds is normal.

"In Scotland, there is no charge for a Church of Scotland funeral. "

 The information given on these pages only relates to the differences between England and Wales and Scotland for burial. For more information relating to Scotland, see pages 63-8 for burials and pages 83-4 for cremations.

inviting them to hold a cord while the coffin bearers take the strain of the lowering. In most areas of the country the cords actually take the weight. Courtesy cords are not used for the burial of cremated remains.

A pad or mattress may be put on top of the coffin as a development of the old custom of putting grass or straw over the coffin to muffle the sound of earth falling on the lid when the grave is filled in.

Burial customs in Scotland vary in different regions. The funeral director will advise on regional customs if the funeral is being arranged by someone who lives elsewhere.

SENDING A BODY ABROAD

There are no formalities connected with the removal of bodies out of Scotland for either cremation or burial in another country, but you should ensure that the death has been registered in Scotland before moving the body out of Scotland. The procurator fiscal does not have to be informed. However, many hospitals in Scotland issue the equivalent of an 'out of England' certificate for the benefit, especially of crematorium authorities elsewhere in the UK. Many procurators will issue a Furth of Scotland (out of Scotland) in cases in which they have been involved, if needed to assist with funeral arrangements.

If the body is being taken to England or Wales for burial, the certificate of registration or the standard death certificate must be produced for the cemetery authority as well as a registrar to obtain a 'no liability to register' there. No formal notice has to be given or permission sought when cremated remains are being taken out of the country.

BRINGING A BODY FROM ABROAD

There is no need to produce evidence for the registrar in Scotland that the death took place elsewhere. If the body is coming from England or Wales, the person in charge of the place of

❝ Unlike in England and Wales, no part of the certificate of registration of death is returned to the registrar. ❞

Useful Scottish government websites include the General Register Office for Scotland (www.gro-scotland.gov.uk) and the Scottish Executive Health Department (www.scotland.gov.uk).

interment or cremation in Scotland will require the coroner's form permitting the body to be removed.

When a body is brought into Scotland to be cremated, the authority of the Scottish government must be obtained before cremation can be carried out. This means applying to the Scottish Executive Health Department (see box on page 97), with any supporting papers, such as a foreign death certificate and the application form for cremation.

Cremated remains brought into Scotland must be accompanied by a certificate of cremation issued by the crematorium.

"If a body is being brought into Scotland to be cremated, the authority of the Scottish Executive Health Department must be obtained first."

The funeral

The content of the funeral can be as formal or informal as you like. Sometimes the deceased will have left specific funeral instructions; but often it is up to the relatives to decide. If you are at all concerned, ask the advice of the funeral director or minister or celebrant, if used.

The ceremony

Depending on the beliefs of the deceased and the family a funeral ceremony can have several functions as described below.

- It may be an essential ritual in determining the passage of the deceased to an afterlife.
- It can reaffirm the faith of the bereaved in the continuing existence of the deceased within the context of their belief system.
- It is a public ritual acknowledging the event of the death.
- It allows other mourners to express their grief in a collective setting and to support the immediate family by expressing solidarity with them in their grief.
- It can be an opportunity for thankfulness and celebration of the impact of the deceased in the lives of others.
- If the funeral immediately precedes or includes the committal (the moment that the coffin usually disappears from view at the crematorium, or is lowered into the ground at the cemetery), it is the final event in which the body of the deceased is present.

The funeral ceremony also requires a number of decisions to be made. In some faiths there is very little latitude for personal choice in a funeral, but for others the funeral has to be planned completely. Advice can be sought from older members of the family regarding any family traditions, and from ministers or elders of a faith community. This will be especially important if someone has responsibility for arranging the funeral of somebody whose faith they do not share.

If someone has died in hospital, the chaplains will have contacts for all the main faiths practised in the local area, and a search of the telephone directory or internet will usually give access to local or national centres for further information. Any funeral director should be able to provide a funeral for someone of any faith, but there are some who specialise in certain styles.

❝ The ceremony might mark the passage to the afterlife or affirm a faith, give an opportunity to express grief or to celebrate a life. ❞

SOME QUESTIONS TO CONSIDER

Taking time to think through the following issues will help to create a ceremony with real meaning and significance for those who attend.

How formal an event is wanted?

Is the tone to be one of sombre quiet reflection or a joyful celebration? This will be influenced by the wishes of the deceased, if known, but perhaps also the nature of the death and who will be present.

Where will the ceremony take place?

Will the entire ceremony take place at the crematorium chapel, or in the cemetery chapel where there is one? Or will there be a main service at a place of worship or other venue, and just the committal at the cemetery/ crematorium? A factor here is that cemeteries and crematorium have timed appointments and a longer appointment may be needed.

Crematoria work to a strict appointments system, so services must be fairly short, unless a special booking is made for a longer period, which will cost extra. Most crematoria allow 30 minutes between appointments, some allow 45 minutes, and a few only 20 minutes. Equally, some people choose to have the committal first and then have a more celebratory event afterwards, without the coffin present.

Who will be invited?

Will everyone be invited to the funeral and committal, or is the committal to be restricted to close mourners?

Who will conduct the funeral?

If the faith of the deceased or the family does not dictate who will conduct the funeral, who will take on this responsibility? There are a number of choices:

- **The funeral director can identify a religious minister** who should meet with the family and discuss the content of the funeral. Many will be very flexible, but will not want to include elements that specifically contradict their faith.
- **A humanist celebrant.** Humanist funerals are truly secular in that they include no reference to god at all. The British Humanist Association will put you in touch with someone in your area who can conduct such services; most funeral directors will be able to refer you to someone, and

 To contact the British Humanist Association, go to www.humanism.org.uk.

some are experienced themselves at conducting such services.

- **A civil celebrant.** Civil celebrants will plan the funeral with the family and will be prepared to include some prayers or religious music if wanted.
- **A member of the family,** or colleague or friend. This is a considerable responsibility to ask someone to take on and everyone present may feel safer if there is someone slightly distanced from the emotion of the event in charge. This will be especially the case if a lot of people are expected who will not know the family, such as work colleagues.

What music will there be?

Although hymns are traditional, if the majority of the mourners are not regular churchgoers, this may not be practical. Many people do not sing regularly and may not be confident enough to sing in a public setting. An alternative is to have recorded hymns, but many other styles of recorded music have become popular, including classical music and modern pop and rock songs. Some crematoria have web-based music systems, but the family can also provide music to be played – these need to be very carefully labelled so the right track is played at the right time.

Will there be readings?

As well as religious texts there are many anthologies of poetry and readings collected specifically around the theme of bereavement. One or more pieces may be written for the event. For example, a school class might all contribute a line each that are then compiled to be read after the death of a teacher.

Will there be a sermon, tribute or eulogy?

A religious funeral might include a short piece of teaching relevant to the event. But, in many funerals a tribute or eulogy has replaced the sermon. It may be given by the person conducting the funeral, put together from information provided by the family, or there may be one or more contributions from family, friends and colleagues. Even if someone is a confident speaker normally, having written notes will be helpful to prevent

❝Hymms are traditional but many people today do not sing such songs regularly and may not be confident to sing in a public setting. ❞

If you are looking for inspiration for choosing music at a funeral, search for 'funeral music' on a music website, such as Spotify. You can't download music for free from this website, but if you find what you are looking for you can then buy it.

them drying up, and they can also be read by someone else if it is too difficult for the planned speaker to read their contribution at the last moment.

What about prayers?

These can be a formal liturgy (prayers that form part of church tradition and used on a regular basis) or written for the occasion. They can be replaced or put together with a period of silence in which people are invited to reflect or pray – this makes the time inclusive for those who have no faith.

Is the style of dress important?

The usual dress for funerals is darker colours, such as black, navy or grey, but it is helpful to mourners if they know that the funeral is formal and black is a definite requirement, or that the preference would be for people to wear bright colours or even the colours of a particular football club.

Recording people's attendance

At some funerals a book of condolence is provided for mourners to sign and record a personal message, or individual cards may be provided for the same purpose. This can be extremely helpful for the bereaved, who may not know many of the people present. It also gives an alternative way of expressing condolences for those mourners who feel unable or think it inappropriate to send a personal card or letter to the bereaved.

MAINTAINING TRADITIONS

Some areas of the country or particular ethnic communities have their own particular traditions. For example, in Scotland, the lowering of the coffin into the grave will often be done by family members and in funerals of people whose families who originated from the Caribbean, it will be men from the family who backfill the grave while the women observe and sing hymns.

AFTER THE CEREMONY

It is helpful if the person conducting the funeral gives out any instructions, such as whether there is to be a collection for charity, whether everyone present is welcome to come to the committal, or any refreshments are being offered. If there is a private committal followed by shared refreshments, mourners will value being told where to assemble and wait for immediate family to join them.

Filming a funeral

Although it is still rare, there are now companies that can provide audio recording or filming or even live web coverage. This can be helpful if a family is very geographically dispersed and travel is difficult or there are a number of people who cannot attend because of infirmity.

MEMORIAL CEREMONIES

A memorial will include most of the elements of a funeral but without the committal. It will often be held some time after the funeral, which allows more time for detailed planning and preparation. Music performed live may be a feature of memorial services.

MEMORIALS

Relatives often want to place a memorial tablet or headstone in a churchyard or cemetery where a coffin or ashes casket has been buried. Both churchyards and municipal cemeteries impose restrictions on the size and type of memorial and on the kind of stone that may be used and the type of lettering inscribed on it. Take care to comply with the regulations of the particular cemetery before a design is finalised. They should be created and placed by accredited companies who belong to the National Association of Memorial Masons (see box on page 108) as there are strict regulations around the health and safety aspects of placing a heavy stone on a grave. In fact, many cemeteries only allow certain accredited companies to do

"Memorials include most of the elements of funerals but without the commital. There is often more time for planning and preparation. "

work in their cemeteries, so do check with the cemetery management or funeral director. Many cemeteries and almost all churchyards prohibit kerbs or surrounds to graves, and memorials are often restricted to a headstone or a plinth and vase set at the head of the grave.

Memorials at crematoria

About a week after a cremation has taken place, the crematorium will usually send a brochure to the next of kin explaining what kinds of memorials are available. These are all optional, are not covered by the fees already paid for cremation, and are subject to the payment of VAT.

The most popular means of memorial at the crematorium is the **Book of Remembrance**. Hand-lettered inscriptions in the book usually consist of the name, date of death and a short epitaph. The crematorium displays the book, open at the right page, on the anniversary of death or of the funeral: the relatives choose which they prefer. Some crematoria sell a miniature reproduction of the entry as a card, or bound as a booklet.

Charges for the erection of memorial plaques or for inscriptions on panels on memorial walls, where available, vary greatly. Some municipal crematoria will allow no memorial other than the entry in the Book of Remembrance.

Some crematoria have a colonnade of niches for ashes called a **columbarium**; the ashes are either walled in by a **plaque** or left in an urn in the niche. Many of these are now full, and where there are spaces, charges are high. Some new crematoria, however, have recently made extensive provision for these and other similar memorials.

Some new or recently refurbished crematoria provide extensive means of memorial in carefully landscaped grounds. Some have made new provision for the storage or burial of ashes caskets, and one or two have created elaborate water gardens with provision for personal memorials to be set in place.

Other crematoria have memorial trees or rose bushes; these are usually arranged in beds, where the memorial bush is chosen by the family, the ashes scattered around it, and a small plaque placed nearby. Costs vary, as does the length of time for which the crematorium will provide maintenance before renewing the charge.

All of these will involve varied charges, and are usually offered to the bereaved a couple of weeks after the funeral. Do not allow yourself to be pressurised into buying a memorial that is not something you really want. Take time to consider all the options and costs, and discuss the matter thoroughly with all involved. You may decide that you do not want any form of memorial at the crematorium.

Memorials in cemeteries

Municipal and private cemeteries are generally less rigorous in legislating about types of stone and the wording of inscriptions than churchyards, but many authorities, faced with increasing difficulties of maintenance, insist that only 'lawn' graves with a simple headstone will be permitted.

The upkeep of a memorial is the responsibility of the person who arranged for it to be placed in the cemetery: this includes the responsibility for ensuring that the memorial is in a safe condition. Several people have been killed or injured in recent years as the result of collapsing memorial masonry. Some older memorials are very unsafe, and their condition causes great concern to

Jargon buster

Book of Remembrance A book in which the name of the person cremated can be entered. It is usually on display in a small chapel whenever the crematorium is open

Columbarium A niche in a wall at a crematorium where ashes can be walled in or left in an urn

Plaque panel A small notice with the name and date of death of the deceased, placed near a memorial rose bush or shrub or attached to a panel on a wall in the crematorium grounds

cemetery authorities. Often the owners cannot be identified, as families or relatives of those buried there cannot be traced. In such cases, cemetery authorities have sometimes had to resort to making such memorials safe by laying the masonry flat on the ground over the relevant grave.

&& If you place a memorial in a cemetery, its upkeep is your responsibility. ,,

Memorials in churchyards

There is no right to a memorial in a churchyard and the rules applying to memorials in churchyards are generally more limited than in municipal or private cemeteries. Normally each diocese publishes guidelines for memorialisation, and incumbents (the rector, vicar or priest in charge) are increasingly coming under pressure to enforce compliance. Usually, there are limitations as to the size of the

---

Cold calling

Bereaved families can suffer from memorial salespeople 'cold calling'. They search the local papers for bereavement notices and attempt to make doorstep sales.

---

memorial, the type of stone and the wording of the inscription. The general rule is that the type of stone used in the memorial must conform to the stone used in the building of the church; thus churches built of Portland stone (or similar) will often restrict memorial stones to either Portland or Purbeck, and will not allow granite or marble; flint churches, on the other hand, will often require granite or similar materials in order to conform to the appearance of the church.

Most churchyards have a maximum permissible size for stone tablets marking the location where cremated remains (ashes) have been buried; sometimes these are as small as 23 x 23cm (9 x 9in), with only a name and date of death allowed as inscriptions. The rules will vary according to traditional practice or the preference of the priest.

Neither reserving a grave in a churchyard by faculty, where this is still possible (see pages 78–80), nor purchasing the exclusive right of burial in a cemetery, automatically provides the right to put up any kind of memorial. For this, approval must be gained from the respective authorities and a fee paid.

Anything other than a simple headstone or inscription requires the granting of a faculty, as does any unusual wording. The wording of an inscription must be approved by the incumbent. Many object to colloquialism and informal descriptions, and will often stipulate that any quotations are either biblical or otherwise religious. The incumbent or funeral director will advise on how to apply for a faculty, and a fee will be charged for this. It should be noted that a change of incumbent in a parish church may result in a different interpretation of guidelines, and local regulations may be relaxed or tightened accordingly. What was allowed before may not be allowed now.

Arranging for a memorial

The funeral director or monumental mason will normally apply to the church or cemetery authorities for permission to erect a memorial; a copy of the entry in the burial register or the deeds of the grave may be required before authority is given. After a burial, allow several months for settlement before any memorial is erected or replaced.

Take time when considering and purchasing a memorial. Names of established local firms of monumental masons can be obtained from the National Association of Memorial Masons.

The cost of memorials varies enormously, depending on the type of stone, size, ornamentation, finish and lettering. Before ordering a memorial, ask for a written estimate, which states clearly the items and total cost, including any delivery or erection charges and cemetery fees. It is normal for the stonemason to ask for a 50 per cent deposit to be paid by the client on confirmation of the order: this may

seem a lot, but if the client changes their mind, there is not much the mason can do with the already inscribed stone.

VAT is charged on the provision of a new headstone or on adding a new inscription to an old one; it is not levied on the removal and replacement of existing memorials. The cemetery fee for the erection of a memorial is also exempt from VAT.

Other memorials

Placing a bench in a favourite place where the deceased often admired the view is a popular choice, or planting a tree is increasingly common. A cup or trophy may be appropriate for a sportsperson. Gifts to charity are now perhaps the most common way to memorialise someone, and allow people to contribute as they are able.

Memorials online

With the rapid increase in the number of people who now have access to the internet and email has come the

❝When choosing a memorial, do your research. Names of firms of established masons are available from the National Association of Memorial Masons. ❞

107

development of an internet memorial business. In addition to websites giving information about grief support services, there are sites that will help you to develop your own web page. Many charities are combining the opportunity to give a donation with a web page memorial to which people can contribute photographs and comments. This allows people to contribute more personal reminiscences than is possible at the funeral, provided it is done with sensitivity and respect. The best sites have security systems that allow the next of kin to control what is accessible to the public and what is password protected.

While these sites will only last as long as the relevant webmaster is in business, they provide the opportunity for posting a much fuller obituary than is possible in national or local papers, and at considerably less cost. Websites may include photographs, video clips and music (see box, below).

 Care should be taken by users of social networking sites that material is not shared posthumously that would cause distress or embarrassment to the close family of the deceased. The different networks have different procedures for closing accounts.

 The website for the National Association of Memorial Masons is www.namm.org.uk and the website for the Association of Burial Authorities is www.burials.org.uk. For adding an obituary to the internet, go to any of these websites: www.in-memoriam-uk.com, www.lovethelife-remembered.com, www.foreveronline.org or www.muchloved.com.

Appropriate services

Most people feel that a funeral service should be intensely personal, and whoever conducts the service will need to talk with the family so that a fitting tribute to the deceased can be created. The person conducting the funeral service does not have to be a minister of religion; increasingly, funeral services are conducted by a humanist or civil celebrant, an experienced funeral director, or a friend of the family.

The following pages give a brief introduction to the main aspects of the main faith groups in the UK. This may be helpful for anyone needing to arrange a funeral of someone of a different faith from their own. However, family and friends of the deceased will usually be generous with information and advice as to how strongly the deceased adhered to their faith.

CHRISTIAN FUNERALS

Traditionally, the cortege (or funeral procession) started at the house where the deceased lived, with the hearse and one or more cars for the mourners travelling by a pre-arranged route to the church or crematorium. This still frequently happens, but it is as common for the hearse to travel directly to the location of the funeral from the funeral director's premises; the mourners will then be brought to meet it by either their own or the funeral director's vehicles. If the funeral director provides cars for the bereaved

relatives, he will marshal the cortege and arrange its departure.

Timing is most important, because cemetery and cremation authorities work to a very tight schedule; if the funeral cortege arrives too early or too late, it will probably interfere with the preceding or following funerals. Should it arrive considerably late, especially at the crematorium, it is possible that the funeral service will have to be drastically shortened, or even postponed, to the great distress of the relatives.

Closing of the coffin

Different parts of the UK and different faith and ethnic communities have diverse traditions as to when the coffin is finally closed. This may be at the house, if the coffin has been brought home, or sometimes it happens during the church service.

The funeral director may walk in front of the hearse as it leaves the deceased's house, and again as it approaches the church or crematorium; this is not only as a mark of respect, but to enable him to direct the traffic and keep the funeral cortege together, especially as it leaves a side street to enter a main road. The coffin is traditionally carried into the church or crematorium on the shoulders of four of the funeral director's staff, although in some places a small trolley is used for moving the coffin. Some local authority cemeteries and crematoria insist that the coffin is wheeled on a trolley rather than carried on the shoulders of bearers. The funeral director or cemetery/crematoria management will advise on local policy.

❝ The coffin is carried into the church or crematorium on a small trolley or on the shoulders of four of the funeral director's staff. ❞

When members or friends of the family are able to act as bearers, this makes for a closer participation in the funeral, and the funeral director's staff will still be on hand to assist and give directions. Occasionally, at more formal funerals, pall-bearers walk alongside the coffin, apparently fulfilling no purpose. Traditionally, these used to carry the 'pall', a heavy fabric canopy that was held over the coffin. Today, the pall may be used to cover the coffin in the hearse if it has to travel some distance between towns before the funeral cortege can gather. It is then removed, and the family flowers are placed on the coffin before it moves off.

Cremation

Traditionally, the funeral service prior to cremation was held in church, with the congregation (or only the chief mourners if the cremation was to be private) travelling to the appropriate crematorium for a brief committal afterwards. Increasingly, funeral services are held entirely in crematorium chapels; the hearse and cars go straight to the crematorium and the bearers carry the coffin into the chapel and place it on the catafalque. Usually, the mourners follow the coffin into the crematorium, led by the minister and funeral director but, increasingly, people prefer to enter the chapel and sit down before the coffin is brought in, or have the coffin brought in before the mourners arrive. This is difficult in crematoria, as access to the crematorium chapel is not possible

---

Register of cremations

Each crematorium has to keep a register of cremations. A copy of the entry in the register is obtainable for a small fee.

until mourners at the previous funeral have left. However, it is usually possible for the coffin to be in place before the main mourners arrive. The coffin must be closed before arriving at the crematorium.

When the words of committal are spoken, the coffin passes out of sight; it will either sink into a recess or pass through a door, or a curtain will move in front of it. Some people prefer the coffin to remain on the catafalque until the mourners have left the chapel; this option is available if requested. During the funeral service, the funeral director's staff take the flowers from the hearse and place them in the floral display area; when the coffin moves out of sight at committal, the flowers on the coffin are retrieved and added to the display. Some crematoria only keep flowers on display for the day following the funeral; others leave them in place for several days, while yet others remove them once a week.

When the coffin moves out of sight, it is taken to the committal room to await cremation. Each coffin is loaded individually into a cremator, once the name on the coffin plate has been checked by the crematorium staff. It is illegal to remove the coffin from the crematorium (other than the flowers), or anything from the coffin, once the

committal has been made. When the cremation process is complete, after two or three hours, the ashes are removed.

When the cremation is complete, the remains are removed. Any metals, such as hip implants are separated out. Each cremater must be cleared before another coffin is inserted. The human remains are placed in a cremulator to create the evenly textured ashes that can then be scattered or interred. The ashes are placed into carefully labelled containers. Some people are anxious about whether ashes returned are of their own relative. Very careful attention is given by crematoria staff to ensure that there is correct identification of the remains throughout the entire cremation process.

"Some people prefer the coffin to remain in sight until the mourners have left the chapel. "

 Most of the information relating to cremations and burials is covered in the preceding chapter – for cremations, see pages 80-3, and for burials, see pages 78-80.

Disposal of the ashes

Cremated remains can usually be obtained from the crematorium on the day following the funeral; however, provided notice is given in advance, ashes may be obtained on the same day if the funeral is taking place before midday.

There is no law regarding the scattering of cremated remains; ashes can be scattered anywhere, provided that this is done respectfully, and with the consent of the owners of private grounds, such as golf courses, and so on. If desired, the funeral director will arrange to scatter the ashes for clients in a chosen location and will not normally charge for this unless considerable time and travelling expenses are incurred.

The crematorium grounds are usually known as a Garden of Remembrance; such ground is not usually consecrated, and the place where ashes are scattered is not normally marked. Some crematoria scatter the ashes around on the surface of the grass or earth; others remove a small portion of turf, pour the ashes on the ground and then replace the turf. Some allow a casket containing the ashes to be buried in the grounds. The family can choose a spot and witness the proceedings if they request to do so; some crematoria charge a fee for this. The burial of a casket is frequently attended by a minister who conducts a brief service of committal. An increasing number of crematoria offer a brief civil ceremony for the scattering of cremated remains.

Burial

Where a burial is preceded by a church service, the coffin is taken into the church by the bearers and placed on trestles or a trolley in front of the altar. In Roman Catholic and some other churches, the coffin may be taken into church before the funeral, often the previous evening, and remain there until the funeral service takes place. Most funeral services in church take about half an hour, although a requiem mass, or the funeral of a well-known member of the church congregation, may take an hour or more. After the service, the bearers will take the coffin from the church, either to the churchyard or, more commonly, to the local cemetery, usually led by the minister and funeral director. If burial is not preceded by a church service, the coffin is carried direct from the hearse to the graveside, where there is normally a short service.

The coffin will be lowered into the grave by the bearers while the words

❝ The ashes can be scattered anywhere, provided that it is done respectfully and with the consent of the owners of private grounds. ❞

Register of burials

A register of burials in the parish is kept by the church; every cemetery has to keep a register of burials and records of who owns a grave plot, and who has already been buried in each grave. A copy of the entry in these registers is obtainable for a small fee.

of committal are said; this part of the funeral service is quite brief, and normally lasts about five minutes. In Scotland, the coffin is usually lowered by members of the family. Sometimes the mourners throw a token handful of earth into the grave, or each drops a flower on to the coffin; they do not normally remain to see the grave filled in – this is done later by the cemetery staff or gravedigger. The exceptions are in Ireland and also families of African Caribbean origin, where backfilling is carried out by the men while the women observe and sing hymns.

When someone is buried in a Church of England churchyard the family is responsible for looking after the grave in accordance with local regulations. The PCC (parochial church council) is responsible for looking after the churchyard generally, and for keeping the paths and unused parts tidy. Some dioceses stipulate that, before a funeral takes place, a contribution must be made towards the upkeep of the churchyard. Municipal and private cemeteries will employ groundsmen

to take care of grounds and graves; this upkeep is often difficult and costly, which is why many authorities now stipulate lawn graves only: graves with a simple headstone in line with other headstones, and no kerbs or surrounds to interfere with mechanical mowing. However, where there are gravestones, whether simple or elaborate, the holder of the grave deeds is responsible for their upkeep; this can become very expensive as stones weather and crack, and ground settles over the years. Upkeep of memorial stones is often neglected – another reason why authorities prefer to stipulate lawn graves only.

"When someone is buried in a churchyard, the family is responsible for looking after the grave of the deceased in accordance with local regulations."

Church of England services

A Church of England funeral service that is held in church may be conducted by the incumbent or, with their permission, by any other clergyman – for instance, the clergyman whose church the deceased normally attended or who is a member or friend of the family.

There is no obligation to hold a service in church; unlike weddings, for which a building or location must be licensed through the registration authority, funeral services may be held in any building, or at the graveside. Increasingly, funeral services involving cremation are held in the crematorium chapel, but if this is not large enough, the service may be held in a village hall or any such suitable building, with only the committal taking place at the crematorium.

It is possible for the whole service, including the committal, to take place at the church or hall; the coffin is then taken away to the crematorium with only one or two direct family members attending as witnesses. Sometimes this procedure is reversed: there is a private committal at the crematorium early in the day, attended by a few family members, and the main funeral service is subsequently held in a church or hall later in the day.

The local vicar or rector will be accustomed to taking funeral services in crematoria chapels, and may be asked to conduct such services in other locations. This may be an advantage if a longer form of funeral service is planned, as services in most crematoria are limited to 20–25 minutes, although double time may usually be booked at an extra charge.

The Church of England, in common with most religious denominations, has a form of funeral ceremony, but again, unlike weddings, there is no secular legal requirement for any form of words to be said. In the UK, unless the dead person had professed another religion,

" The whole service can take place at a church or hall and the coffin subsequently taken to the crematorium with only one or two family members. "

or the relatives have made specific requests, one of the Church of England orders of funeral service will probably be used at the funeral. Most rituals can be adapted according to the preferences of those concerned. For instance, the main part of the service can be held in the church or some other suitable building, with only a few words of committal at the graveside or crematorium, or the whole service can be held where the committal is to take place. A funeral address may be given either in the church or outside, or not at all.

Many people give a lot of thought to planning the kind of funeral service they would like for their deceased relatives, with readings, poetry and particular pieces of music (see page 102). Services held in a Church of England church may be more limited due to the liturgical constraints felt by some of the clergy.

An old Church of England tradition from an age in which fewer people had easy access to transport is for the funeral service to take place in the church and the words of committal are said at the lych gate (the covered gateway often found at the entrance to old churchyards). No further ceremony is needed at the crematorium and this may be especially suitable for very rural areas with long distances to the nearest crematorium.

Roman Catholic services

For a practising Roman Catholic, it is usual to arrange for the priest to say a requiem mass in the local parish church and for him to take the funeral service. A requiem mass in a Roman Catholic church will follow a very precise order. There are no set fees laid down for Roman Catholic priests to charge for funeral services, but it is usual for the deceased's family to make an offering to the church. Cremation is no longer discouraged for Roman Catholics, and crematoria have Roman Catholic priests on their rota, where such rotas are used.

 Denominational burial grounds usually insist on their own form of service. If you are arranging the funeral of someone of a faith different from your own, get in touch as soon as possible with the local minister or priest of that denomination to find out what needs to be done.

BUDDHISTS

Buddhism is a common religion in many Far-Eastern countries such as Burma, Nepal and Japan, but it is still relatively rare in the UK. After death, Buddhists will have the deceased person wrapped in a plain sheet and prepared for cremation. Buddhists of different nationalities have widely varying funeral customs depending on the teacher followed, and nothing can be assumed to be held in common.

HINDUS

Hindus do not normally insist on one approved funeral director to handle funerals; there is no central authority for those who adhere to this religion, and rites and customs vary enormously.

There are thousands of Hindu deities, which are all held to be manifestations of the same God. The three main deities are Brahma, the Creator; Vishnu, the Preserver; and Shiva, the Destroyer. Hindu belief in reincarnation means that most individuals face death in the hope of achieving a better form in their next incarnation. Death is therefore relatively insignificant, although there is likely to be open mourning with much weeping and physical contact by the family and friends.

Hindus are always cremated (with the exception of babies and small children), and never buried. Prior to the cremation, most Hindus bring their dead into a chapel of rest, where the body must be wrapped in a plain sheet and placed on the floor. Most light lamps or candles, and those who come to view will probably burn incense sticks. There are normally no objections to the body being handled by non-Hindus, but this and all burial rites are capable of great variation. The family concerned will be explicit about the rites required by their form of Hinduism. Many families arrange repatriation of the ashes to India to be scattered in the river Ganges. The river Soar in Leicestershire has also been approved for scattering of Hindu and Sikh ashes instead of the Ganges. Your funeral director will advise if a river near to you has been authorised for the purpose.

❝ Hindus are always cremated and never buried. ❞

JEWS

Scattered from their homeland by the Roman army in AD 70, the Jews dispersed across the world and adopted many different practices and interpretations of the Mosaic Law, yet always maintaining their essential unity. Orthodox Jews believe that the Law was literally handed to Moses by God, while Progressive Jews (divided into Reform, Liberal and Conservative groups) believe that the Law, while inspired, was written down and influenced by many different authors. Orthodox Jews are therefore

If a secular Jew is appointed as executor, or is responsible for making funeral arrangements, it is essential that enquiries are made into the religious background of the deceased, so that the appropriate rabbi may be contacted.

extremely strict on the observation of funeral rites, while other Jews vary in their attitudes.

When a Jew dies, the body is traditionally left for eight minutes while a feather is placed on the mouth and nostrils to give any indications or signs of breathing. Eyes and mouth are then closed by the oldest son, or nearest relative. Many Jews follow the custom of appointing 'wachers': people who stay with the body night and day until the funeral, praying and reciting psalms. The dead are buried as soon as possible. No Orthodox Jew will accept cremation, although it is increasingly chosen by other groups. Orthodox rabbis will sometimes permit the burial of cremated remains in a full-sized coffin, and say Kaddish (the mourner's prayer) for the person concerned.

If a man subscribes to a synagogue burial society, he and his wife or his dependent children will be buried, free, by the society in its cemetery. The funeral and coffin will be very simple, and there will be no flowers. Orthodox Jews are never cremated, and postmortem examination, embalming or bequeathing a body for medical purposes is not allowed. Reform non-orthodox Jews are more flexible, and permit cremation. The coffin and funeral will always be simple, but flowers may be allowed.

Jewish funerals are usually arranged by a Jewish funeral agency (such as United Synagogues (www.unitedsynagogue.org.uk)). Otherwise, the local Jewish community will arrange a contract with a Gentile funeral service, under which all Jewish funerals will be carried out according to strict rabbinical control. A man may be buried with his own prayer shawl or the burial society may provide one.

A Jewish burial society may agree to carry out the funeral of a Jew who was not a member of a synagogue and had not been subscribing to any burial society, but his family will be charged for the funeral and the cost will be considerable. There is rarely any difference between the funeral of members of the same synagogue; all are simple.

If a Jew dies when away from home, it is the responsibility of the relatives to bring the body back at their own expense for the synagogue burial society to take over.

The Jewish Bereavement Counselling Service (www.jvisit.org.uk/jbcs/index. htm) offers support to those who have lost loved ones.

MUSLIMS

Muslims live according to the teaching of the Qur'an, which has specific instructions concerning death and burial. There are different forms of Islam, each with its own variation of funeral rites, but in the UK the majority are Sunni Muslims, and the remaining are mostly Shia Muslims.

Muslims are always buried, never cremated. Traditionally, there is no coffin – the body is wrapped in a plain white sheet and buried within 24 hours of death in a simple grave, which must be raised between 10 and 30cm (10 and 12in) from the ground, and must not be walked, sat or stood upon. Most cemeteries in Britain, however, require a coffin for burial or cremation. Many British cemeteries insist on levelling the graves as soon as possible, which has led to some authorities providing special areas for Muslim burials; where

❝ Muslims are never cremated, but always wrapped in a white sheet and buried within 24 hours of death in a simple grave. ❞

there is none, families can suffer great distress. Because of the need for haste in burials, requests for postmortems and organ donation are usually, but not always, refused.

Muslims believe that the soul remains for some time in the body after death, and the body remains conscious of pain. Bodies must therefore be handled with great care and sensitivity, and disposable gloves worn at all times by those handling the body: the body must never be touched directly by a non-Muslim. Embalming is not normally practised, but is permissible where the body has to be conveyed over long distances.

The funeral service will take considerable time. There will be ritual washing, at least 30 minutes of prayer at the mosque, possible return to the family home, prayers at the graveside

Muslims and laying out

Normally, the family will attend to laying out the body, and they will turn the head over the right shoulder to face Mecca, which in the UK is roughly to the southeast. The body will be wrapped in a plain sheet and taken home or to the mosque for ritual washing: men will wash male bodies, and women female. Camphor is normally placed in the armpits and body orifices, and the body will be dressed in clean white cotton clothes or a special white shroud brought back personally from Mecca.

> **❝ Muslims must be buried facing Mecca, with the head over the right shoulder, so graves lie northeast/southwest. ❞**

and the filling in of the grave. Relatives and friends will carry the coffin at shoulder height, passing it from one to another, and they will want to see the face of the deceased after the final prayer at the graveside. Muslims must be buried facing Mecca, with the head over the right shoulder; hence graves must lie northeast/southwest, with the head at the southwest end. The family will normally perform all rites and ceremonies, together with the imam, the spiritual leader of the local mosque.

 For more information on funeral customs of all forms of religion, go to www.funerals-and-flowers.com/death-and-funeral-customs.html.

SIKHS

After death, men are dressed in a white cotton shroud and turban; young women are dressed in red, and older women in white. The family will almost always want to lay out the body, and will want cremation to take place as soon as possible – in India, it would normally be within 24 hours.

Sikhism developed from Hinduism in the 15th century and has much in common with it, but with a strong emphasis on militarism. There is a common belief in reincarnation, and the fact of death is normally accepted calmly.

Sikhs are always cremated, never buried; the Sikh family will insist in every instance that their dead are cremated with all five 'K symbols' present. Considerable diplomacy may be required to satisfy both family and crematorium authorities.

The coffin will normally be taken home and opened for friends and family to pay their last respects and will then be taken either to the gurdwara, for the main funeral service, or direct to the crematorium, where the oldest son will, instead of lighting the traditional funeral pyre, press the crematorium button or see the coffin into the cremator. The ashes will be required for scattering in a river or at sea; it is not unusual for one member of the family to take them to India to scatter them in the Punjab.

Stillborn babies, by exception, are usually buried.

❝ Sikhs are never buried, always cremated. The ashes are scattered in a river or sea, sometimes in the Punjab region. ❞

The Sikh symbols of faith

There are five symbols of faith, which are vitally important to every Sikh.

- The Kesh is the uncut hair, which, for men, is always turbaned.
- The Kangha is a ritual comb to keep the hair in place; this is never removed.
- The Kara is a steel bracelet worn on the right wrist (or left if left-handed).
- The Kirpan is a small symbolic dagger, which may actually vary in size from a brooch to a broadsword - and the Sikh will never be separated from it.
- The Kaccha are ceremonial undergarments, which are never completely removed, even while bathing.

NON-RELIGIOUS SERVICES

There is no necessity to have a religious ceremony, or indeed any kind of funeral ceremony at all. It is possible for a cremation or burial to take place with no one present, although this is unusual. However, because some kind of ceremony is customary, if you do not want one or the dead person had made it clear that he or she did not want one, it is important that the executor or whoever is in charge of the arrangements is aware of this and they will probably want to make this fact known among close associates of the deceased.

If a body is to be buried in a churchyard without a religious ceremony, or with a ceremony held by an officiant of another denomination, you should give the incumbent of the parish 48 hours' notice in writing; in practice, it should be possible to make the necessary arrangements in a telephone conversation. The usual parish regulations and fees still apply, and additional fees for the officiant may be involved.

If a body is to be buried in a cemetery or cremated at a crematorium without a religious ceremony, tell the funeral director or the authorities at the time the funeral is being arranged. There will normally be no difficulties, provided it is clear that the proceedings will be properly conducted. Where there is not going to be a religious ceremony, whoever is in charge of the funeral arrangements must also make arrangements for the details of the ceremony.

If you want a non-religious ceremony without an officiant, on the lines of a Society of Friends (Quaker) meeting, you must make sure that those present either know already how such a ceremony works or are told at the beginning. The funeral director or the cemetery or crematorium staff will be able to assist with explaining the practicalities of such an event.

More commonly, people choose to have an officiant or celebrant who prepares and conducts the ceremony instead of a religious minister. This may be a member of the family or a close friend, or a professional celebrant from a non-religious organisation. The only qualification is some experience of handling meetings. It is helpful if the person has some experience of speaking in public and is confident that the responsibility of conducting the ceremony will not be too emotionally overwhelming for them.

Humanist funeral officiants accredited by the British Humanist Association can conduct a funeral (see

The British Humanist Association website is www.humanism.org.uk and their national helpline number is 020 7079 3580, or see the book *Funerals without God: Practical Guide to Nonreligious Funerals.*

box, below left). Most humanist officiants do not permit any reference to a god within the ceremony so this will be a comfortable choice for atheists, but may be more difficult for people with a more tenuous faith or who are agnostic. There are also civil celebrants who create a ceremony completely according to the wishes of the family, which may include some religious content.

The Institute of Civil Funerals (www.iocf.org.uk) provides training and accreditation to civil funeral celebrants who may work independently, be employed by a civil ceremonies provider or a local authority.

It will also be possible in some areas for an experienced funeral director to conduct the service. In the circumstances surrounding a funeral arrangement, trusting relationships are often formed very quickly, and some people feel they would rather be helped in this way by the funeral director than someone who they do not know.

The form of a non-religious ceremony

A non-religious ceremony may take any form, provided it is decent and orderly. Clearly 'decent and orderly' is a matter of personal perception and especially if you are not using a funeral director, it is wise to discuss what is planned with the cemetery or crematorium management. In a cemetery it is particularly important to give some consideration to the needs of other bereaved who may be visiting graves at the same time as the funeral is taking place.

The usual procedure is for the officiant to explain the ceremony, after which there may be readings of appropriate prose or poetry, tributes either by the officiant or others present, and the playing of appropriate music. It is common to allow a time of silence when the deceased may be remembered personally, and religious people may offer silent prayers. These

❝ Civil celebrants will create a ceremony according to the wishes of the family, which may or may not include some religious content. ❞

Burial or cremation without a ceremony

If you want no ceremony at all, you may choose to have a few members of the family or close friends to attend the committal in silence or with some music being played. The alternative is to have no one present, in which case mourners may choose to have an alternative ceremony elsewhere.

ceremonies are not intended to oppose religious funerals, but are alternatives for people who would feel it hypocritical to have a religious service, or who want a respectful celebration of the death that has occurred without a religious emphasis.

OTHERS

There are a great variety of religious groups that originated in Christianity but have diverged from it, which include the Mormons, Jehovah's Witnesses, Christadelphians, Christian Scientists, Scientologists, the Unification Church and the Children of God. For most, while differences in doctrine are held to be immensely important, there is little deviation from orthodox Christian practice as far as funerals are concerned. Funerals may well take longer, however, which may cause difficulties in fitting in with crematorium schedules.

Some groups, such as Baha'i and Hare Krishna have their roots in Hinduism, and may adhere more closely to Hindu funeral rites than any other.

Some New Age culture also includes aspects of eastern faiths, such as Hinduism, and those who practise yoga or transcendental meditation may adopt the Hindu philosophies that lie behind them, which will, in due course, affect the funeral arrangements that will need to be made.

PAGANS

Woodland burials are particularly attractive to people who describe themselves as pagans, deriving their faith from pre-Christian religions, such as Druidism and forms of animism.

❝ Woodland burials are particularly attractive to people who describe themselves as pagans. ❞

Obtaining probate

Sorting out the affairs of a person who has died can appear to be a bewildering task; certainly, at first there may be a lot to do, but taken one step at a time, it should be fairly straightforward. This chapter leads you carefully through each stage.

Applying for probate

The term 'probate' (or 'probate of the will') means a court order issued to one or more people ('the executors') by the Probate Registry authorising them to deal with an estate. The Probate Registry must grant probate and, until this is done, none of the deceased's property should be sold, given away or disposed of.

If the deceased has not made a will, the next of kin will usually have to apply to the Probate Registry for a document called 'letters of administration'. The flow chart overleaf sets out the essential steps of applying for probate of the will.

When you apply for probate of the will (as executor) or letters of administration (as administrator) you must establish that you are legally entitled to do so. Once granted – known as the **grant of representation** – that document is legal proof that you are entitled to claim the assets of the deceased, not for yourself but in your capacity as personal representative. You must then administer the estate according to the law – either following the will or the rules of intestacy.

A certified copy of the death certificate is required to apply for probate. Probate may be obtained using a coroner's interim certificate, but the estate should not be distributed until the conclusion of the inquest and the death is registered.

DO I NEED TO APPLY FOR PROBATE?

If all the property of the deceased passes automatically to a beneficiary, probate may not be necessary. It is, however, normally required by the asset holder, such as a bank, if the value of the estate exceeds £5,000, but the Administration of Estates (small payments) Act 1965 allows some small estates to be administered without obtaining probate.

Probate will be required in order to sell or transfer any property held only in the name of the deceased. It would not be needed if the only asset was a

 Your local probate registry is your first point of contact. Either phone the helpline 0845 302 0900 or go to website www.hmrc.gov.uk/inheritancetax/index.htm and follow the links to probate. From here you will find links to all relevant websites. The form PA2 - How to obtain probate, which is available from www.hmcourts-service.gov.uk - is a useful guide to get hold of immediately.

Accounting to HM Revenue & Customs

If the value of the estate is low-value (meaning no more than £325,000 (2009-10), or exempt (meaning that the estate is valued at no more than £1 million but there is no tax to pay because of bequests to a surviving spouse or civil partner or charity), you only need to deliver a simplified account to HM Revenue & Customs (HMRC).

house held jointly as beneficial joint tenants. Probate is needed if the deceased held property as one of two or more tenants in common.

A house or flat could be advertised for sale soon after the death of the owner, but remember that contracts should not be exchanged before probate has been granted.

A lay executor who distributes the assets of an estate without obtaining probate might miss the obligation to submit an account to HM Revenue & Customs (HMRC) for Inheritance Tax (IHT) purposes, especially where a substantial gift had been made in the seven years prior to the death or for a longer period if there had been a reservation of interest. This failure could result in serious consequences for the executor.

When and why letters of administration are needed

If someone dies intestate – that is, without making a will – the rules of

❝You must be legally entitled to apply for probate of the will or letters of administration. ❞

intestacy say who can be the administrator and who should benefit from the estate (see pages 161–2). As an administrator you have to apply for letters of administration for exactly the same reasons as an executor has to apply for probate. You may run into difficulties if someone else in the family is equally entitled to apply for letters of administration and you cannot agree who should apply. It could also make it hard to decide who will arrange the funeral and who will take charge of the house. Generally speaking, the grant is made to the first applicant but, in the case of a dispute between equally entitled administrators, consult the Registrar of the Probate Registry.

 For more information on how to obtain probate, contact the Probate and Inheritance Tax Helpline on 0845 302 0900 or go to website www.courtservice.gov.uk and click on the 'Forms and Guidance' tab or search for 'probate'.

Applying for probate: the procedure

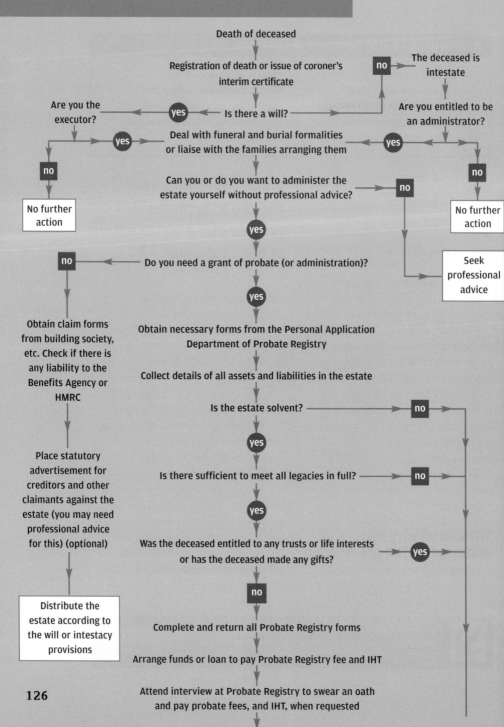

Death of deceased

Registration of death or issue of coroner's interim certificate → no → The deceased is intestate

Is there a will? → yes → Are you the executor? / no → Are you entitled to be an administrator?

Deal with funeral and burial formalities or liaise with the families arranging them

Are you the executor? → yes ↑

Are you entitled to be an administrator? → yes ←

no → No further action

no → No further action

Can you or do you want to administer the estate yourself without professional advice? → no → Seek professional advice

yes

Do you need a grant of probate (or administration)? → no → Obtain claim forms from building society, etc. Check if there is any liability to the Benefits Agency or HMRC

yes

Obtain necessary forms from the Personal Application Department of Probate Registry

Collect details of all assets and liabilities in the estate

Place statutory advertisement for creditors and other claimants against the estate (you may need professional advice for this) (optional)

Is the estate solvent? → no

yes

Is there sufficient to meet all legacies in full? → no

yes

Was the deceased entitled to any trusts or life interests or has the deceased made any gifts? → yes

no

Distribute the estate according to the will or intestacy provisions

Complete and return all Probate Registry forms

Arrange funds or loan to pay Probate Registry fee and IHT

Attend interview at Probate Registry to swear an oath and pay probate fees, and IHT, when requested

126

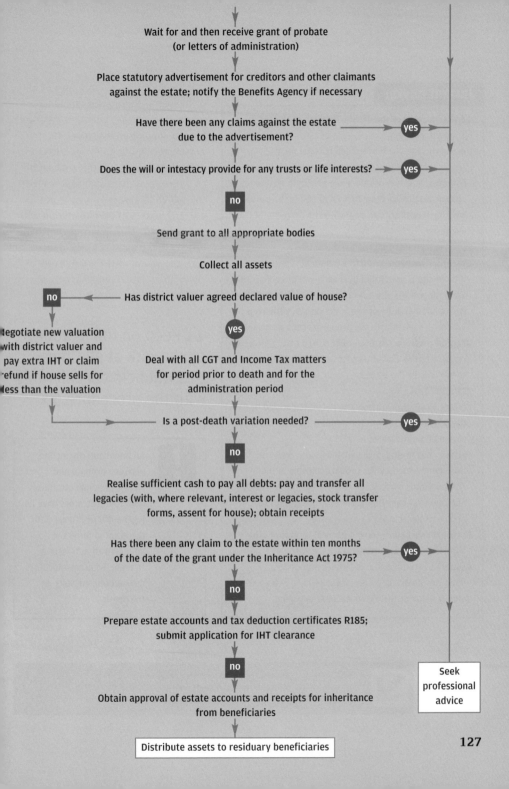

Wait for and then receive grant of probate
(or letters of administration)

Place statutory advertisement for creditors and other claimants
against the estate; notify the Benefits Agency if necessary

Have there been any claims against the estate
due to the advertisement? → yes →

Does the will or intestacy provide for any trusts or life interests? → yes →

no

Send grant to all appropriate bodies

Collect all assets

no ← Has district valuer agreed declared value of house?

Negotiate new valuation with district valuer and pay extra IHT or claim refund if house sells for less than the valuation

yes

Deal with all CGT and Income Tax matters
for period prior to death and for the
administration period

Is a post-death variation needed? → yes →

no

Realise sufficient cash to pay all debts: pay and transfer all
legacies (with, where relevant, interest or legacies, stock transfer
forms, assent for house); obtain receipts

Has there been any claim to the estate within ten months
of the date of the grant under the Inheritance Act 1975? → yes →

no

Prepare estate accounts and tax deduction certificates R185;
submit application for IHT clearance

no

Obtain approval of estate accounts and receipts for inheritance
from beneficiaries

Distribute assets to residuary beneficiaries

Seek
professional
advice

127

Jargon buster

Administration of the estate The task of the executor or administrator

Administrator The name given to a personal representative if not appointed by a valid will. The administrator will usually have to obtain letters of administration to show that he or she is the person with legal authority to deal with the property of the deceased

CGT Capital Gains Tax

Executor The name given to a personal representative if he or she is appointed by a valid will or codicil. The executor will usually have to apply for probate of the will to show that he or she is the person with legal authority to deal with the property of the deceased

Grant of probate The document issued by the probate registry to the executors of a will to authorise them to administer the estate

IHT Inheritance Tax

Letters of administration The document issued by the probate registry to the administrator of the estate of an intestate

Letters of administration with will annexed The document issued by the probate registry to the administrator when there is a will but the will does not deal with everything, for example, it fails to appoint an executor

Personal representatives A general term for both administrators and executors

Residue Everything that is left once all debts, liabilities, taxes, costs and legacies have been paid

Solvent Value of the assets exceeds any debts

If a will deals with part but not all of the administration (for instance, where the will says who gets what but fails to appoint an executor), the person entitled to apply for letters of administration makes the application to the registrar. The applicant, called the **administrator** in this case, is granted '**letters of administration with will annexed**'. The applicant can then distribute the estate in accordance with the will or, if the will fails to cover an essential point, in accordance with the rules of intestacy.

> ❝ Keep on top of your paperwork at all times; this will help considerably with the procedure. ❞

 An important distinction between probate and letters of administration is that administrators have no legal authority to act until the grant of letters of administration is issued to them, whereas executors may act immediately on the death.

 Who can apply for letters of administration? See page 161 for a list setting out in detail the order of those entitled to apply for letters of administration.

Checklist for personal representatives

In cases where the house has to remain empty after the death of its owner it is important for the executor to safeguard the house and its assets. Do not go alone or you may be accused of taking items or money that other beneficiaries believe the deceased had in their possession.

- **Check the insurance** on the house is adequate and valid.
- **Remove any valuables** for safe keeping (don't forget to notify your own insurers if you are looking after the valuables). Make sure the other beneficiaries know what you are doing.
- **Advise the police** and see if a neighbour is willing to keep an eye on the house for you.
- **You may wish to keep the services running** but you might find that you have to turn off the water to maintain insurance cover through the winter. Discuss the situation with the insurers to make sure you are as fully covered as possible.

- **If there is a car,** it will cease to be covered by the deceased's policy although, as a short-term measure, the insurers may agree to fire and theft cover if it remains in a garage.
- **Arrange with the post office** that all mail will be redirected to one of the executors. An application form can be obtained from any post office. A fee is payable depending on the number of months the service is needed. This forwarding service is useful where a house will be standing empty.
- **Reduce junk mail** by registering the deceased on the Bereavement Register or Mailing Preference Service (see useful addresses).

Executors not willing to act

There may be a number of reasons why someone might not want to be an executor: for instance, a relative or friend who had had no contact with the testator for a long period, or someone who simply does not want to be troubled with the chore and responsibilities of the administration. If you have no wish to take part in the administration, you can renounce probate (obtain a **form of renunciation** from OyezStraker, see box below). Alternatively, you can take a back seat but remain a potential executor by allowing your fellow executor to apply

To contact OyezStraker go to website www.oyesformslink.co.uk, and for the Probate Office, go to www.courtservice.gov.uk. In Northern Ireland you will need to contact the Probate Office: www.nidirect.gov.uk.

for probate with 'power reserved' to you. To do this they must serve notice on you (obtain a **power reserved letter** from the Probate Registry).

If one of the executors renounces, the substitute (if one is named in the will) automatically comes in, unless that person also renounces.

It is possible for a person named as executor in the will to appoint an attorney for the purpose of obtaining the grant; the attorney then acts as if they had actually been named as the executor in the will. (The appropriate form for this can also be obtained from the Oyez shops.)

A personal representative who has obtained a grant can appoint an attorney to act for him or her in the rest of the administration. Usually the power lasts for one year and relieves a personal representative of the form-signing part of the administration. It can be useful where the executor is abroad or infirm. The rules are complicated, and, if any question of incapacity through old age or mental illness arises, you should seek legal advice.

DO-IT-YOURSELF

There are examples of people sorting out legal problems themselves and conducting quite complicated cases without legal help. Some 'litigants in person', as they are called, have taken cases to court alone, and many people have bought or sold a house without a solicitor. Whereas a litigant in person and a do-it-yourself house-buyer cannot expect special treatment from the other side, a personal representative will find that special arrangements are in place at the Probate Registry to help him or her to obtain probate without a solicitor. See the chart on pages 132–7 for a step-by-step breakdown of what needs to be done. The Probate Registry form for guidance to apply for probate without a solicitor is PA2. Download it from the London Probate Registry website (see below).

WHEN TO USE PROFESSIONAL ADVICE

There are, however, some good reasons as to why it might be worth employing legal help from a solicitor or specialist probate service:

- **Any number of complexities** can arise in connection with the administration of an estate.
- **Often the personal representatives** are busy people, without the time to cope with the legal side of an administration and would not contemplate administering an estate without employing a professional adviser.

 The London Probate Registry website is www.courtservice.gov.uk: use the search box to find form PA2. The Bereavement Advice Centre also produces a free article to carrying out probate: go to www.bereavementadvice.org.

- **Professionals carry insurance** in case a mistake is made. An executor without a legal background might make a mistake and would be personally liable.
- **A good knowledge of the law** is essential when the deceased owned their own business, for instance, or was a partner in a firm, or was involved in an insurance syndicate, or where there is agricultural property, or when family trusts are involved.
- **The same applies** where, on an intestacy or under the will, some of the property is to pass to children who are under the age of 18. Their rights are called minority interests and particular legal problems can arise regarding them.
- **Another situation** that usually requires legal advice is one in which, on an intestacy, some long-forgotten relative is entitled to a share in the estate. The problems involved in tracing relatives who have apparently disappeared generally require careful handling, as does the situation if they are not found.
- **Homemade wills,** particularly on printed forms, sometimes contain ambiguities or irregularities that can create difficulties, and legal help about the interpretation may be needed to avoid errors. An executor who wrongly interprets a will and fails to distribute to a lawfully entitled beneficiary may well become financially liable for the consequences of that mistake.
- **The will** creates a life interest – for example, a family member is entitled to remain in the home for the remainder of their lifetime although ownership has passed to someone else.
- **A professional** should also be consulted if there is a possibility of anyone seeking a share, or a larger share, of the deceased's estate under the Inheritance (Provision for Family and Dependants) Act 1975.

Negligence by executors and administrators

If the administration is being conducted by an executor who is also a solicitor, or if you have instructed a solicitor to deal with the administration for you, that person is liable at law if there is any negligence. A solicitor must hold insurance to cover this possibility.

If you are a lay executor, always take advice when a problem crops up that you do not understand. Otherwise you may be personally liable if things go wrong. If you act on advice from a solicitor (preferably in writing) and the advice is wrong, the solicitor is liable.

If the estate is insolvent – if the debts exceed the value of the assets – care is required. The same applies where, although the estate is solvent, there is not sufficient to pay all the legacies in full or there is no residue. If you arrange a funeral but there is no money in the estate to cover it, you will have to foot the bill.

Legal fees

Legal fees for dealing with an estate are paid out of the deceased's property. They are a legitimate expense, like the funeral expenses and the IHT. The personal representatives do not have to pay them out of their own pockets: along with any other debts and taxes, legal costs are usually paid first from the assets of the estate, after which the remaining monies are distributed to the beneficiaries.

Solicitors should charge fees in accordance with the Solicitors' (Non-Contentious Business) Remuneration Order 1994. This sets out the elements that can affect the final fee, including the time spent, the complexity of the estate and its value. The order also sets out the rights of clients to information and interest.

Clearly, the charges will be considerably less for a straightforward administration than for one in which complicated matters arise, although the professional may not know about them at the outset.

If the will states that a bank is to be the executor, it is worth talking to the bank at an early stage if you wish to challenge its fee scales, as banks still tend to calculate their charges according to a percentage of the gross estate. Typical charges would be 5 per cent of the first £75,000, with 3 per cent levied on the next £50,000, and 2 per cent on any balance over £125,000. If the estate is under £10,000, a minimum charge of £500 may be levied, but there can also be additional fees.

Probate specialist companies (who often employ solicitors) will give you details of their charging schedules and terms and conditions.

The application for probate

There is a Personal Application Department in each of the Probate Registries, which has special staff, forms and procedures designed to smooth the path of the inexperienced layman.

The help and advice given by the Personal Application Department of a Probate Registry is confined to getting the grant of probate or letters of administration, and the personal representative has to take responsibility for the rest of the administration.

In cases where IHT is payable, the Capital Taxes Office (a branch of HM Revenue & Customs) is geared up to help the layman, but great care is needed to ensure that a mistake or omission does not have financial consequences that fall on the shoulders of the personal representative. You must have a clear understanding of what you are doing and what your obligations are.

> **❝ In cases where IHT is payable you must take great care to ensure no mistakes are made. ❞**

OBTAINING A WILL

If the will is lodged in the bank, the executor has to sign for it or acknowledge its safe receipt in writing if it is sent by post. Where several executors are named in the will, the bank should ask for all their signatures before releasing the will to one of them on the understanding that in due course all the executors will sign an acknowledgement.

Sometimes the will may be held in a professional's office safe. There should be no need for the professional to keep the will, and they should release it to the executors against their signatures if they all sign a receipt for it. If the professional is also one of the executors, they will expect to be involved in the administration. The professional can be asked to renounce, but will charge for this and is not obliged to agree. If the firm is to deal with the administration of the estate, make sure you are clear about the basis on

 Having trouble finding your local probate registry? Go to website www.direct.gov.uk and search for 'probate'.

which the firm will charge (see Legal fees on page 132). If the professional who was appointed an executor has left the firm concerned, or has retired, he must be contacted. The professional may be prepared to renounce as executor, leaving you free to administer the estate without having to use a particular firm of solicitors or other professional advisers.

The reading of a will

A formal reading of the will to the family after the funeral is a ritual that now happens mostly (though not entirely) in the world of fiction. It is usual for the executor or administrator to inform the beneficiaries of the contents of the will as it affects that individual at an early stage although you should remember that anyone can see a copy once probate has been obtained. There is a small risk that the will might be found invalid, or a later will might be found, or that there is not enough in the estate to pay out all the legacies, so that no legacy can be confirmed until after probate is granted and the estate administered. That might be a reason to wait but, otherwise, the beneficiaries might become upset if the contents of the will are kept from them.

AN EXECUTOR'S FIRST ACTIONS

Executors have to make sure that all the testator's wishes are carried out as far as is possible. They owe a duty of the utmost faith not only to the deceased but also to the probate court, the creditors of the estate and the beneficiaries. They are under an obligation to realise the maximum benefit from the estate and can be challenged by the beneficiaries or the creditors if they fail to meet their obligations. They must therefore keep all matters of the administration of the estate entirely separate from their own personal affairs and be able to show, later on, by the preparation of estate accounts, that all the assets of the estate could be accounted for.

There are a few things that you should do early on in the proceedings:

- **Once the death** has been registered, obtain copies of the death certificates (see page 49).
- **Establish from the will** that you have full authority to act as an executor, either singly or jointly. If you are a joint executor, decide who is going to do what and get this down in writing. Even if you divide responsibilities, you will still both have to sign the probate

" A formal reading of the will to the family after the funeral is now something that mainly belongs to the world of fiction. "

Provisional details of a sample estate

Leave a column at the right-hand side blank so that you can fill in the actual figures alongside the estimates as they become known. Put this provisional list of assets right at the front of a file for easy access.

Assets	£ estimated value	£ actual value
Cash, including money in banks, building societies and National Savings		
Household and personal goods		
Stocks and shares quoted on the Stock Exchange		
Stocks and shares not quoted on the Stock Exchange		
Insurance policies, including bonuses and mortgage protection policies		
Money owed to the person who has died		
Partnership and business interests		
Freehold/leasehold residence of the person who has died		
Other freehold/leasehold residential property		
Other land and buildings		
Any other assets not included above		
SUB-TOTAL		

Liabilities		
The funeral		
Household bills		
Building Society mortgage		
Probate fees and expenses (approx)		
SUB-TOTAL		

Approximate net value of the estate (assets less liabilities)		

Estimated Inheritance Tax

Net value of estate		
Less nil-rate band	325,000	
Estimated IHT @ 40% =		

documents and claim forms. You are both legally responsible for the proper administration of the estate.

- **Search the contents** of the deceased's deed box, if it exists. Many important documents might be stored in there, such as a life insurance policy, NS&I Certificates, a building society account book, Premium Bonds and share certificates.

- **Get organised.** It's worth setting up a large file with different sections for each organisation you will be contacting, e.g. bank, insurance company, building society. Take a copy of the will for the file, too. If the original gets damaged in any way, the Probate Registry might raise queries about it.

- **Start preparing a list** of assets, with an estimate as to the value of each (see page 135).

- **Open an executor's account.**

 Provided you keep the necessary receipts and a separate note of the amounts involved, executors are entitled to recover any expenses reasonably incurred in the administration of the estate. On the other hand, you cannot claim payment for time spent.

❝Important documents might be stored in a deed box, so if there is one, make this your first port of call.❞

Valuing of the assets

Now that you have a good idea of what is likely to be involved in administering the estate, write to all the banks, building societies and insurance companies to find out the precise value of each asset.

In these letters you are requesting a **claim form for signature by the executors** and you should include:

- The relevant account or policy number.
- A description of the asset.
- The fact that you are the executor of the will of the deceased (name in full).
- The name of the co-executor, if there is one, and give their address.
- A death certificate.
- The fact that you will be able to send a copy of the grant of probate once you have received it.
- An enquiry as to whether it is a certificated holding (if you have no certificate).

66 After notification of someone's death, the bank will return cheques marked as 'drawer deceased'. **99**

BANK ACCOUNTS

In addition to obtaining the bank account details, establish if the deceased kept a deposit account at the branch and, if so, the balance at the date of death and the interest accrued to the date of death but not yet added to the account. The deceased might also have kept a deed box at the branch, or otherwise deposited any documents there, and this, too, is worth establishing now.

When a bank is given notice of a customer's death, cheques drawn on that account are returned unpaid with a note 'drawer deceased', and all standing orders or direct debit mandates cease.

- Any cheques drawn by the deceased (other than as a gift) but not met on presentation because notice of death has been lodged at the bank should be regarded as a debt due from the deceased to the payee.
- If any payments are to be made to the account, the amounts will be held by the bank in a suspense account for the time being.

Cut all plastic cards in half so that they cannot be used fraudulently.

Normally, a bank must not disclose to other people the details of how much is in a customer's account and what securities, deeds or other papers or articles are held, let alone hand them over. The exception is where the information is needed by the executors or administrators after a death so that the IHT accounts can be completed.

❝ The only time a bank can disclose other people's account details is when information is needed by an executor or administrator. ❞

Direct debits

Contact the companies concerned to explain there has been a death and that therefore any direct debits will cease. Let them know that you will settle any outstanding payment when the probate has been granted (if the estate is solvent).

Joint bank accounts

When assets are held in joint names, it may be that the holders intended that, in the event of a death, that person's share would pass to the survivor.

If it is impossible to show who contributed what, or if the items in the account are too numerous or complicated to make it possible to distinguish the sources, the balance might be considered to be held equally by its joint holders.

However, where the joint account holders are husband and wife, it is presumed that, even if all the money came only from the husband or only from the wife, it is held by them equally. Therefore, half the balance on the date of death would be taken as the value belonging to the spouse who has died. Circumstances may also show that a joint account held by an unmarried couple is owned equally between the joint account holders. It is best to settle any dispute in this area by agreement as the law can be vague on joint ownership disputes.

A joint account held by a couple has the advantage that the survivor can continue to draw on the account even though the other account holder has died. As it can take weeks or even months to get a grant of probate, this allows the survivor to have continued access to ready cash.

The balance in a personal joint account will usually pass automatically to the survivor and so bypasses the will (unless it is a trust account or some other specific agreement was made between the joint account holders). Nevertheless, the share of the deceased is included as an asset of the estate for IHT purposes – unless the survivor is the surviving spouse or civil partner, in which case it is an IHT-exempt transfer.

With any assets held jointly – building society accounts, savings bank accounts and investments, for instance – similar principles apply.

BUILDING SOCIETY ACCOUNT

When you write to a building society, enclose the passbook, if there is one, so that a note of the death can be made on it and to ensure there is no possibility of a fraudster making withdrawals on the account.

The amount shown in the book might not necessarily be the current balance of the account because of subsequent payments in or withdrawals, so it is best to ask for confirmation of:

- The capital balance at the date of death.
- Interest due but not added to the account at that date.
- What interest was credited to the account in the last tax year ending 5 April.

NATIONAL SAVINGS & INVESTMENTS (NS&I)

If there are any NS&I products, such as Savings Certificates and Premium Bonds, to realise, obtain claim form NSA 904 (2001 02) (Death of a holder of National Savings) from the NS&I website: www.nsandi.com.

Valuations of the various assets will be returned to you together with repayment/transfer forms, depending on how you indicate the assets are to be dealt with.

Where the value of all NS&I Savings accounts or bonds (including interest and any Premium Bond prize won since the date of death – see

❝ A joint account held by a couple has the advantage that the survivor can continue to draw on the account even though the other account holder has died. **❞**

box, below) is £5,000 or less, it may normally be paid out without any grant having been obtained. NS&I will, however, ask if a grant is being obtained and, if so, may refuse to pay without sight of it unless the savings were held jointly or in trust.

INSURANCE POLICY

Check through any insurance policy to establish what type it is. If the policy has a named beneficiary, it will not form part of the estate. However, if there is no named beneficiary and the policy is with-profits, an additional sum will be paid to you, the executor, by the insurance company. In this instance, when you write to the company, you should ask for confirmation of the amount payable on death in addition to the sum assured.

VALUATION OF PROPERTY

Most people have some idea of the current value of the properties in their locality. It is not essential in the first instance to obtain a professional valuation from a firm of surveyors and valuers.

Whether you have a professional valuation or not, if the estate is large enough to incur IHT, your estimate will be checked sooner or later by an official called the **district valuer**. The district valuer knows the value of every sale in their district so there is no point in trying to understate the value of a house. However, for possible saving on IHT, at this stage you may decide to put down your lowest reasonable and justifiable estimate of value. The district valuer may query your figure later on if it is too low, but perhaps not if it is on the high side. If there is IHT to pay on the estate, you would be wise to bring in a professional valuer to prepare a valuation in case the district valuer should challenge your valuation.

Premium Bonds

Premium Bonds do not need to have an official valuation, but you should nevertheless notify NS&I of the bondholder's death as soon as possible by filling in form NAS 904 (www.nsandi.com or telephone 0845 964 5000). Premium Bonds retain their face value, and no question of interest arises. They cannot be nominated and cannot be transferred to beneficiaries but may be left in the prize draws for 12 calendar months following the death, and then cashed. The money can be reinvested in new bonds in the name of the beneficiary but these will have to wait three months before becoming eligible for inclusion in the prize draw.

Where it happens that a prize warrant has been paid into the deceased's bank account after the date of death but before either the bank or the Bonds and Stock Office has been notified to freeze the account or stop payment, the Bonds and Stock Office will ask for the prize to be returned so that a new warrant can be sent to the executors after probate has been registered.

"If the estate is large enough to incur Inheritance Tax, your estimate of the value of any property will always be checked by an official called the district valuer."

However (particularly in an estate where there is no IHT payable), pushing for a higher estimated value could mean less tax in the long run if there is a possibility that any future sale might be subject to Capital Gains Tax (CGT – see pages 148–9). The established value for IHT purposes will be the beneficiary's base cost for CGT, so a low IHT value on death might mean a larger gain on any future sale.

Where a house is not going to be sold, it is possible to agree a value for the house with the district valuer before applying for probate, but this can delay matters.

If the property is jointly owned

There are two different ways in which people may own a house or land jointly: as beneficial joint tenants or as tenants in common. Married couples and civil partners usually hold property as joint tenants, and business partners as tenants in common, but this isn't always the case.

- Where a house is owned by **joint tenants**, the share of the first to die passes to the survivor automatically on death. The survivor of joint tenants acquires the other half-share merely by surviving, irrespective of anything the will may say.
- In the case of **tenants in common**, however, the share of the first to die passes according to the will or intestacy. It could pass to the co-owner under the will, but that is not the same thing as the share passing

If you live in Scotland, Scottish law is different in certain places to the law of England and Wales, so turn to pages 173-7 for changes in the law that you need to be aware of.

to the survivor automatically, as happens when it is a joint tenancy, and it may go to someone quite different.

- If the property is held as tenants in common, you will have to know the proportions in which it is held (this could be unequal) in order to estimate the value of the share of the deceased at the date of death.
- For joint tenants, it will be half and half (or equal shares if there are more than two joint tenants).

❝ If there is an outstanding mortgage on the property, this must be taken into account when calculating IHT. ❞

 If there is any doubt as to whether the property is in the deceased's name alone or in joint ownership as a joint tenancy or tenancy in common, you must check what the deeds (or title) says.

Calculating the share of the house for IHT

Whenever a house is held in the joint names of two people (whether married or not) the value of the deceased person's share has to be declared for IHT purposes.

The vacant possession value at the date of death is the starting point in calculating the value of the deceased's share of the house for IHT. Suppose it is the figure of £200,000. In the case of a joint tenancy or a tenancy in common held in equal shares, that figure must be divided by two to determine the share of the one who has died. This would give a figure of £100,000.

Except where the joint owners are husband and wife or civil partners, HMRC accept that the value of a part share in jointly held property is usually worth less than simply the relevant share of the vacant possession value. This is because on the open market it will generally be hard to find a buyer willing to buy just a part share, especially if the surviving co-owner(s) have the right to stay in the property.

As a starting point, HMRC allow you to reduce the value of the deceased's share of a property by 10 per cent. In the example above, therefore, the £100,000 share of the £200,000 house would be reduced to £90,000 for IHT purposes. However, if the surviving owner has the right to stay in the property, the Revenue should accept a 15 per cent reduction. So, in this example, the value of the deceased's share would be £85,000.

When the property is owned jointly by husband and wife

Valuation officers do not allow any such reduction in the value because of what is called 'related property' provisions, which apply under the Inheritance Tax Act. However, if before the death the property was jointly owned by, say, brothers and sisters, or two or more friends, or parent and child, or any two people not married to each other, you should claim the reduction in the valuation.

❝ If the surviving owner has the right to stay in the property, the Revenue should accept a 15 per cent reduction in the value of the deceased's share of the property. ❞

Outstanding mortgage debts

Account must also be taken of any outstanding mortgage debt on jointly owned property. Suppose that it is £20,000; then the deceased's share of this debt would normally be half, that is £10,000. The result would be that the value of the deceased's share of the house (see main text, opposite) less the mortgage debt would be £75,000, assuming 15 per cent discount.

If there is any outstanding mortgage on the property, you need to obtain an exact figure from the mortgage lender showing the position at the date of death. If there is an endowment mortgage, you need to establish its position, too. You must also check when a house is given to the beneficiary. Is the gift free of the mortgage or subject to it?

 For the Which? report on Inheritance Tax, go to the Which? website: www.which.co.uk. Some of the content on the website is only available to subscribers - information for how to subscribe is given on the website. See also the Which? book *Giving and Inheriting* by Jonquil Lowe.

SHARES AND UNIT TRUSTS

For shares and unit trusts, you need to establish what their value was on the day of death.

You can find a rough estimate of what they were worth by looking up the closing prices in the paper. But for IHT purposes, it is necessary to work out their exact price, for which there is an accepted formula for all shares that have been bought and sold on the London Stock Exchange:

- On any particular day, there are sales of shares in nearly all the big companies (or plcs), and the prices often vary depending on the prevailing circumstances. At any one time two prices are quoted – the higher is that at which people buy and the lower at which people sell. The closing prices are the two prevailing prices of the share at the time in the afternoon when the stock exchange has closed dealing for the day.
- To work out the value that is officially recognised for probate purposes, you need to know the closing prices on the day of the deceased's death. *The Stock Exchange Daily Official List* (SEDOL – see below) gives the closing prices.

- Take as the figure a price that is one-quarter up from the lower to the higher figure. If, for example, the two figures in the quotation column are 100p and 104p, then you take 101p as the value; if the two prices are 245p and 255p, then you take 247.5p as the value. The prices quoted in the official list are often prices for every £1 share held; the nominal value of a share may be 20p, 25p, £1, or any one of many other amounts. It bears no relation to the actual value of the holding.

If there is a long list, it is probably better to write to the bank (but you might be charged for the valuation). Alternatively, a stockbroker would be able to provide this information quite easily, either on the telephone in the case of a few quotations, or by letter if there are more. When a stockbroker

Death at a weekend

If the death was at the weekend, prices from the official list for the Friday or for the Monday may be used and you may mix the Friday and Monday prices to the estate's advantage.

 You may be able to access the Stock Exchange Daily Official List (SEDOL) at your local reference library or a very large branch of a bank. You can also buy it for a relatively small sum from FT Information Services: www.ftid.com.

makes a valuation, his charge is based on a percentage of the value of the shares.

Checking the holdings

Check you have the correct holdings by writing to the registrar of each company concerned. The address of the registrar usually appears on the counterfoil of the dividend warrant. The counterfoil also acts as a certificate of Income Tax paid, so it is likely that these have been kept in a safe place. If you can't find the counterfoils, it may be because the deceased didn't keep them, or they may be at the bank if the dividends were credited there directly from the company, or they may be at the deceased's accountants. If, after further searching, you still can't find the certificate(s), make a note to get hold of a copy once you have been granted probate. To do this, you will have to contact the relevant company registrar (see box, below) and you will probably have to pay a fee. You also need to remember that some holdings may have a certificate while others may be uncertificated holdings.

Write the standard letter as outlined

 Bear in mind that you might later have to account to HM Revenue & Customs for Income Tax on any income from the securities that you receive while administering the estate.

on page 137 and ask for confirmation of the relevant holdings and whether there is any unclaimed dividend or interest payment held at the offices.

When a company does not want to distribute its dividend but wishes to retain the cash within the company, it will sometimes 'capitalise' the dividend and instead issue additional shares (called a **bonus, or scrip, issue**).

A **rights issue** is when a company offers its shareholders further shares at less than the market price. If, at the date of death, payment for a rights issue is due, contact the registrar to see if they will agree to postpone payment until probate is received. If not, the funds would have to be raised elsewhere (from the bank or by a loan from the executors or

Finding a company registrar

There is a book called the *Register of Registrars*, kept in some reference libraries, which gives details of the registrar of each company quoted on the stock exchange. Alternatively, you could telephone the head office of the companies concerned to find the proper address for the registrar.

beneficiaries to the estate), because the payment may secure a valuable asset to the estate. If payment is not made as required, the rights will be lost.

The same point could arise if a deceased person had just acquired shares in a newly privatised company. Sometimes the original subscription will be for only part of the price, and the balance will be payable by the owner of the shares some months later. If the date is missed, the share can be forfeited

Ex-dividend

If a price for shares has the letters 'xd' beside it, this means that the price was quoted 'ex-dividend'. This means that if the shares are sold, the seller – not the buyer – will receive the next dividend on these shares. The price the buyer pays is therefore lower than he would otherwise pay, to the extent of the dividend he is foregoing. This is because the company prepares the actual dividend cheques in advance in favour of the owner at that time, so if the shares are sold before the company sends out the cheque on the day the dividend is due, it will still go to the seller. This usually happens about six weeks before the date for payment of dividends.

Because the price does not reflect the full value of the shares, the dividend must be included as another asset in your list. Phone the registrar of the company to find out what the dividend is to be paid on each share. You can then calculate the total. The answer must be included as a separate asset in the HMRC account of the estate.

or lost, so it is important to ensure that the money is available from some source. It is always wise to check the correct procedure with each company's registrar because practice can vary from company to company.

Unit trusts

If you own shares in one company, you do not know how well that company is going to perform and therefore what profits it will earn, which directly affects the value of the shares. Many people consider it sensible to spread the risk by owning shares in a number of larger companies.

Some investment managers have specialised in this, and it is possible to buy units in a pool of investments in which the investment managers specifically aim to spread the risk. With unit trusts, you do not buy and sell specific shares in companies but buy and sell a specific number of units. This 'unit trust' industry is itself very specialised; investment managers now specialise in different funds so that units can be bought in a portfolio consisting, for example, of property companies, of UK companies or of overseas companies.

If the deceased owned such unit trusts, ask the trust manager to confirm the closing prices on the date of death together with the value of the holding.

Private companies

Although older 'Ltd' certificates are still valid, companies whose shares are quoted on the stock exchange are usually registered with the words 'Public Limited Company' or 'plc' at the end of the name. Private companies, whose shares are not quoted on the stock exchange (and which cannot always be freely sold), all have the word 'Limited' or 'Ltd' at the end of their name.

Valuing shares in a private company not quoted on the stock exchange requires expert help. Sometimes the secretary or accountant of the company concerned can state the price at which shares have recently changed hands, and this may be accepted for probate purposes. If not, detailed and possibly difficult negotiations may have to be undertaken and, unless the shares are of comparatively small value, it would be worthwhile to get an accountant to handle the matter. The basis of valuation is different depending upon whether the interest in the company is a minority or a majority shareholding.

❝Valuing shares is not straightforward - ask the relevant trust manager or company secretary to confirm closing prices on the day of death. ❞

PENSIONS

Quite often a pension scheme provides that a capital sum should become payable on the death of one of its members. For instance, if a member were to die while still an employee – that is, before retirement – the scheme might provide for the return of the contributions that had been made over the years by the member, and from which no benefit had been erived, because that person did not survive to collect the pension.

- If the lump sum that represents this return of contributions were part of the deceased's estate, it would have to be declared for IHT.
- However, in most schemes nowadays it would be paid 'at the trustees' discretion' and not be subject to IHT.
- Such schemes provide that the trustees may select who is to receive the capital sum (but they are bound by the rules of the particular scheme, and some are quite restrictive). However, schemes usually ask their members to fill in an 'expression of wish' form setting out the person or people they would like to receive the lump sum and the trustees will normally take this wish into account.
- Provided the payment is made genuinely at the trustees' discretion (and so the executors have no legal right to enforce the payment), there is normally no IHT regardless of to

whom the payment is made. In very limited cases - for example, where the member was terminally ill and has deliberately acted to increase the death benefit lump sum they leave - IHT could be due but not where the lump sum is left to a surviving spouse, civil partner or dependents.

Whatever the circumstances, it is probably best, where the deceased belonged to a pension scheme, to get a letter from the secretary of the pension fund to confirm the exact position regarding what the estate (as distinct from a dependent) is entitled to receive under the scheme. Even if it is only the proportion of the pension due for the last few days of life, obtain a letter to provide written confirmation for the purpose of IHT.

State benefits

If the deceased was receiving state retirement pension and/or other state benefits, such as attendance allowance, winter fuel payment, pension credit or income support, report the death to the Pension Service or Jobcentre Plus using the certificate of registration of death (BD8 in England and Wales, form 334/SA in Scotland and form 36

in Northern Ireland), which will be given to you by the registrar when you register the death.

The Pension Service or Jobcentre Plus will work out if any arrears of payments are due. These form part of the estate. They have to be declared for IHT and included in the probate paperwork.

INCOME TAX AND CAPITAL GAINS TAX (CGT)

Income Tax is usually based on a person's income received in the tax year that runs from 6 April to 5 April the following year. PAYE works so that a person's tax allowances are spread over the whole year and tax is deducted week by week, or month by month on the assumption that the taxpayer will go on having income throughout the year. If that person dies during the year, the PAYE assumptions are upset because the taxpayer did not live to receive the income throughout the tax year, and a tax repayment will be due because the full year's allowances can then be set against the income to the date of death. Where the deceased paid tax through self-assessment rather than PAYE, too little or too much tax may have been paid through their payments on account up to the date

For further information on benefits and allowances, see pages 199-203. Also, go to the Department of Work and Pensions (www.dwp.gov.uk), HM Revenue & Customs (www.hmrc.gov.uk), Jobcentre Plus (www.jobcentreplus.gov.uk) or the Pension service (www.pensionservice.gov.uk).

of death. Also, if the taxpayer was not liable for tax because their income did not exhaust the allowances due, the executor may be entitled to a tax repayment if the deceased received bank interest from which tax had been deducted. Any tax rebates must be included as part of the value of the estate.

You should explain the situation fully to the local inspector of taxes and, if necessary, go to see the inspector about any repayment that may be due because too much Income Tax was levied on the deceased during the tax year in which that person died. Although tax is claimed only on the amount of income received up to the date of death, tax allowances (such as a single person's or a married person's personal allowance) are granted for the full year, even if the death took place early in the tax year.

If the deceased had an accountant, it might be more convenient to ask the accountant to complete the tax return to the date of death.

Depending on the circumstances, you are likely to receive a tax return or a tax claim for completion.

 You are given no personal allowances to set against the estate income, but you can set off against the income any interest paid on a loan raised to pay the IHT.

a certificate (R185) showing what tax has been deducted from the income being passed on to any beneficiaries – see page 190.

Strictly speaking, you should notify HM Revenue & Customs within six months of the relevant year-end and complete a tax return. However, HM Revenue & Customs has recently extended its informal procedure to cover straightforward estates whose income for the administration period does not exceed £10,000. In these cases, the personal representatives can submit a simple computation of the tax liability. In other cases, a self-assessment return will be required.

Income received after the date of death

Where income is received after the date of death, you, as the personal representative, will be taxed, either by prior tax deduction or by assessment in the normal way. You will not pay the higher tax rate but, on final distribution, you need to provide

❝ If the deceased had an accountant, it might be more convenient to ask the accountant to complete the tax return to the date of death. ❞

CONTENTS OF PROPERTY AND PERSONAL ASSETS

The next item requiring valuation is the furniture and effects, known as 'the chattels'. This includes furniture in the property, household goods of all kinds, jewellery, clothes, the car and all personal possessions.

It may not be necessary to prepare a complete list, or to state the respective values of different kinds of articles – but the Capital Taxes Office (who deal with IHT) are becoming more interested in the value of personal belongings and household contents.

Where the person who has died was sharing the house with a husband (or wife) or any other person, it is important to realise that it is only the deceased's household goods, effects, furniture and so on, which need to be included in any valuation for IHT

included. If the deceased owned any particular items outright, the full value of those items will have to be included. (There may be specific items bought by the husband or the wife particularly for themselves, or acquired by way of inheritance from their own respective families. Such items could quite possibly have been regarded by them as belonging to one or the other, not owned by the two of them jointly.)

You should discuss with the other person concerned to ascertain what was owned by the deceased, what was owned by the other person and what was owned jointly.

It will usually be assumed that, in the case of a husband and wife, the items are owned jointly. If property is held by joint tenants who are not married or in a civil partnership, it will become owned by the surviving owner regardless of the provisions of the will or intestacy, although part of the value will have to be declared for tax purposes. In the case of other people, for example an unmarried couple, it is usually assumed that the person who paid for an item owns it. Obviously, the provisions in a will (or indeed, intestacy) can operate only on the property that is found to be part of the deceased's estate, and no tax is payable on anything owned by someone else.

> **❝If property is held by joint tenants, it will become owned by the surviving owner regardless of the provisions of the will.❞**

purposes. A husband and wife may have regarded all of the property as being jointly owned by the two of them so that, on the death of either, it becomes wholly owned by the survivor. In such a case, one-half of the value of all the contents should be

Valuing a car

The make and age of the car are the principal factors that affect its value;

its condition is another consideration. A study of the prices being asked for second-hand cars by local garages or dealers will give an indication of the value to within about £50. Do not forget to deduct any outstanding loan. If the car is on hire purchase, contact the hire purchase company to obtain its consent to sale (see also box, page 152).

Valuing jewellery

For probate purposes, it is the value for which jewellery could be sold that is needed; insurance value would be the cost of replacement, which is often considerably higher. You will have to pay a valuation fee, for which the jeweller will give you a receipt at the same time as the official valuation certificate. The fee can be included in expenses recovered from the estate due to you as probate representative.

Valuing paintings

When making a calculation of the total value of the effects, it is better to

Photographic evidence

HM Revenue & Customs pays particular attention to the estimated open-market values given for household and personal goods, so be ready to support your estimates with written and photographic evidence. It even looks at car registration numbers for additional value.

put a separate valuation on items of particular value, such as, say, paintings worth more than about £100. This can be reasonably easy to establish, perhaps because they were recently purchased or had been valued by an expert for insurance (although the insurance value is unlikely to be the same as the probate value). If not, you can obtain a verbal estimate of their value by taking them to a local auction house.

❝ It is better to put a separate value on any painting that is worth over, say, £100. This can be reasonably easy to establish. ❞

General valuation

More difficult to fix is a value for the great bulk of the household furniture and effects. How do you decide what the tables, chairs, beds, linen, cups and saucers, carpets, TV set, clothes and all the rest of it are actually worth? You have to decide what price they would get if sold to best advantage on the day of death. In practice, this means what they would fetch at an auction. Of course, the second-hand value of the great majority of items is considerably less than the cost when new.

Hire purchase

If there are any items being bought on hire purchase, it is sufficient to take a common-sense attitude by valuing the article as if it had been part of what the deceased owned, along with everything else, and then to treat any outstanding instalments as a debt due from the estate. Where the figures are large, as for example on a car, it might be better to declare the net value as an asset after deducting the outstanding debt, rather than bringing this in as a separate debt.

For IHT, you do not consider the cost of replacement, but the price they would fetch if sold second-hand. The Capital Taxes Office of HMRC does not expect you to provide an expert's valuation, or one that is accurate to within a few pounds, but a valuation that is honest and sensible, and says what the executor really thinks the items are worth. If the estate is liable to IHT expect the revenue to question the accuracy of estimated values.

DEBTS AND LIABILITIES

If anyone owes money to the deceased, include it in the list declared for IHT, as these count as assets. They are debts that are due to the estate. The items that fall within this category include the dividend on any shares, pensions due to the date of death and any Income Tax repayment.

Debts due from the deceased have to be listed, too. Any money that is owed reduces the estate for the purpose of calculating the total value: the liabilities are deducted from the assets. These debts can consist of almost anything: fuel bills, tax, telephone account, amounts due on credit cards or credit accounts, hire-purchase debts, an overdraft, for example. In addition, the funeral expenses are deducted (but not your expenses for administering the estate).

You will need to contact any companies and individuals that are owed money, explaining that they will be paid soon after probate has been granted.

Don't forget the cash

Cash is an asset – don't forget to gather any together and add it to your calculations.

 On page 135 there is a chart to show the provisional details of a sample estate. Continue to refer to it and fill in for your own needs as it gives you prompts for such things as deducting funeral expenses and household bills.

Not enough to meet the debts

In some cases, debts can be a big problem in administering an estate. If you discover that the estate is insolvent, do not continue with the administration and take advice immediately from an insolvency adviser or from a Citizens Advice Bureau (see box, below), an accountant or a solicitor. It may be necessary to petition the court immediately for a trustee to be appointed to administer the estate – otherwise, you may become personally liable for the administrative costs and the funeral expenses if you authorised them.

MOVING TOWARDS APPLYING FOR PROBATE

As you receive answers from your letters to the bank, building society, etc., you can start filling in the right-hand column of the deceased's list of assets and liabilities. Once you've heard from everyone – this could take at least a month – you can complete the forms that enable you to apply for the grant of probate. First, though, open an executor's account at your bank, so that you have somewhere specific to transfer money relating to the estate, which is separate from your own bank account.

❝If you discover that the estate is insolvent, do not continue with the administration: stop what you're doing and take immediate advice. ❞

x

 To find your nearest Citizens Advice Bureau (CAB) see your local phone book or go to www.adviceguide.org.uk.

Probate application forms

Do not be deterred by the many forms and booklets listed below relating to applying for probate. They are all clearly laid out and designed to make the job as straightforward as possible. If you have any queries, contact the Probate Registry or HM Revenue & Customs (see box, below).

There are several forms to obtain when applying for probate. From the Probate Registry you need:

- Form PA1: The probate application form
- Form PA1A: Guidance notes
- Booklet PA2: A guide to help a person applying for probate without a solicitor
- Form PA3: A list of probate fees
- Form PA4: A list of probate registries and interview venues.

If the value of the estate is more than £325,000 (2009–10) (including the deceased's share of any jointly owned assets, the value of assets held in trust and any gifts made within the last seven years), from the Capital Taxes Office at HMRC you need the following forms.

- IHT400: The Inland Revenue account
- IHT421: Probate summary
- IHT400 Notes: To help fill in IHT400, which contains supplementary pages
- IHT400 Calculation – worksheet
- IHT422: To obtain a tax reference
- IHT 14: A booklet that sets out the responsibilities of Personal Representations
- C4: Corrective account
- IHT 30: Clearance certificate

If the value of the estate is no more than £325,000 (2009–10) (or no more than £1 million and left largely to your spouse, civil partner and/or charity), from the Capital Taxes Office at HMRC you need different forms:

- IHT 205: Return of estate information

 The forms from the Probate Registry can be obtained from www.hmrc.gov.uk/inheritancetax/index.htm or telephone the helpline 0845 302 0900. The HM Revenue & Customs forms can be downloaded from the same site.

- IHT 206: Notes to help fill in IHT 205.
- **Filling in the probate application form (PA1):** Use the guidance notes from PA1a. This is an interactive form and can be filled in on-screen.
- **Filling in the return of estate information (IHT205):** Use the guidance notes from IHT206. If you can't determine the exact value of all items, reasonable estimates are acceptable (mark as 'estimated').
- **Filling in Inland Revenue account (IHT400):** Use the guidance notes that come with it. You can either assess any tax due yourself or ask HMRC (Capital Taxes) to do it for you.

SENDING OFF THE FORMS AND PAYING IHT

The back page of the probate application form PA1 sets out a checklist of forms to be sent to the Probate Registry but, where IHT is payable, form IHT400 must be sent to the Capital Taxes Office. If there is no IHT to pay, send form IHT 205 to the Probate Registry. The flowchart overleaf shows the sequence of events.

If there is IHT to be paid, this has to be done before the grant of probate can be issued, but a tax reference number must be obtained first. IHT is liable to be paid on the value of an estate over £325,000 (2009–10). It may be possible to increase the figure of £325,000 by using transferable, unused allowance from the estate of a spouse (or civil partner) who died previously. It is 40 per cent of the excess.

So if, for example, an estate is worth £400,000, the executor would have to pay 40 per cent of £175,000 (£400,000– £325,000), which is £30,000. It is payable to HM Revenue & Customs.

❝ The Inland Revenue no longer exists. It is now known as HM Revenue & Customs instead. ❞

 You don't have to work out the IHT due yourself. You can submit all your figures to HM Revenue & Customs and they will work out the figure for you - but see page 158 for which forms to send where.

 Some forms and guidance booklets differ in Scotland and it is important to obtain the correct set of forms or guidance booklets for the estate you are dealing with. Full details are obtainable from www.hmrc.gov.uk.

Steps involved in the granting of probate

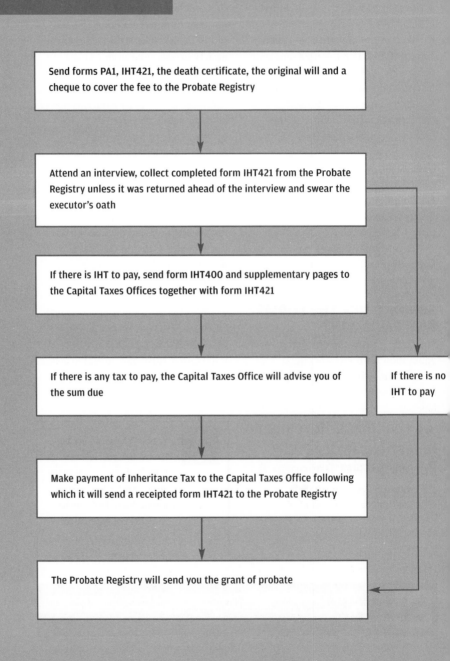

Send forms PA1, IHT421, the death certificate, the original will and a cheque to cover the fee to the Probate Registry

Attend an interview, collect completed form IHT421 from the Probate Registry unless it was returned ahead of the interview and swear the executor's oath

If there is IHT to pay, send form IHT400 and supplementary pages to the Capital Taxes Offices together with form IHT421

If there is any tax to pay, the Capital Taxes Office will advise you of the sum due

If there is no IHT to pay

Make payment of Inheritance Tax to the Capital Taxes Office following which it will send a receipted form IHT421 to the Probate Registry

The Probate Registry will send you the grant of probate

Raising money to pay IHT

Generally, assets cannot be dealt with before there is a grant of probate (or letters of administration). But if the person who died had a bank or building society account, it is possible that the bank or society will release money from the account for the purpose of providing finance for IHT (and funeral and probate fees). A cheque will be issued not to you, as executor or administrator, but made payable to HM Revenue & Customs for the IHT and to the Paymaster General for the probate fees.

If the person who died had a Girobank account, you may, subject to satisfactory identification, borrow for the purpose of paying IHT, so that a grant of probate may be obtained. The borrowing is limited to solvent estates and to the amount of the credit balance in the deceased's account.

The Capital Taxes Office provides form IHT423 on which to apply to a bank for the IHT to be paid out of the deceased's account. The notes that accompany the forms explain how to fill them in and what to do with them (see the foot of page 159).

If this arrangement is not available, you will have to persuade a bank to give you a loan to cover the tax, which can then be repaid once probate has been granted. This can prove difficult if you do not have a friendly bank.

In theory, you can be faced with an odd dilemma. On the one hand, no bank or insurance company that holds money belonging to the estate is willing to hand any of it over to you until a grant of probate is obtained and produced to them; the probate is the only authority that can allow them to part with the money. On the other hand, you cannot obtain a grant of probate until you have actually paid the IHT, or at least most of it. How can you pay the tax without being able to get your hands on the wherewithal to pay it?

Obtaining probate

Paying the IHT on property by instalment

If there is property to sell that makes up a significant part of the value of the estate, this can reduce the tax payable before getting probate because land and houses are eligible for an instalment option. This means that the IHT due on the value of a house can be paid by ten equal instalments over ten years. Interest is payable but the first payment does not have to be made for six months. As a result, you may not have to raise a loan from the bank, although you will have to pay IHT on the value of the rest of the estate before you get the grant of probate which gives you access to the assets of the estate. If the house is sold within ten years, all outstanding IHT must be paid.

- **If there are funds** in National Savings & Investments accounts (and funds cannot be made available from anywhere else), these can be used to pay the IHT.
- **Also you can use:**
  - NS&I certificates
  - Yearly-plan and Premium Bonds
  - British savings bonds
  - Government stocks on the UK Debt Management Office (DMO) register, administered by Computershare
  - Money from save-as-you-earn contracts.
- **A special system** operates between the Personal Application Department of the Probate Registry and NS&I, which enables this to be done. (For obtaining payment from a building society, see page 139.)

IHT payment forms

If you want the Capital Taxes Office to work out the IHT, forms need to be submitted in a different order and to different offices, which are explained on the relevant forms. In addition, if you are submitting form IHT421 to a bank or building society, there are other steps that have to be taken:

- Send forms PA1 and IHT421 (see page 156) to the Probate Registry together with the original will and an official copy of the death certificate and a cheque for the appropriate amount made payable to HM Paymaster General (the probate fees are £130 and you will also

need sealed copies of the probate – ten copies should do – each at £1).
- Following an interview at the Probate Registry (see opposite), form IHT421 with Section A is returned, completed by the Probate Registry.
- Complete form IHT421 and send it to the Capital Taxes Office together with form IHT 200 and the supplementary pages. You will then be advised how much IHT is due to be paid. (If you elect to pay the IHT arising on a property, this figure will not be included.)
- To pay, send form IHT421 to the relevant bank or building society. Once payment has been made, the Capital Taxes Office will receipt form IHT421 (to show IHT has been paid) and send it back to the Probate Registry. Probate will then be granted following an interview at the Probate Registry.

Fees

The probate fees are charges made by the Probate Registry for dealing with the papers and issuing the grant of probate. Form PA4 gives a list of the fees, as a guide. It would be wise, however, to confirm the actual amount payable before you attend the interview at the Probate Registry to swear the papers as this is when you need to pay it. Payment can be made by cheque, banker's draft, postal order or in cash.

AT THE PROBATE REGISTRY

Once the application for probate is submitted, you will be given an appointment for an interview at the Controlling Probate Registry or Interview Venue that you requested on form PA1. This is to confirm the information sent in the application and should last no longer than 15 minutes, and you will need two separate forms of identification, such as a passport and a utility bill showing your current address.

All the information that you have supplied will have been translated on to a formal printed legal document, known as the executor's oath. The commissioner will ask you to check the forms to ensure the details are correct – as personal representatives, the executors are responsible for checking that everything is accurately stated (it's worth taking your file of papers with you).

Once you are satisfied, sign the oath in the space provided at the end. You will also need to sign the original will and swear an oath (or affirm) the contents of the documents are true. It is a serious offence if you swear or affirm that the contents of the documents are true when you know they are not.

If IHT is payable, you will be given form IHT421 to send with form IHT 200 to the Capital Taxes Office. If all this is in order, they will advise you what to pay. Once the tax is paid, the receipted IHT421 will be sent to the Registry, who will then issue probate.

If no IHT is payable, the grant will be posted to you, usually within ten working days of the appointment, together with copies that you have paid for.

THE GRANT – PROBATE OR LETTERS OF ADMINISTRATION

While there may be an interval of several weeks between lodging the probate papers and being asked to come to the Probate Registry to sign and swear them, after that things tend to move quickly. If there is no IHT to be paid, the grant of probate (or letters of administration) will be issued within a few days. If arrangements have to be made to pay the IHT, matters might take a little longer.

Any property that passes by survivorship does not 'devolve to' the personal representatives but goes to the survivor. This is why it is excluded from the value of the personal estate even though it is not excluded from calculations for IHT, where applicable.

The Capital Taxes Office is a department within HM Revenue & Customs – see the website www.hmrc.gov.uk/inheritancetax/index.htm, where you can download all relevant forms, such as IHT421 and IHT 200 mentioned above.

At the end of the grant, the value of the gross and net estate (that is, before and after deduction of debts) is stated, but the amount of tax is not disclosed. The press often publish the value of the estates of famous people who have died. It is seldom a true indication of their wealth because it takes no account of any jointly owned property nor of any trusts to which they are entitled, nor, for that matter, of the IHT to be paid out, which will reduce the estate.

Attached to the grant of probate will be a photocopy of the will, accompanied by a note that briefly explains the procedure for collecting in the estate and advises representatives to obtain legal advice in the event of any dispute or difficulty.

You are now entitled to deal with the deceased's property, pay his or her debts, and then distribute the property in accordance with the will – see pages 180–1.

Remember that the will is a public document in the sense that anybody, including any beneficiary, and even the press, can obtain a copy of it or of the will from the Principal Registry of the Family Division for a small fee. Copies of the will or the grant can also be obtained at the Probate Registry where they were issued.

❝ When the value of an estate of a famous person is published in the newspapers, it is seldom a true indication of that person's wealth. ❞

Intestacy

This section looks at the thorny issue of intestacy and how a person's estate is distributed when there is no will.

LETTERS OF ADMINISTRATION

When a person has died leaving no will (and recent research shows this is more than half the population), the people who administer the estate are called administrators (as opposed to executors, who are named in a will). The procedure adopted by administrators applying for a grant of letters of administration is broadly the same as that adopted by executors applying for a grant of probate, but if the estate is insolvent, a trustee is usually appointed to administer the estate anyway – see page 162.

The nearest relatives, in a fixed order, are entitled to apply for the grant. If the nearest relative does not wish to apply, he or she can renounce his or her right to do so, in which case the next-nearest becomes entitled to be the administrator, and so on, down the line of kinship as set out in the list below.

If none of these comes forward, the application can be made by the Treasury Solicitor on behalf of the Crown or by a creditor of the deceased.

Order of entitlement

The order of entitlement to apply for letters of administration where the deceased has died intestate (that is, leaving no partially effective will) is:

- The deceased's spouse.
- The children of the deceased or their issue* (if over 18), if a child of the deceased has died before the deceased.
- The parents of the deceased.
- The brothers and sisters of the whole blood or their issue, if any of the brothers and sisters have died before the deceased.
- The brothers or sisters of the half-blood* or their issue (as above).
- The grandparents.
- The uncles and aunts of the whole blood or their issue (as above).
- The uncles or aunts of the half-blood or their issue (as above).

* 'Issue' means your children and all subsequent generations arising from them, that is, your grandchildren, your great-grandchildren and so on. Half-blood means sharing only one parent.

No distinction is made between legitimate, adopted or illegitimate relationships. They are all treated equally. Normally, a court order would be required to prove a link between an illegitimate child and the child's father if the father was not a signatory to the birth certificate. However, the advances in blood and DNA analysis have made such proof easy to obtain. It is in the fields of artificial insemination by donor, embryo donation and surrogate motherhood where the issues become complicated, not forgetting the distinction between brothers and sisters of the whole blood and brothers and sisters of the half-blood.

An adopted child is deemed to be the legal child of his or her adoptive parents and has exactly the same inheritance right as the adoptive parents' other (natural) children, but adoption removes any rights they may have had in law to their natural parents' estate. Similarly, the natural parents of an adopted child lose their right to claim against that child under intestacy laws. (However, a natural parent can, of course, still leave property to such a child in their will and vice versa.)

Step-children who have not been formally adopted do not inherit.

Distribution on intestacy

When it comes to distributing the estate, administrators must apply the intestacy rules laid down in the Administration of Estates Act 1925.

The division of the net estate where a person has died without leaving a will depends on the value of what is left and what family survives. The net estate is what remains of the estate after paying the debts, the funeral expenses, the expenses of getting letters of administration and administering the estate.

IHT will be payable on the basis of the distribution of the property according to the intestacy rules, that is, no tax is payable on anything that goes to the surviving spouse. IHT is payable on the balance, once the nil-rate band has been used up.

 Specific laws apply for the distribution of an intestate estate. Anyone considering making a claim under the Inheritance Act (on an intestacy or also where there was a will) should certainly take advice on current entitlements for any estate over £250,000.

Confirmation in Scotland

Inheritance Tax (IHT) and its exemptions, including the 'seven-year rule' regarding lifetime gifts and gifts with reservation, apply in Scotland. In other ways, there are considerable differences in law, practice and procedure between the Scots law of wills and succession and the law as it applies in England and Wales.

INTESTACY IN SCOTLAND

The rules of intestacy are set out in the Succession (Scotland) Act 1964 and represent what Parliament then considered to be a reasonable distribution for the average family. Since then, society has changed greatly and the Family Law (Scotland) Act 2006 makes changes to the law to try to take some account of modern lifestyles. For example, cohabitees who are not married to each other (opposite sex relationships) or are in civil partnership with each other (same sex relationships), now have a right to apply to the Sheriff court for a discretionary financial provision from the estate of their deceased partner, if intestate. This right must be exercised within six months of the deceased's death and can be either an award of a capital sum or of a transfer of property. A number of factors have to be taken into account by the court when determining what level of award is appropriate, but a surviving cohabitant will never be better off than if the cohabitant had been married to the deceased. If the deceased left a will, then a surviving cohabitant's right to make a claim in the Sheriff court is defeated.

Under the 1964 Act as amended, the law does not discriminate between children born in or out of marriage or between natural or adopted children. A divorced person or a former civil partner cannot inherit from their ex-spouse or ex-civil partner and, where a person with a child later marries or enters into civil partnership, the child cannot inherit from his or her step-parent.

The Scottish Law Commission proposed extensive reform of succession law in Scotland in April 2009. It is not yet known which changes will be adopted by the Scottish Parliament. Until any change is made, the 1964 Act continues to apply.

ADMINISTRATORS IN SCOTLAND

All executors have to be officially 'confirmed' by the sheriff court before they can start collecting in the estate. However, confirmation of assets is not always needed. The rules for payments of smaller balances by organisations such as the Department for National Savings are the same in Scotland as in England and Wales. If the only item in the estate is a bank account, it is worth asking the bank for details of its own small estates procedure. Most will pay up to about £10,000 against a formal receipt and indemnity. Confirmation is also unnecessary in the case of joint property where title is subject to a survivorship destination. On death, the deceased's share of the property passes to the other automatically, bypassing the executor.

If confirmation is required for even one item, all assets (cash, personal effects, furniture, car and similar items) have to be entered in an inventory for confirmation. They do not need to be professionally valued, however, and may be valued by the executor. Unless the title to the property contains a survivorship destination (when the share is disclosed for tax purposes only), the deceased's share of joint property must also be confirmed.

Declining to be an administrator in Scotland

If an executor-nominate does not wish to act, he or she can decline to be confirmed. A simple signed statement to that effect is all that is needed. You cannot decline but still reserve the right to apply later. If a sole executor-nominate declines, the family may have to apply to the court for another executor to be appointed. In this case, it is quicker and cheaper for the nominated executor to bring someone else in as co-executor and then decline, leaving the co-executor to be confirmed and act alone.

 Useful websites for executors in Scotland include: www.hmrc.gov.uk (HM Revenue & Customs Capital Taxes (Scotland)), www.ros.gov.uk (Registers of Scotland) and www.scotcourts.gov.uk (Sheriff Clerks' Office).

ADMINISTRATOR OF AN INTESTATE ESTATE IN SCOTLAND

For a person who dies intestate, the court appoints an '**executor-dative**'. In this case a member of the family, often the surviving spouse, normally (except for small estates, whose value before deduction of debts does not exceed £30,000) has to petition the court in the place where the deceased was domiciled for appointment as executor-dative. Such petitions are best put in the hands of a solicitor. The court normally handles them within two weeks.

If you are an executor-dative appointed by the court, you are required to supply a guarantee that you will carry out your duties as executor properly before confirmation is issued. This guarantee is called a 'bond of caution' (pronounced 'kayshun') and is usually provided by an insurance company. In recent years the insurance companies have become more difficult about issuing these bonds and the premiums quoted can be quite high. This is an area where almost certainly an executor will require professional help, as the insurers are reluctant to issue bonds to inexperienced executors. Instead of an insurance company, you can, in theory, have an individual as a cautioner but the court would need to be satisfied that, if called upon to do so, the individual is rich enough to pay the sum due. In practice this course is not an option.

Losses caused by the negligence or fraud of an executor are made good by the cautioner in the first instance, with the cautioner then seeking to recover the money from the executor personally.

A bond of caution is not required if you are a surviving spouse and you inherit the whole estate by virtue of your prior rights.

❝Losses caused by the negligence or fraud of an executor are first made good by a cautioner who then seeks to recover the money from the executor.❞

 For more information about intestate estates, see pages 161–2.

FIRST FORMALITIES FOR EXECUTORS IN SCOTLAND

Executors, whether nominated in the will or appointed by the court, have limited powers before confirmation. In this period, they should confine themselves to safeguarding and investigating the estate. They should not hand over any items to beneficiaries. Any person who interferes with the deceased's property may be held personally liable for all the deceased's debts, however large. This liability of confirmed executors for debts is limited to the overall value of the estate, providing they acted prudently and within their legal authority before confirmation.

Confirmation forms in Scotland

In addition to the forms outlined on page 154, **form C1** has to be filled in for confirmation of assets and liabilities. All forms can be downloaded from the HMRC website (www.hmrc.gov.uk). Also, printed copies can be obtained from the Capital Taxes Office or the Commissary Department of the Sheriff Clerks' Office (www.scotcourts. gov.uk). There are no special forms for lay applicants.

Once you, the executor, have all the information regarding the valuation of the assets in the estate and the deceased's debts, you are ready to fill in form C1 for obtaining confirmation. When there is more than one executor, one of them applies on behalf of all. If there is disagreement among the persons entitled to apply, the sheriff can be asked to make a ruling. An executor appointed by the will who does not wish to act must sign a statement to this effect. This accompanies the application for confirmation.

Post or deliver the form at the Sheriff court for the place where the deceased was domiciled at the time of death. If you are in any doubt, ask your local Sheriff court to advise you. At the same time as you lodge the will, you pay the fee for confirmation. For estates over £5,000, the fee is £195. Please note that these fees are liable to be increased without warning.

For an estate with a range of assets, ask for certificates of confirmation for individual items of estate. These cost £5 each if ordered when you apply for confirmation. You can collect the assets simultaneously, using the appropriate certificate of confirmation as evidence of your right to demand and receive them.

 If you think you need to pay IHT, there are special forms to be filled in. See pages 154–5 for which forms you need and also pages 157-8 for more information on IHT.

Transfer of a property

If the title deed contained a survivorship destination, the executor is not involved in transferring the house of the person who died. The deceased's share of the house is automatically transferred to the surviving co-owner. In other cases, the house must be transferred to a beneficiary under the will or the rules of intestacy and this work should be done by a solicitor. At the same time as the title is transferred, and if money is available, any building society loan can be discharged. Otherwise, arrangements need to be made for the loan to continue under the new owner's name or for a new loan.

After a week or so, if everything is in order, the confirmation is sent to you by post and the will is also returned, the court keeping a copy for its records.

PROCEDURE FOR SMALL ESTATES

To reduce the expense of obtaining confirmation, special procedures apply to small estates, which, before deduction of debts, have a gross value of less than £30,000. For a small estate with no will, you do not have to petition the court for appointment of an executor, and the necessary forms are completed for you by the staff at the Sheriff court. Whether or not a will exists, you apply to any convenient Sheriff court by post or in person. You subsequently take (or send) to the court:

- A list of all assets and their values
- A list of debts (including the funeral account)
- The deceased's full name and address, date of birth and date and place of death
- The will, if there is one.

The sheriff clerk then prepares the appropriate form for you to sign then and there or to return in a few days' time. The fee for confirmation is payable on signing the form. No fee is charged if the estate is below £5,000. Above that figure, the fee is currently £195. A few days after you have signed the form, confirmation is sent to you by post or to the executor-dative appointed by the court. The will is returned, with the court keeping a copy for its records.

" Confirmation is always sent to the executor through the post together with the will. A copy is kept with the court for its records. "

167

Probate in Northern Ireland

The law on wills and probate in Northern Ireland is similar to that in England and Wales. In fact, the law relating to wills is almost identical, following legislation passed on 1 January 1995. This legislation generally applies to wills made both before and after this date, regardless of when the testator died. As for probate, the laws also vary between England and Wales and Northern Ireland and these differences are covered here.

The Administration of Estates Act 1925 does not apply in Northern Ireland. The equivalent legislation is the Administration of Estates Act (Northern Ireland) 1955. Likewise, the Trustee Act 2000 does not apply in Northern Ireland. However, the Trustee Act (NI) 2001, which is very similar to the Trustee Act 2000, came into force on 29 July 2002.

One major difference between England and Wales and Northern Ireland has been created by the 1995 legislation. In Northern Ireland, provided the will is actually signed after 1 January 1995, a married minor or minors who have been married can now make a valid will. However, it is not possible for a married minor in England and Wales to make a valid will.

After someone dies and probate has been obtained, anyone can apply to see it or obtain a copy of it at the Probate Office, Royal Courts of Justice (see below). If it is more than five years since the grant was obtained, application should be made to the Public Record Office of Northern Ireland (see also below).

❝After probate has been attained, anyone can apply to see it. ❞

 The website for the Royal Courts of Justice is www.courtsni.gov.uk, or to get in touch with the Public Record Office of Northern Ireland, go to www.proni.gov.uk.

DIFFERENCES BETWEEN ENGLAND AND WALES AND NORTHERN IRELAND

Use the basic information already given for England and Wales on pages 124–62, but take into account the special conditions in Northern Ireland relating to the issues discussed below.

Death of husband and wife

In Northern Ireland, the common-law presumption of simultaneous deaths in cases where it is not certain who died first still applies.

Solicitors' fees

There is no recommended scale of fees for solicitors. However, the profession in Northern Ireland tends to follow these guidelines:

- On the first £10,000 of the gross value of the estate: 2½ per cent
- On the next £20,000: 2 per cent
- On the next £220,000: 1½ per cent.

Where the gross value of the estate includes the principal private dwelling house, the house's value is normally reduced by 50 per cent for the purpose of calculating fees. In addition to these 'standard' fees, the time spent by various members of staff in the solicitor's office is also costed and charged.

Executor not wishing to act

Only if the executor resides outside Northern Ireland or is incapable of managing their own affairs and a controller has been appointed by the Office of Care and Protection, can a person named as an executor in a will appoint an attorney. So, when you make your will, make sure that your nominated executors are willing to serve.

Advertising for creditors

The special procedure for formally advertising for creditors in Northern Ireland requires both an advertisement in the *Belfast Gazette* and an advertisement twice in each of any two daily newspapers printed and published in Northern Ireland. If the assets include land, the advertisements should be in the *Belfast Gazette* and in any two newspapers circulating in the district where the land is situated.

❝If assets include land, advertising for creditors needs to be done in a different way to assets not including land, as explained above.❞

Fees due for probate applications

• Net estate under £10,000:	nil
• Net estate of £10,000 and upwards:	£200

Applying for probate forms

Personal applications should be made to the Probate Office, Royal Courts of Justice in Belfast, or the District Probate Registry in Londonderry.

If the deceased had a fixed place of abode within the counties of Fermanagh, Londonderry or Tyrone, application may be made to either address. If the deceased resided elsewhere in Northern Ireland, the application must be made to the Belfast office (for contact details, see below). The fees in all applications are based on the net value of the estate (see box, below).

❝ The fees due for probabe applications used to be banded, but now they simply fall into two categories. ❞

There is no additional fee to be paid for a personal application. Personal applications must be made in person – that is, not by post. The fees increase from time to time with little prior warning, so it is best to check with the appropriate Probate Office before writing the cheque.

IHT payments

The cheque for IHT due should be made out to 'HM Revenue & Customs' and the cheque for the Probate Office fees should be made out to 'Northern Ireland Court Service'.

Form PA1

In Northern Ireland, it is not necessary to serve a notice on an executor who is not acting and who has not renounced. It is therefore possible for one executor to obtain probate, without another executor even being aware that that is the case.

Transfer of a property

While property is registered or unregistered as in England and Wales,

 The website for the Probate Office in Belfast is www.nidirect.gov.uk. The Royal Courts of Justice is also at www.courtsni.gov.uk. To contact the Londonderry District Probate Registry, telephone 028 7126 1832.

land law legislation generally in Northern Ireland is very different from that in England and Wales.

In the case of registered land, the executors or administrators complete assent **form 17**. The completed form 17 is then sent to the Land Registers of Northern Ireland in Belfast, together with the land certificate, the original grant of probate or letters of administration and **form 100A** (Application for Registration). Both forms are available from the Land Registers (see below). The fee is £75. If the property is subject to a mortgage, the certificate of charge with the 'vacate' or receipt sealed by the bank or building society should be lodged at the same time. Cheques should be made payable to 'DFP General Account'.

Unregistered land is, in fact, registered in the Registry of Deeds, held at the Land Registers. Although no particular form of words is required in order to vest property in a beneficiary, the wording varies both as to whether the title to the property is freehold, 'fee farm grant', or leasehold, and as to whether the property has been specifically bequeathed or forms part of the residue.

In these cases, ask a solicitor to prepare an assent for unregistered land. The solicitor can arrange for a memorial of the assent to be registered in the Registry of Deeds, for which the Registry charges a fee of £13. The memorial is an extract of the assent giving the date, names of the parties executing the deed, the address of the property and whether the property is freehold or leasehold.

❝ Wording varies on a title deed when land is unregistered. If you see the words 'fee farm grant', this means the property is freehold. **❞**

 The website for the Land Registers of Northern Ireland is www.lrni.gov.uk. Once you've registered on the website you have direct access to the Land Registers of Northern Ireland.

Distribution on intestacy

The main difference between English and Northern Irish law about wills and probate relates to the rules on intestacy. In Northern Ireland, unlike in England and Wales, no life interests are created on intestacy. As in England, the nearest relatives in a fixed order are entitled to apply for the grant of letters of administration (see page 161) and, if the nearest relative does not wish to be administrator, that person can renounce the right to do so, in favour of the next nearest.

The surviving spouse normally becomes the administrator. Where there is a surviving spouse, that person is always entitled to the deceased's personal effects, no matter how great their value. For all other circumstances of an intestate estate, consult a solicitor.

❝ Even for an intestate will, where there is a surviving spouse, he or she is always entitled to the deceased's personal effects. ❞

Completing the administration

Applying for and receiving probate can take many months of preparation and correspondence, but by this stage the end is in sight. As soon as probate is granted all creditors can be paid, tax affairs finalised and beneficiaries given their dues.

The administration

This chapter describes what happens after the grant of probate.

GATHERING THE ASSETS

Enclosed with the grant will be the number of sealed copies of it that you requested. This enables you to proceed with the administration more quickly because instead of having to send the probate in turn to each organisation requiring to see it, you can send a copy to all interested parties at the same time. Write to each company or bank (see pages 137–40) sending the completed claim form and a copy of the sealed office copy probate – and remember to ask for the probate to be returned once the details have been entered in their records, which is often referred to as 'registering the probate'.

As a rule, banks do not allow the credit on the deceased's bank account to be treated as available until probate is obtained. As a result, you may be faced with paying overdraft interest to a bank even though there is money available in the same bank, which will only be paid to the executor when probate has been granted.

Premium Bonds are not transferable and must be repaid, though the other National Savings and Investments (NS&I) products do not have to be encashed but can be simply transferred to beneficiaries after probate. On some types of NS&I products there is a limit to the total amount any one person is allowed to hold, but this limit can be exceeded if the excess is the result of transferring to the inheritor the savings held by the deceased. NS&I Certificates are exempt from Income Tax.

After you have followed up all the organisations, all the money due to the estate will be paid into the executorship account at your bank.

 It is not advisable for the inexperienced to sell shares direct without a broker. When it is done through a bank, it is the bank's broker who does the actual selling. If a broker is used, find out his or her commission rates before giving dealing instructions. Selling through a bank's broker attracts a commission just as selling through any other broker does, often with a minimum fee of, say, £15 per holding. The bank may also charge a dealing fee.

PAYING OFF CREDITORS

Once there are no further assets to collect in, you need to pay all creditors before distributing the rest of the estate to the beneficiaries. During this time, you might want to consider putting some of the money, leaving enough to pay creditors, into a deposit account to earn more interest.

The most likely bills to be paid are:

- Funeral director
- A mortgage company
- Gas
- Electricity
- Telephone
- Credit card
- Any hire purchase agreements
- Income Tax (see pages 176–7)
- and, if it takes more than six months from grant of probate to sell a property, council tax.

(see pages 176–7)

Finding unknown creditors

A personal representative is obliged to make full enquiries to discover what debts the deceased had. In addition, there is a procedure that involves advertising for creditors. After obtaining probate, put an advertisement in the *London Gazette* and a local newspaper announcing that all claims against the estate should be made by a certain date, which should be at least two months after the appearance of the advertisement. When this is done in the official way, you, as the personal representative, will be quite safe to distribute the assets of the estate on the basis of

the debts known to you on the date by which claims have to be made. Failure to do this could make you liable to pay creditors who apply for payment after you have paid the beneficiaries.

> **❝ Paying off creditors is a big step towards completion of your duties as executor. ❞**

Income Support

If the deceased was receiving Income Support, contact the Benefits Agency as a refund may be due to the Agency if the deceased had not disclosed all his or her capital to it.

IHT rectification

When there has been no agreement with the district valuer about the value of a house, the first contact with him or her is likely to be after probate has been obtained. Where this happens, the value of the house as finally agreed with the district valuer may be higher than the value included in the HM Revenue & Customs account. This results in a further payment of IHT having to be made. If that happens (or values in the original should be reduced), you will have to notify the Capital Taxes Office on a corrective account form C4. You will then get a revised assessment of IHT payable (or a refund). If the sale of a house is concerned, it may be prudent to wait, because then the question of value can be re-opened.

INCOME TAX RETURN

As an executor, there are now two questions to answer: first, is a tax return necessary to settle the tax affairs of the deceased up to the date of death and, second, is a tax return necessary to deal with the income received by you during the administration of the estate? Delay could result in a penalty.

" In some instances, the deceased may be owed a tax refund. "

The tax affairs of the deceased

Generally, any income of the deceased received before the death should be included in a tax return. If the deceased kept up to date with tax returns and paid tax through PAYE, the final return prepared by the executors will usually have to cover only the period from 6 April before the death to the date of death. In some instances, depending on the date of death, two tax returns covering the last two tax years may have to be completed.

The full amount of personal reliefs, however, will be available to set against the income and capital gains received or realised in that period. As a result, a refund may be due. This can affect the IHT payable.

Income received by the executors

Executors have to pay basic or lower-rate (20 per cent) tax on any income or 10 per cent on dividend income they receive. You then pay the remaining net income to the beneficiary with an R185 certificate giving details of the tax that has already been paid on that income.

Although you do not receive any personal reliefs to set against income received during the administration, you do not pay higher rate tax. However, there is one permitted deduction: if you had to take out a loan to pay IHT, the loan interest could be deducted. Technically, HM Revenue & Customs could object to a deduction of interest for probate fees, as opposed to IHT, but some inspectors do not take this view.

You are also liable for CGT on chargeable gains realised on the sale of assets (including houses) in the

If you are in any doubt as to the calculation of a tax return, consult an accountant or get in touch with HM Revenue & Customs at www.hmrc.gov. uk for advice.

For more information on CGT, see pages 179-81. At this stage, it is worth double checking that you have contacted everyone that you initially got in touch with, as outlined on pages 137-40.

estate if the difference between the probate value and sale value exceeds available allowances. In this case, you are allowed the same exemption as an individual for the year in which the deceased died, and the following two years (then no exemption in subsequent years), although the rate of tax is now 18 per cent.

Where an asset is passed direct to a beneficiary (rather than being sold by the estate), the beneficiary acquires the asset at its value at the date of death. If the beneficiary subsequently sells, they are liable for CGT based on their own allowance and tax rate. Therefore, when you are considering whether to distribute assets or cash from their sale, you might want to consider whether more or less tax would be paid according to whether any assets were sold by the estate or by a beneficiary. If land is sold by the executor within four years of the death at a lower figure than the probate value, that lower figure can be substituted for the probate value and a refund of IHT can be obtained.

THE DISTRIBUTION

Once all the debts are settled and the tax paid, you are free to distribute the assets in accordance with the will. Some can be handed over directly to the beneficiaries, in return for a receipt. Other assets, such as shares and a house, if they are not being sold, have to be transferred by deed or other document to the beneficiary.

Expenses

All the expenses involved in the administration of the estate will be paid out of the executorship account at the bank. These expenses might include:

- **The cost of the grant** and obtaining copies of it
- **The bank's charge** on the transfer of shares and the Land Registry fees on the transfer of a house
- **Your out-of-pocket expenses,** such as postage and fares to visit the Probate Registry. Personal representatives are not entitled to be paid for the time they devote to the administration, unless the will specifically says so.

Legacies

Any legacies can also now be paid although a legacy for a person under 18 cannot be paid directly to that child. The executors, therefore, have to invest the money until each child, on becoming 18, can receive their share (plus the interest it had earned meanwhile). You might also want to

Paying legacies

Wills usually provide that a legacy is clear of tax (which then comes out of the residue unless the legacy is tax free). However, the actual wording must be checked. Interest at an appropriate rate can be claimed if the executor has not paid the legacy within one year of the death. The executor should take care to get a receipt.

consult an independent investment adviser on how best to invest a legacy to comply with the provisions of the Trustee Act 2000.

When an administration is long and complicated, the legacies might not be paid for several years. When it is then paid, the legatee is entitled not only to the actual amount of the legacy but also to interest (currently at 0.3 per cent per annum) from the date one year after the date of death until payment of the legacy. This is taxable as income in the hands of the recipient, but it is also deductible against any income that is earned in the administration for Income Tax purposes.

Shares

It is often necessary to sell some or all of the shares held by a person who has died in order to pay the debts, IHT or the legacies or to meet the expenses of administering the estate. When this happens, it is then the remaining shares that are divided according to the will.

When shares or unit trust holdings are sold within a year of a death for less than the value on the date of death, the total of the gross selling price of all such investments (you cannot pick and choose the under value sales) can be substituted as the value for IHT. The sale has to be made by the executors, but once the shares have been transferred into the names of the beneficiaries, it is too late to claim a reduction of IHT.

Adjustment is made by a corrective document. If the market for shares has fallen, this can be a valuable relief if some shares have to be sold.

Whether the shares are sold or not, it is necessary for each company in which shares are held to see a copy of the grant (see box at the bottom of page 145). In a case where a sole executor is also the person entitled to the shares under the will, the company will usually provide its own form in order to complete the transfer. Whether the shares are to be sold or transferred direct to the beneficiaries entitled to have them under the will,

Dividing shares

If shares remain unsold and they are passed on to beneficiaries, it is possible to divide each existing holding between them, equally or otherwise – always get a written confirmation of the division from the interested parties. If no agreement is possible, all the shares should be sold and the beneficiaries should get their entitlement in cash. Then there can be no argument about who gets what, but from an investment point of view this may not be the most advantageous thing to do.

To affect a division, you can employ the bank or stockbroker. All they will need are the holding certificates, and any fees (ranging from nothing to between £2 and £6 per share) will be debited from the executorship account.

it is usually possible to send the probate to the registrar of the company at the same time as sending the transfers of the shares to be dealt with by him or her.

Transfer of a property

Where a mortgage is outstanding at the time of death and there is nothing in the will about having it paid off out of the residue, the house may have to be sold so that the mortgage can be repaid from the proceeds of the sale and the beneficiaries would get the balance of the money. However, many people nowadays have a mortgage protection policy or a mortgage backed by an endowment policy, so that the mortgage can be repaid automatically on the death of the borrower.

Be very careful if a property with a mortgage is left to a beneficiary. Does the will say that the mortgage is to be repaid from the residue or is the gift made subject to the mortgage?

Where the house is to be transferred outright into the name of a beneficiary, the building society may be prepared to let the beneficiary continue with the existing mortgage. That person can, of course, apply to any source for a new mortgage if that gives a better deal. The title of the house will also have to be transferred to the beneficiary. Contact the mortgage company or Land Registry for advice on how to do this, but don't forget to pass on the obligation to observe covenants if the property is subject to them. There will be different procedures to follow depending on whether or not the property is registered at the Land Registry.

 Where there are any complications, such as a lease or restrictive covenants on the property, take legal advice to make sure that, as executor, you are not left with any personal liability.

> ❝If a mortgage is outstanding, the house may have to be sold so that the mortgage can be repaid.❞

CAPITAL GAINS TAX (CGT)

Capital gains can arise when assets are sold or transferred for more than they cost when they were bought or more than their probate value (that is, their value at the time of the owner's death). Take professional advice as to how to minimise CGT.

For the Which? report on captial gains tax, go to the Which? website: www.which.co.uk. Some of the content on the website is only available to subscribers – information on how to subscribe is given on the website.

FINAL STEPS

Once all the debts have been paid, there are no outstanding claims and all other property has been distributed, all that remains is to distribute the remaining cash. Before doing this, though, personal representatives should consider carefully everything they have done on the account.

Double check every asset in the estate and look at each debt and expense to see that everything has been done properly. This is important if several people are sharing the residue, and it would be more important still if there had been any dissent within the family. All executors should have checked and approved the administration papers, too. Once you are happy with everything, prepare the estate accounts.

Accounts

These accounts don't have to take any particular form as long as they are clear and accurate (for an example, see page 182-3). It is useful to have a separate note of the income received, so that the calculation of the tax credit due to each beneficiary is more straightforward.

The final balance on the accounts should match the closing balance at the bottom of the last bank statement. If these figures are not the same, something is wrong, and you then have to look at everything – starting with the adding up.

It is, of course, unlikely that the values of all the assets shown in the IHT 400 or IHT 205 at the date of death will match exactly the money received when the accounts are closed or transferred. Interest will have accrued and shares may have risen or fallen in value.

Some estate accounts show the value of the assets at the date of

Income Tax again

The only other matter to deal with is the Income Tax deduction certificates in form R185. Complete this form (which can be obtained from HM Revenue & Customs) when income, which has already had tax deducted from it, is being paid to beneficiaries. The beneficiaries disclose the income on their tax returns, but they will be given credit for the tax already paid when HM Revenue & Customs makes an assessment on the beneficiaries' income for the year.

 The website for HM Revenue & Customs is www.hmrc.gov.uk where you can download most of their forms.

death and then the transactions taking place during the administration.

Send a copy of the accounts to each of the beneficiaries for their approval, asking them to sign and return the accounts to you. At the same time, you can send the cheques for the final amount owing together with an R185 form, if necessary (see box, opposite), and ask each recipient to sign a formal acknowledgement. If you are worried that a beneficiary might challenge the accounts, you could arrange for them to be professionally audited as a precaution.

When the cheques are cleared, you can close the executors' account, although there may be a small amount of residue left to distribute after closure because interest accrues to the last day. The administration is now finished. Bundle together all the papers, including the original probate and the signed copy of the accounts, and put them in a large envelope to be kept in a safe place, theoretically for 12 years (where there are any life interests under any trusts in the will, the papers should then be kept for 12 years after final distribution following the death of anyone with a life interest). You might choose to keep the probate as a family document.

❝ If you are worried that a beneficiary might challenge the accounts, you could always arrange for them to be professionally audited. ❞

Example of how the final accounts might look

CAPITAL ACCOUNT

Assets

Property		227,500.00
Endowment policy		85,300.00
Life policy		9,100.00
Building Society		81,000.00
Bank		1,900.00
National Savings Certificates		5,000.00
Premium Bonds		4,000.00
1,500 units Investment Fund (sold)		2,730.00
£50,000 5% Treasury Stock 2008 (sold)		51,000.00
Retained shares		85,550.00
Jewellery (valued)		1,500.00
Car (estimated)		4,000.00
Contents (estimated)		11,000.00
Private pension arrears		200.00
State benefit arrears		78.00
Cash		80.00
		569,938.00

Liabilities

Funeral account		2,200.00
Household bills		320.00
Mortgage on a property		25,400.00
Probate fees		140.00
Executor's expenses		200.00
Land Registry fees		70.00
Guarantee for missing shares		35.00
Inheritance Tax (1st payment)	54,408.70	
payment on a property	32,358.50	
final adjustment	960.00	86,767.20
Balance transferred to distribution account		454,805.80
		569,938.00

INCOME ACCOUNT

Received	Tax	Net
Building society	25.00	100.00
Dividend from shares	44.00	396.00
Interest – executor's bank account	7.50	30.00
Transfer to distribution account	76.50	526.00

THE DISTRIBUTION ACCOUNT

Received

Balance from Capital Account made up as follows:

Any property	227,500.00	
Retained shares	85,550.00	
Jewellery	1,500.00	
Car	4,000.00	
Contents	11,000.00	
Cash balance	125,255.80	
		454,805.80
Balance from income account		526.00
		455,331.80

Distribution

Legacies e.g. grandchildren (£500 each)	1,500.00
– a charity	100.00
1st beneficiary: a car	4,000.00
the contents of a property	11,000.00
a property	227,500.00
The residue: 2nd beneficiary: $1/2$ shares (value)	42,775.00
$1/2$ balance	62,840.90
3rd beneficiary: $1/2$ shares (value)	42,775.00
$1/2$ balance (including jewellery, valued at £1,500)	61,340.90
	455,331.80

In the capital account, include the capital balance in the building society account at the date of death and interest accrued to that date. The income account includes any interest accrued after the date of death. The other interest payment represents the further interest due to the date of closing of the executor's deposit account.

In the income account, include the receipts of all the income received after the date of death, so they are excluded from the capital account to avoid recording the same item twice.

Problems and disputes

It is a sad fact that the death of a family member can trigger a dispute within the family. The first sign of trouble is often preceded by the remark 'It's not the money that I'm bothered about. It's the principle of the matter.' Another sad fact is that the cost of a dispute can reach astronomical levels and consume the value of the estate that is in dispute.

However, disputes do arise and have to be dealt with. They fall into two main categories. First, there are disputes over the will. Was it valid? Was it fair? Was it forged? Second, disputes can arise over the administration of the estate of the deceased person. Are the executors or administrators acting improperly or failing to do what they should be doing? Have they paid out to the wrong person or are they refusing to tell the beneficiaries what they have done? This section first deals with both kinds of problems, and then discusses other common issues.

If you are involved in a dispute over a will or administration, the best advice you will get is to try to settle it as quickly as possible, and perhaps to have a word with the Probate Registry (see below). If that cannot be done, you will almost certainly need to instruct a solicitor who knows their way around court procedures.

> **❝If you are involved in a dispute over a will or its administration, try to settle it as quickly as possible. The next step would be to instruct a solicitor. ❞**

 To contact the Probate Registry, go to www.courtservice.gov.uk. Their helpline phone number is 0845 302 0900, and there are plenty of articles on the website that might address your particular problem.

PROBLEMS WITH THE WILL

Executors responsible for an estate and getting probate for it before distribution to the beneficiaries are strictly regulated by law. They also commonly face problems which can impede progress and can also mean, at the worst, that the rules of intestacy apply.

No will can be found

The deceased person may never have made a will, but what if one of the family believes that the deceased did make one and it cannot be found? If a thorough search of papers and possessions fails to discover the will, one step is to write to local firms of solicitors and banks who might have been employed to make or keep a will on the deceased's behalf. If all enquiries fail, the rules of intestacy apply.

Was it signed properly?

The will should be carefully checked to ensure that it has been signed by the testator and that the testator's signature has been witnessed by two witnesses (who must not be beneficiaries to the will). Both witnesses must have been present when the will was signed. As executor, if you have any doubts about the signing of the will, check with the witnesses. If the will has not been properly signed and witnessed, the Probate Registrar may declare it invalid or at the very least require a sworn affidavit to explain the irregularity.

Was the will dated?

If it is not dated, you have a problem. Do the witnesses remember when it was signed? If so, the Probate Registry will require an affidavit to explain the lack of a date. Sometimes, it is apparent that a will has been changed or that some other document has been attached. Take all the documentation you have to the Probate Registrar, who can advise whether any of it should be counted as part of the will.

Is it the last will?

Even if you find a will that is properly dated and witnessed, it may not necessarily be the last will the deceased made. The older the will, the greater the chance that a later will or a codicil exists changing its terms. Always make further enquiries to be sure. Remember, too, that even an apparently valid will may have been wholly or partly invalidated by a subsequent marriage or divorce.

Remarriage automatically revokes any earlier will unless that will was specifically stated to be made in contemplation of the marriage. In particular, if there are children and a new will wasn't made following a remarriage, the rules of intestacy will automatically operate after death.

PROBLEMS WITH THE TESTATOR
Did the testator have 'testamentary capacity'?

In order to make a valid will, a testator must understand what is owned, understand the effect of the will and recognise individuals to whom the testator might have responsibilities – for instance, a wife with young children. As executor, if you believe the testator lacked testamentary capacity, you need medical evidence to support your case and should take legal advice.

> **"** Probate actions can be very expensive, transferring a large proportion of the estate to the solicitor and barristers involved. **"**

Was the testator threatened or improperly influenced?

Anyone wishing to challenge the will on these grounds must show that the testator was induced to make it by force, fear or fraud or that in some other way the will was not made voluntarily. Legal advice should be taken before attempting to challenge a will on these grounds.

If someone decides to challenge the will, it is necessary to apply to the Probate Registry for a 'caveat'. This prevents an application for probate being made. It covers all registries and lasts for six months. If not renewed, it lapses. While it is in force, probate cannot be issued. If a caveat has been registered, as executor, you first have to resolve the problem with the applicant. If you cannot, you have to issue a warning to the Probate Registry, which has the effect of beginning a court action to settle the dispute. This is an area requiring specialist knowledge, so seek legal advice at an early stage.

Is the will or distribution on intestacy unfair?

If it is generally agreed by the beneficiaries that the will (or intestacy) has not made reasonable provision for all the interested parties, they can enter into a deed of variation. This has the effect of rewriting the will or intestacy rules. This step must be taken within two years of the death. If the variation reduces the share of a beneficiary who is under 18, the court's approval must be obtained. If you wish to make such an agreement, take legal advice. If there is no agreement and the matter remains in dispute, the only recourse is to take the dispute to court. Probate actions can be very expensive, in effect transferring a substantial proportion of the estate from the beneficiaries to their solicitors and barristers. If there is no alternative, the claimant has to take proceedings under the Inheritance (Provision for Family and Dependants) Act 1975.

OTHER PROBLEMS
Bankrupt beneficiaries
If you suspect that a beneficiary is bankrupt or about to be made bankrupt, you should make further enquiries, including a search on form K16 at the Land Charges Registry. Any payments due to a bankrupt must be made to that person's trustee in bankruptcy who must produce an S.307 notice under the Insolvency Act 1986. Under these circumstances, consult a solicitor.

Missing beneficiaries
Use what detective qualities you have. In addition to family networks and newspaper advertisements, you could use the internet to track down missing people. Genealogists can be engaged on a 'no-find no-fee' basis – check that their finding fee is a reasonable proportion of the sum involved. You can also look at the possibility of insurance (don't forget to allow for interest on the bequest), failing which obtain a court order permitting distribution on the assumption that the beneficiary has died without issue, or pay the money into court under the provisions of the Trustee Act 1925.

Problem executors or administrators
If it appears that a personal representative is unsuitable or failing to carry out his or her duties, an application for removal can be made to the High Court. It is wise to ask the Probate Registrar or a solicitor with specific experience for advice.

Claims by ex-spouses, dependents and family members
If there is an ex-spouse to whom maintenance is still being paid following a divorce or separation, that person is entitled to make a claim against the estate, so remember to take this possibility into account. The extent of the claim will depend upon the size of the estate and the other claimants. Similarly, a cohabitee or child of the deceased who considers the will to be unfair can make a claim against the estate under the provisions of the Inheritance (Provision for Family and Dependants) Act 1975. Under the Act, the claimant has to file a claim no later than six months after the grant of probate or letters of administration. If there is any risk of a claim being made, executors should limit any distribution made during that six-month period.

Having the right to claim does not mean that a person automatically wins the case if a claim is made, especially where the applicant has not been dependent on the deceased. Legal costs

 For an outline of the rules of intestacy, see pages 161-2, which might help throw light on your particular case.

of the action are a matter for the court to decide. Such a person is not paid automatically by the estate nor are the costs paid automatically from the estate.

Court of Protection

If the affairs of the person who has died have been administered by the Court of Protection (in cases of mental incapacity, for example), there are formalities to go through with the court before the assets of the deceased can come under the control of the personal representatives. This usually requires the deputy to file final accounts at the Court of Protection but, if all parties agree, that requirement can be waived. The receiver is the person appointed by the court to look after the financial affairs of people who cannot look after themselves, known as 'patients'.

Foreign property

Generally speaking, if a deceased person owned property or land in

 Other probate disputes can end up in the Probate or Chancery Divisions of the High Court. In either, the proceedings will be costly and you will need advice. They are not DIY territory.

another country, the laws there determine what happens to the property at death and overrule what is said in the English or Welsh will. Seek advice from a solicitor with specific knowledge of the relevant law of the country involved. The Law Society can provide names of suitable solicitors.

Foreign domicile

If the deceased person had a foreign domicile (that is, the country which was recognised as their permanent home), the law of the country of domicile applies to the administration of the estate although probate (or letters of administration) will be required to deal with English and Welsh property they owned.

Caveats and citations

If you wish to prevent the issue of a grant of probate because you believe the will is invalid or that the applicant has no right to apply, you may file a caveat at the Probate Registry. This prevents probate being issued while the problem is resolved. If you simply want to know when probate is issued, you should make a standing search. If the caveat is challenged by a warning, that has the effect of commencing a probate action. A citation is a formal request to the Probate Court to get someone to do something.

 For advice about buying a home overseas, see the Which? Essential Guide *Buying Property Abroad*.

Pensions and other benefits

Pensions and benefits divide into those that are payable because someone has reached state retirement age, those that are payable in certain circumstances (such as severe disability or unemployment) and those that are paid to people who are assessed as having a low income.

The rules are complex as some benefits take into account National Insurance contributions (NICs) paid by the claimant, and others by NICs paid by a spouse. Some benefits cannot be paid if another benefit is already being paid, some are taxable and some take pre-existing savings into account and others do not.

In England, Wales and Scotland all benefits are the responsibility of the Department for Work and Pensions (DWP), delivered through different agencies. In Northern Ireland, the Department for Social Development is responsible. In addition, in England, Wales and Scotland, benefits for those over state retirement age are coordinated by the Pensions Service and others by Jobcentre Plus or the Disability and Carers' Service. (For contact details of each of these organisation, see below.)

There are a huge range of benefits available, and this book gives an introduction only to those directly related to the event of a death. It is not uncommon for a death to result in a significant drop in income for the remainder of the immediate family. Because probate, if required, can take a matter of months or even longer, it is appropriate to make a claim for low-income benefits, even if this is expected to be a fairly short-term requirement. The Pension Service can make home visits if needed to assist with advice and the Jobcentre Plus can advise for people of working age. The Citizens Advice Bureau (CAB) can also advise on entitlements.

> **❝It is not uncommon for death to result in quite a a significant drop in the income of the deceased's immediate family. ❞**

To find out more about what benefits might be available, go to www.directgov.uk and www.dsdni.gov.uk. To find your nearest Jobcentre Plus, go to www.jobcentreplus.gov.uk and the Pensions Service website is www.direct.gov.uk/pensions.

BEREAVEMENT BENEFITS

There are three benefits you may be entitled to if your husband or wife dies:

- **Bereavement Allowance:** a taxable weekly benefit paid for 52 weeks after your husband or wife or civil partner dies, if you are aged 45 and also under state retirement age.
- **Widowed Parent's Allowance:** a taxable weekly benefit.
- **Bereavement Payment:** a tax-free payment of £2,000 paid to you as soon as you are widowed.

Bereavement Allowance/Widowed Parents Allowance

To qualify for these benefits or allowances, your deceased husband or wife must have paid the required number of National Insurance contributions (NICs) – your own NICs do not count. These are available to both widows and widowers and civil partners.

You need to have been married at the time of death to qualify – you will not be entitled to claim if you are divorced. You also lose your entitlement if you remarry or live with someone else as husband and wife as if you are married to them during the period of the benefit.

You can make a claim for bereavement benefits on form BB1, available from any Social Security office or from the DWP. Leaflet GL14 is also available from the DWP and is a basic guide to benefits and tax for women and men who have been widowed. Both documents can be downloaded from the DWP website.

You should claim the Bereavement Allowance as soon as possible to make sure you do not lose any of the benefits. Note that payments cannot normally be backdated for more than three months from the date of the application.

❝Claim your bereavement benefits as soon as you possibly can to make sure you don't lose out.❞

 Information about the Disability and Carers' Service can be found at the DWP website: www.dwp.gov.uk. See also CAB's website: www.citizensadvice.org.uk.

You cannot claim for Bereavement Allowance and Widowed Parents Allowance, but you can claim Widowed Parents Allowance if you are bringing up a child for who you are receiving Child Benefit. You can also claim if you are expecting the baby of the person who died (including a civil partner who is the parent by fertility treatment). Also claim if your spouse or civil partner died as a result of their work, even if they have not paid NICs.

Bereavement Payment

This is a once-only tax-free payment that must be claimed within 12 months of the death, also using form BB1 – details as above. This is only payable to bereaved husbands, wives and civil partners under state retirement age, with the exception of a few pensioners. When a bereaved spouse or civil partner over retirement age notifies the Pension Service of the death, the Pension Service routinely checks whether the surviving person qualifies for the bereavement payment.

The surviving pensioner should also ask for their own position to be reviewed as they may have become eligible for income-related benefits, especially if the State Pension is their only source of income.

Changes at short notice

The government, the DWP and HM Revenue & Customs may make substantial changes to benefits and the qualifications for them at short notice. The information given here is accurate at the time of writing (2009), but if you are considering claiming any benefits or tax credits, contact your local Social Security office, Jobcentre Plus office, the DWP or HM Revenue & Customs to get accurate and up-to-date information and advice. You should also make sure you have the latest edition of any leaflet, and ask if anything has changed since it was published. You may lose some benefits if you do not do this.

❝ Child Benefit is not affected by income or savings and you need to claim in your name. ❞

WAR WIDOW'S PENSION

To qualify for a war widow's pension, the death usually has to be related to injury incurred during military services. The Service Personnel and Veterans Agency can advise.

 The Veterans Agency Helpline is on freephone 0800 169 22 77 or go to the Veterans Agency website at www.veterans-uk.info/.

CHILD BENEFIT

If you are bringing up a child, you can claim Child Benefit even if you are not the parent. Child Benefit is not affected by income or savings, and you need to claim in your name for each child under 16 or 19 if in full-time education. This is paid by HMRC, so you need to contact your local tax office.

GUARDIAN'S ALLOWANCE

A person who takes an orphaned child into the family may be entitled to a Guardian's Allowance. Although the payment is called a Guardian's Allowance, it is not necessary to assume legal guardianship to qualify. Usually the allowance is paid only when both parents are dead, but it can sometimes be paid after the death of one parent – for instance, where the other is missing or cannot be traced or is detained in prison or hospital, or where the parents were divorced (and certain conditions apply). The allowance is not awarded unless one of the child's parents was born in the UK or had been resident in the UK for a specified length of time, or is a national or member of a family of an EU country and insured under UK Social Security legislation. It is paid only if the guardian qualifies for child benefit for the child.

Claims for the allowance should be made on form BG1, obtainable from the DWP or Jobcentre Plus. A claim should be made straight away as you may lose your benefit if you delay (it can be backdated only for up to three months or to the date of the award of Child Benefit).

" It is not necessary to assume legal guardianship to qualify for Guardian's Allowance if you take an orphaned child into your family. "

The experience of grief

Grief is the collection of physical and psychological reactions to the death of someone we care for. This chapter gives you an idea of what you might expect to feel over time.

The process of grief

Each relationship that is interrupted by death is unique and so it follows that each individual's experience of grief is unique.

How we express grief very much depends not only on our own personality and the relationship that we had with the deceased, but also the society in which we have grown up and the one in which we live if the two are not the same. The circumstances of the death can also affect how we react. There is no right or wrong way to grieve. There is also no set timetable for how long grief lasts. There are still European cultures where widows wear black for the remainder of their lives.

" There is no right or wrong way to grieve. It varies with personality, relationships and maybe also the circumstances of the death. "

OTHER PEOPLE'S EXPERIENCES

Over the last 40 years or so there has been a great deal of research into the experiences of the bereaved. What has been described has then sometimes been used in a prescriptive way to suggest how one should grieve. It is possible to read lists of feelings that can seem like a tick list and leave us feeling that we have not grieved properly if we have not ticked all the boxes in the right order. However, what is good about this work is that it has helped us to understand that many of us share similar feelings and experiences after a death. The main reservation with this research work is that, until recently, most of it has been carried out within white European/North American communities so may have limited usefulness for those from other backgrounds.

However, it is clear that many people find it very helpful to read

 Cruse Bereavement Care is an organisation that supports bereaved people in the UK (see page 197). Its website is full of helpful advice. Go to www.crusebereavementcare.org.uk.

of the experiences of others who have been bereaved and sometimes to have contact with others who have had similar bereavements either face to face, on the telephone or by email. For others, the opportunity to talk with people who have been trained to listen carefully and help people understand their own experiences without judgement (counsellors) is invaluable.

STRENGTH OF FEELINGS

Many people find themselves surprised and even shocked by the overwhelming nature of their feelings after the death of someone close to them. The emotions are so strong that they are often experienced and described in terms of physical sensations. Shock, numbness and disbelief are understandable and perhaps protective in the early days as it takes time for the full pain of the loss to be felt. The intensity of anguish reflects the strength of the love and affection someone had for

❝ Shock, numbness and disbelief are perhaps protective in the early days, but there may also be a strong sense of relief if the deceased had suffered a long illness. ❞

the person who has died and their importance to the bereaved – heartache or heartbreak are ways of describing the physical sensation often experienced at this time as well as a seeming never-ending supply of tears.

It is also hard for the people who are trying to be supportive at this time as there is very little that they can do except some of the practical things, such as household chores, and to be there as an often silent presence and listen, listen and listen again. Telling the story of what has happened and the stories of the person's life helps reassure the bereaved that the person who has died was real and their influence or legacy of memories will not just disappear, even if the person is no longer physically present.

It can also be very difficult and lonelier for people whose feelings do not follow this pattern. There may be a strong sense of relief if the deceased had suffered a long and difficult illness, such as dementia, and there has been an extended period of grieving as the person who was known gradually succumbed to the illness. Relief may also be experienced by people who have been long-term carers, together with a sense of disorientation as their lives have been dominated for so long by the needs of the person cared for who has now died.

Grieving is exhausting and a period of apathy and withdrawal is common. Someone may have to keep going to look after children or a surviving parent, but this can be extremely hard work.

It is important to remember that bereavement is not an illness. Although often desperately sad and hard, it is the natural and normal response to the death of someone who was very significant.

66 Accepting support from friends, family and maybe professional people and support groups should be seen not as weakness but rather as wise self-awareness. 99

GETTING HELP

Most people navigate this bereavement journey, as many people describe it, with the support of remaining family and friends. The person who has died is not forgotten and is always missed. Eventually most bereaved people find themselves gradually becoming able to look forward to the future and to rediscover an enthusiasm for living.

Some people do appreciate more organised support from others during this period of their lives. This should not be regarded as weakness but rather wise self-awareness. The following list gives the options available. Not all services are available in all areas and in some cases there may be a waiting list.

Your local hospital

If there are outstanding questions and concerns about the circumstances surrounding the death, it can be helpful to make an appointment with senior medical staff. A hospital Patient Advice and Liaison Service (PALS) or the bereavement office, if there is one, is a good place to start.

Your GP

For emotional support, a visit to the general practitioner is always a good start. Many surgeries have a counsellor on staff and, for some people, bereavement may trigger depression that can be helped by counselling or by medication. A local surgery will also have information about other local services. Talk to the practice manager so that an appointment can be made that is of a suitable length rather than during normal surgery time.

Local services

Many church parishes have a bereavement visiting team who can be contacted via the telephone number on the church noticeboard or a once-a-month coffee morning for bereaved people. Some funeral directors now also provide bereavement support services. Libraries and council one-stop shops often have information about local services.

Self-help groups

A number of these have grown to become national charities and often help people who have experienced a particular type of bereavement, such as the death of a child, a suicide or murder or the death of a young person from cardiac disease or epilepsy. Most offer telephone support, some have local groups and many now have internet forums. A number of these are listed in the useful addresses section at the end of the book.

Cruse

This is the largest national organisation supporting bereaved people in the UK. The services they provide vary slightly across the country, but most provide one-to-one support by trained volunteer bereavement support workers who also receive supervision (this is a system whereby counsellors in return receive support). Cruse does not charge for its time, but it welcomes donations from those who are able to make them.

Services for children

Many counties have their own local charity for the support of bereaved children. As well as Cruse there are a number of national charities that either support children directly or, perhaps even more importantly, provide support to adults caring for bereaved children. It is now recognised that children grieve in ways that are appropriate to their developmental age. They often understand far more than adults

realise and it is very important that they are given information about what is happening and choices about participating in events such as seeing the person who died and the funeral. The Child Bereavement Charity and Winston's Wish have excellent websites and helplines.

❝ Cruse is the largest national organisation supporting bereaved people in the UK, offering one-to-one support by trained workers. ❞

Support for bereaved people with learning disabilities

The needs of people with learning disabilities who are bereaved have been neglected in the past but resources are beginning to be available especially via the internet for both people with a learning disability and for those who support them. The following sites may be helpful with downloadable resources for people with learning disabilities and their carers:

- www.bereavementanddisability. org.uk/
- www.heron.nhs.uk/specialist_ directory/bereavement/ld_ bereavement.htm

- Down's Syndrome Scotland publish a book about death and bereavement, which can be ordered from the publication list on their website: www.dsscotland.org.uk/resources/order_form.htm
- Mencap have a helpline on 0808 808 1111.

Mental health services

The vast majority of people who are bereaved will not need to use formal mental health services, but for people who have experienced mental ill health previously, it can be helpful to get back in touch with a community psychiatric team at a time when one may be more vulnerable.

Private counselling

Private counsellors charge for their services. Some practitioners offer a sliding scale of fees determined by the income of their potential client. Please ensure your counsellor is accredited by the British Association of Counselling and Psychotherapy. This ensures they have undergone extensive training and adhere to a rigorous code of practice.

The first year after the death of someone close can seem an endless stream of anniversaries of 'this time last year …' memories. The first anniversary of the death itself is often very difficult. Adjusting to life without someone special takes courage, time and often having to learn new practical skills as well as coping with emotional turmoil. However, most people are remarkably resilient and we do have the ability to deal with the challenges of bereavement.

 For contact information for each of the organisations and charities included in the private counselling list, see the useful addresses section on pages 203-9.

Glossary

Administration of the estate: The task of the executor or administrator.

Administrator: The name given to a personal representative if not appointed by a valid will. The administrator will usually have to obtain a grant of letter of administration to show that he or she is the person with legal authority to deal with the property of the deceased.

Attesting registrar: An interim register office, which passes all relevant information to the receiving registrar.

Bequest: A gift of a particular object or cash (as opposed to 'devise', which means land or buildings).

Book of Remembrance: Popular means of memorial at a crematorium.

CGT: Capital Gains Tax.

Certificate for cremation: Certificate issued by a coroner if a postmortem has been ordered.

Certificate of no liability to register: A registrar's certificate, issued under certain circumstances such as a death overseas, confirming that a death is not required to be registered.

Chattels: Personal belongings: for example, jewellery, furniture, wine, pictures, books, even cars and horses not used for business. Does not include money or investments.

Child (referred to in a will or intestacy): Child of the deceased including adopted and illegitimate children but, unless specifically included in a will, not stepchildren.

Citation: A document issued by the Probate Registry (upon application) calling on a person to explain why he or she has not taken a certain step, for example, why has there been no application for probate if that person is shown in the will to be an executor.

Co-habitee: An informal partner of the deceased who may be able to claim a share of the estate. The term 'common law wife' has no legal force.

Columbarium: A niche in a wall at a crematorium where ashes can be walled in or left in an urn.

Common grave: When the burial authority has the right to bury another person in the same plot.

Confirmation the document issued to executors by the sheriff court in Scotland to authorise them to administer the estate.

Deed of grant: Confirms the existence of a private grave (see exclusive right of burial).

Demise: a grant of a lease.

District valuer: The district valuer is employed by HM Revenue & Customs but the job has little to do with taxes as such. He or she is concerned with the valuation of land, houses, factories, shops, offices and so on for many official purposes. He or she is an expert on valuation.

Estate: All the assets and property of the deceased, including houses, cars, investments, money and personal belongings.

Exclusive right of burial: When a plot is leased for x number of years.

Executor: The name given to a personal representative if he or she is appointed by a valid will or codicil. The executor will usually have to apply for probate of the will to show that he or she is the person with legal authority to deal with the property of the deceased.

Executor-dative: An administrator appointed by court for a person who dies intestate.

Executor-nominate: The Scottish term that used in place of the English term 'executor'.

Faculty: Authority for work in a churchyard – in this case, for a grave or memorial.

Family grave: A specific grave where only members of the family can be buried.

First offices: When a funeral director prepares a body for burial of cremation.

Form BD8: A free form supplied by the registrar for claiming Social Security benefits, or form 334/SA in Scotland and form 36 in Northern Ireland.

General Register Office (GRO) for England and Wales: Part of the Identity and Passport Services. GRO Scotland and GRO Northern Ireland are the responsibility of the devolved administrations. All administer the registration process in their respective areas.

Grant of probate: The document issued by the probate registry to the executors of a will to authorise them to administer the estate.

Green certificate: The official certificate provided by the registrar authorising a burial or cremation to take place.

Informant: The person who registers a death.

Inheritance tax (IHT): The tax that may be payable when the total estate of the deceased person exceeds a set threshold (subject to various exemptions and adjustments).

Intestate: A person who dies without making a will.

Issue: All the direct descendants of a person, that is, children, grandchildren, great-grandchildren and so on.

Lawn grave: When grave consists of a headstone with mown grass around it.

Laying out: The initial preparation of a body for burial or cremation.

Legacy: A gift of money.

Letters of administration: The document issued to administrators by a probate registry to authorise them to administer the estate of an intestate.

Letters of administration with will annexed: The document issued by the probate registry to the administrator when there is a will but the will does not deal with everything e.g. it fails to appoint an executor.

Mausoleum: A large, brick-built construction including graves.

Minor: A person under 18 years of age.

Moveable estate: Property other than land and buildings in Scotland.

Next of kin: The person that is entitled to the estate when a person dies intestate.

Order for burial: Certificate issued by a coroner if a postmortem has been ordered.

Personal estate: All the investments and belongings of a person apart from land and buildings.

Personal representative: A general term for both administrators and executors.

Plaque Panel: A small notice with the name and date of death of the deceased, placed near a memorial rosebush or shrub or attached to a panel on a wall in the crematorium grounds.

Probate of the will: The document issued to executors by a probate registry in England, Wales and Northern Ireland to authorise them to administer the estate.

Proving the will: Making the application for probate to a probate registry.

Probate registry: The Government office that deals with probate matters. The Principal Probate Registry is in London with district registries in cities and some large towns across the country.

Real estate: Land and buildings owned by a person.

Receiving registrar: The register office where the death must be registered. It must be in the sub-district in which the death took place or where the body was found.

Registrar General: The Government official who is responsible for the registration of births, deaths and marriages.

Residue: What is left of the estate to share out after all the debts and specific bequests and legacies have been paid.

Rigor mortis: A stiffening of the muscles, which usually begins within about six hours after death and gradually extends over the whole body in about 24 hours; after this it usually begins to wear off. Rigor mortis is less pronounced in the body of an elderly person.

Solvent: Value of the assets exceeeds any debts.

Specific bequests, particular items gifted by will. They may be referred to as 'specific legacies'.

Testator: A person who makes a will.

Will: The document in which someone states what is to happen to your possessions on your death.

Useful addresses

Age Concern Cymru
Ty John Pathy
13–14 Neptune Court
Vanguard Way
Cardiff CF24 5PJ
Tel: 029 2043 1555

Age Concern England
Astral House
1268 London Road
London SW16 4ER
Information line: (0800) 0099 66
www.ageconcern.org.uk

Age Concern Northern Ireland
3 Lower Crescent
Belfast BT7 1NR
Tel: 028 9024 5729
www.ageconcernni.org

Age Concern Scotland
Causewayside House
160 Causewayside
Edinburgh EH9 1PR
Information line: 0845 833 0200
www.ageconcernandhelptheaged
scotland.org.uk

Association of Burial Authorities
Waterloo House
155 Upper Street
London N1 1RA
Tel: 020 7288 2522
www.burials.org.uk

Bereavement Advice Centre
Ryon Hill House
Ryon Hill Park
Warwick Road
Stratford-upon-Avon CV37 0UX
Tel: 0800 634 9494
www.bereavementadvice.org

Bereavement Register
Tel: 0800 082 2233
www.bereavementregister.org.uk

BRAKE
PO Box 548
Huddersfield HD1 2XZ
Tel: 0845 603 8570
www.brake.org.uk

Britannia Shipping Company for Burial at Sea Ltd
Unit 3
The Old Sawmills
Hawkerland Road
Collaton Raleigh
Sidmouth
Devon EX10 0HP
Tel: 01395 568028
www.burialatsea.co.uk

British Association of Counselling
and Psychotherapy
BACP House
15 St John's Business Park
Lutterworth LE17 4HB
Tel: 01455 883300
www.bacp.co.uk

British Humanist Association
1 Gower Street
London WC1E 6HD
Tel: 020 7079 3580
www.humanism.org.uk

Child Bereavement Charity
Aston House
High Street
West Wycombe HP14 3AG
Tel: 01494 446648
www.childbereavement.org.uk

Citizens Advice Bureau
Look in your local phone book or go to
www.adviceguide.org.uk

Commonwealth War Graves
Commission
2 Marlow Road
Maidenhead
Berkshire SL6 7DX
Tel: 01628 634221
www.cwgc.org

Compassionate Friends
53 North Street
Bristol BS3 1EN
Helpline: 0845 123 2304
www.tcf.org.uk

Coroners in England and Wales
For contact details for coroners and their
officers contact your local police station
if you have not been given the number
by a doctor or the hospital.

Coroner in Northern Ireland
Mays Chambers
73 May Street
Belfast BT1 3JL
Tel: 028 9044 6800
www.coronersni.gov.uk

Cremation Society of Great Britain
1st Floor
Brecon House
16–16a Albion Place
Maidstone
Kent ME14 5DZ
Tel: 01622 688292/3
www.cremation.org.uk

Cruse Bereavement Care
PO Box 800
Richmond
Surrey TW9 1RG
Helpline: 0844 477 9400
www.crusebereavementcare.org.uk

Cruse Bereavement Care Scotland
Riverview House
Friarton Road
Perth PH2 8DF
0845 600 2227
www.crusescotland.org.uk

Dignity Funeral Plans
Plantsbrook House
94 The Parade
Sutton Coldfield
West Midlands B72 1PH
Tel: 0800 38 77 17
www.dignityfuneralplans.co.uk

Directgov
www.directgov.uk

Driver and Vehicle Licensing Agency (DVLA)
Swansea SA6 7JL
Tel: 0300 790 6801
www.dvla.gov.uk

The Federation of Burial and Cremation Authorities
41 Salisbury Road
Carshalton
Surrey SM5 3HA
Tel: 020 8669 4521
www.fbca.org.uk

Foreign and Commonwealth Office (FCO)
King Charles Street
London SW1A 2AH
Tel: 020 7008 1500
www.fco.gov.uk

Foundation for the Study of Infant Deaths (FSID)
11 Belgrave Road
London SW1V 1RB
Tel: 0808 802 6868
www.fsid.org.uk

Friendly Societies Co UK
www.friendlysocieties.co.uk

Funeral Planning Authority (FPA)
Knellstone House
Udimore
Rye
East Sussex TN31 6AR
Tel: 0845 601 9619
www.funeralplanningauthority.com

General Register Office
www.gro.gov.uk
www.directgov.uk/gro

General Register Office for Scotland
New Register House
3 West Register Street
Edinburgh EH1 3YT
Tel: 0131 334 0380
www.gro-scotland.gov.uk

Golden Charter Funeral Plans
Head Office
Canniesburn Gate
10 Canniesburn Drive
Bearsden
Glasgow G61 1BF
Tel: 0800 111 4514
www.goldencharter.co.uk

Golden Leaves Funeral Plan
299–305 Whitehorse Rd
Croydon CR0 2HR
Tel: 0800 85 44 48
www.goldenleaves.co.uk

Help the Aged
Head Office
York House
207–221 Pentonville Road
London N1 9UZ
Tel: 020 7278 1114
www.helptheaged.org.uk

HM Revenue & Customs
Look in the phone book or use the website for your local tax office or HM Revenue & Customs Centre
Probate helpline: 0845 302 0900
www.hmrc.gov.uk

Home Office
Direct Communications Unit
2 Marsham Street
London SW1P 4DF
Tel: 020 7035 4848
www.homeoffice.gov.uk

Identity and Passport Service
(includes General Register Office)
www.ips.gov.uk

Institute of Cemetery and Cremation
Management
ICCM National Office
City of London Cemetery
Aldersbrook Road
Manor Park
London E12 5DQ.
Tel: 020 8989 4661
www.myonlinedata.co.uk/iccm/

INQUEST
89–93 Fonthill Road
London N4 3JH
Tel: 020 7263 1111
www.inquest.org.uk

Institute of Civil Funerals
6 Nene Road
Bicton Industrial Park
Kimbolton
Cambridgeshire PE28 0LF
www.iocf.org.uk
0845 0048608

Land Registry of England
and Wales
Tel: 020 7917 8888
www.landregistry.gov.uk

Land Registry of Scotland
www.ros.gov.uk

Law Society of England and Wales
The Law Society's Hall
113 Chancery Lane
London WC2A 1PL
Tel: 020 7242 1222
www.lawsociety.org.uk

Law Society of Northern Ireland
96 Victoria Street
Belfast BT1 3GGN
Tel: 028 9023 1614
www.lawsoc-ni.org

Law Society of Scotland
26 Drumsheugh Gardens
Edinburgh EH3 7YR
Tel: 0131 226 7411
www.lawscot.org.uk

Mailing Preference Service (MPS)
DMA House
70 Margaret Street
London W1W 8SS
Tel: 0845 703 4599
www.mpsonline.org.uk

Marine and Coastguard Agency
Tel (for deaths at sea): 02920 448800
www.mcga.gov.uk

Marine Environment Team
Marine and Fisheries Agency
Area 4D
Ergon House
Horseferry Road
London SW1P 2AL
Tel (for burial at sea): 020 7270 8664
www.mfa.gov.uk

Ministry of Justice
www.justice.gov.uk

Miscarriage Association
c/o Clayton Hospital
Northgate, Wakefield
West Yorkshire WF1 3JS
Tel: 01924 200799
www.miscarriageassociation.org.uk

National Association of Funeral
Directors (NAFD)
618 Warwick Road
Solihull
West Midlands B91 1AA
Tel: 0845 230 1343
www.nafd.org.uk

National Association of Memorial
Masons
1 Castle Mews
Rugby
Warwickshire CV21 2SG
Tel: 01788 542264
www.namm.org.uk

National Association of Widows
3rd Floor
48 Queens Road
Coventry CV1 3EH
Tel: 0845 838 2261
www.nawidows.org.uk

National Council for Voluntary
Organisations
Regent's Wharf
8 All Saints Street
London N1 9RL
Tel: 020 7713 6161
www.ncvo-vol.org.uk

National Savings & Investments
(NS&I)
See website for correct address for each
product
Tel: 0500 007 007
www.nsandi.com

National Society of Allied and
Independent Funeral Directors (SAIF)
3 Bullfields
Sawbridgeworth
Hertfordshire CM21 9DB
Tel: 0845 230 6777
www.saif.org.uk

Natural Death Centre
In the Hill House
Watley Lane
Twyford
Winchester SO21 1QX
Tel: 0871 288 2098
www.naturaldeath.org.uk

NHS Choices
www.nhs.uk

NHS Direct
Tel: 0845 4647 (England, Wales and
Northern Ireland)
www.nhs.uk
www.wales.nhs.uk (Wales)
www.healthandcareni.co.uk (Northern
Ireland)

NHS 24 (for Scotland)
Tel: 08454 242424
www.nhs24.com

NHS Organ Donor Registration Service
Tel: 0300 123 23 23
www.organdonation.nhs.uk

207

The Pension Service
Tel: 0845 606 0265
www.directgov.uk

Northern Ireland Land and Property
Services
Lincoln Building
27–45 Great Victoria Street
Belfast BT2 7SL
Tel: 028 9025 1555
www.lpsni.gov.uk

Perfect Choice Funeral Plans
Beaufort House
Brunswick Road
Gloucester GL1 1JZ
Tel: 0800 633 5626
www.perfectchoicefunerals.com

Probate/Confirmation services
www.hmcourts-service.gov.uk/
infoabout/ civil/probate/registries.htm
(England and Wales)
Helpline: 0845 302 0900 (for probate
and Inheritance Tax)
www.courtsni.gov.uk/en-GB/AboutUs/
ContactDetails/ (Northern Ireland)
www.scotcourts.gov.uk/sheriff/index.asp
(Scotland)

Probate Office
Royal Courts of Justice
PO Box 410
Chichester Street
Belfast BT1 3JF
Tel: 028 9023 5111
www.nidirect.gov.uk

Register Offices
Search on direct.gov.uk for your local
register office

Registrar General (Northern Ireland)
General Register Office of
Northern Ireland
Oxford House
49–55 Chichester Street
Belfast BT1 4HL
Tel: 028 9025 2163
028 9025 2000 (credit card line)
www.groni.gov.uk

RoadPeace
Shakespeare Business Centre
245a Cold Harbour Lane
London SW9 8RR
Tel: 0845 4500 355
www.roadpeace.org

Royal National Institute for the Blind
(RNIB)
105 Judd Street
London WC1H 9NE
Tel: 020 7388 1266
Helpline: 0303 123 9999
www.rnib.org.uk

Samaritans
Helpline: 0845 790 9090
www.samaritans.org
Look in your telephone book for local
branch

Service Personnel and Veterans Agency
Norcross
Thornton Cleveleys FY5 3WP
Tel: 08001 692 277
www.veterans-uk.

Stillbirth and Neonatal Death Society (SANDS)
28 Portland Place
London W1B 1LY
Helpline: 020 7436 5881
www.uk-sands.org

Support after Murder and Manslaughter (SAMM)
L&DRC
Tally Ho
Pershore Road
Edgbaston
West Midlands B5 7RN
Helpline: 0845 872 3440
www.samm.org.uk

Survivors of Bereavement by Suicide (SOBS)
The Flamsteed Centre
Albert Street
Ilkeston DE7 5GU
Tel: 0844 561 6855
www.uk-sobs.org.uk

The WAY Foundation
Suite 35
St Loyes House
20 St Loyes Street
Bedford MK40 1ZL
Tel: 0870 011 3450
www.wayfoundation.org.uk

Winston's Wish
Westmoreland House
80-86 Bath Road
Cheltenham
Gloucestershire GL53 7JT
Tel: 01242 515157
www.winstonswish.org.uk

Index

Index

211

Index

213

which?

Which? is the leading independent consumer champion in the UK. A not-for-profit organisation, we exist to make individuals as powerful as the organisations they deal with in everyday life. The next few pages give you a taster of our many products and services. For more information, log onto www.which.co.uk or call 0800 252 100.

Which? magazine

Which? magazine has a simple goal in life – to offer truly independent advice to consumers that they can genuinely trust – from which credit card to use through to which washing machine to buy. Every month the magazine is packed with 84 advertisement-free pages of expert advice on the latest products. It takes on the biggest of businesses on behalf of all consumers and is not afraid to tell consumers to avoid their products. Truly the consumer champion. To subscribe, go to www.which.co.uk.

Which? online

www.which.co.uk gives you access to all Which? content online and much, much more. It's updated regularly, so you can read hundreds of product reports and Best Buy recommendations, keep up to date with Which? campaigns, compare products, use our financial planning tools and search for the best cars on the market. You can also access reviews from *The Good Food Guide*, register for email updates and browse our online shop – so what are you waiting for? To subscribe, go to www.which.co.uk.

Which? Legal Service

Which? Legal Service offers immediate access to first-class legal advice at unrivalled value. One low-cost annual subscription allows members to enjoy unlimited legal advice by telephone on a wide variety of legal topics, including consumer law – problems with goods and services, employment law, holiday problems, neighbour disputes, parking, speeding and clamping fines and tenancy advice for private residential tenants in England and Wales. To subscribe, call the membership hotline: 0800 252 100 or go to www.whichlegalservice.co.uk.

Which? Money

Whether you want to boost your pension, make your savings work harder or simply need to find the best credit card, *Which? Money* has the information you need. *Which? Money* offers you honest, unbiased reviews of the best (and worst) new personal finance deals, from bank accounts to loans, credit cards to savings accounts. Throughout the magazine you will find tips and ideas to make your budget go further plus dozens of Best Buys. To subscribe, go to www.which.co.uk.

Which? Computing

If you own a computer, are thinking of buying one or just want to keep abreast of the latest technology and keep up with your kids, there's one invaluable source of information you can turn to – *Which? Computing* magazine, *Which? Computing* offers you honest unbiased reviews of new technology, problem-solving tips from the experts and step-by-step guides to help you make the most of your computer. To subscribe, go to www.which.co.uk.

Which? Local

Using a trader can be a bit hit and miss. But using one who has been recommended can help ensure a more reliable service. Which? Local is an easy-to-use website with thousands of recommendations for local traders across the UK reviewed by Which? members. From plumbers to builders, tree surgeons to hairdressers, Which? Local's listings have saved members time and money. If you're already a Which? member or want to find out more, visit www.which-local.co.uk. To find out how you can become a member, call 01992 822 800.

Which? Books

Which? Books provide impartial, expert advice on everyday matters from finance to law, property to major life events. We also publish the country's most trusted restaurant guide, *The Good Food Guide*. To find out more about Which? Books, log on to www.which.co.uk or call 01903 828557.

" Which? tackles the issues that really matter to consumers and gives you the advice and active support you need to buy the right products. **"**

Which? Books

Other books in this series

Pension Handbook
Jonquil Lowe
ISBN: 978 1 84490 025 1
Price: £9.99

A definitive guide to sorting out your pension, whether you are deliberating over SERPs/S2Ps, organising a personal pension or moving schemes. Cutting through confusion and dispelling apathy, Jonquil Lowe provides up-to-date advice on how to maximise your savings and provide for the future.

Care Options in Retirement
Margaret Wallace and Philip Spiers
ISBN: 978 1 84490 053 4
Price: £10.99

Care Options in Retirement is the definitive guide to navigating the many financial and legal considerations of care and accommodation for older people. The book provides vital information on the many types of housing and care available, from care at home and retirement housing to respite care and care homes. Regional differences in Scotland, Wales and Northern Ireland are highlighted as well as special considerations for meeting specific religious and mental health needs. Whether you need to know about benefits, support services, renting or buying retirement housing or want advice on how to interpret a care home's inspection report, you will find useful tips and information.

Wills and Probate
Jonquil Lowe
ISBN: 978 1 84490 070 1
Price: £10.99

Wills and Probate provides clear, easy-to-follow guidance on the main provisions to make in a will and the factors you should consider when drafting these. You will also find advice on probate, making the process as straightforward and trouble free as possible. By being aware of key changes and avoiding the common problems and pitfalls, you can limit delays, avoid disputes and save tax. The book also includes an exclusive discount on a Which? online will.

Which? Books

Other books in this series

Save and Invest

Jonquil Lowe
ISBN: 978 1 84490 044 2
Price: £10.99

Save and Invest is a detailed guide to all saving and investment avenues suitable for those approaching the markets for the first time and those seeking to improve their portfolio. Jonquil Lowe, an experienced investment analyst, introduces the basics of understanding risk and suggests popular starter investments. Many types of savings accounts are closely analysed, along with more complex investment options, such as venture capital trusts, high-income bonds, hedge funds and spread betting.

Make the Most of Your Money

Nic Cicutti
ISBN: 978 1 84490 062 6
Price: £10.99

Make the Most of Your Money is a no-nonsense, hassle-free guide designed to help you work out your financial priorities, grow your cash and kick-start your journey to good financial health. Utility bills are rising, credit is limited, property prices are falling and good investments are harder to come by. Getting your finances on track means learning how to cope with these changes and maximising the funds you do have.

Giving and Inheriting

Jonquil Lowe
ISBN: 978 1 84490 032 9
Price: £10.99

Inheritance Tax (IHT) is becoming a major worry for more and more people. *Giving and Inheriting* is an essential guide to estate planning and tax liability, offering up-to-the-minute advice from an acknowledged financial expert. This book also features information on equity release, trusts and lifetime gifts.

Which? Books

Other books in this series

Divorce and Splitting Up

Imogen Clout
ISBN: 978 1 84490 034 3
Price: £10.99

Divorce, separation, dissolution of a civil partnership or simply splitting up with a partner is never easy – the emotional upheaval, legal complexities and financial implications make even the most amicable parting a demanding business; when children are involved, couples are in dispute and property needs to be divided the whole process can be fraught with difficulties. *Divorce and Splitting Up* offers comprehensive, clear, step-by-step guidance through the whole process, explaining how the law works, drawing attention to key considerations and looking at ways of minimising unnecessary conflict and costs.

Buy, Sell and Move House

Kate Faulkner
ISBN: 978 1 84490 056 5
Price: £10.99

This best-selling property guide covers the latest changes to HIPs and analysis of the property market. From dealing with estate agents to chasing solicitors and working out the true cost of your move, this guide tells you how to keep things on track and avoid painful sticking points.

Finance Your Retirement

Jonquil Lowe
ISBN: 978 1 84490 057 2
Price: £10.99

Finance Your Retirement is the essential step-by-step guide to a secure retirement, providing advice on saving for your pension, whether to opt for an annuity, how to access your money if you retire abroad and the basics of Inheritance Tax. There are helpful tips for maximising your budget using state benefits and investments, such as unit trusts and OEICs, plus guidance on how to make your property work for you.

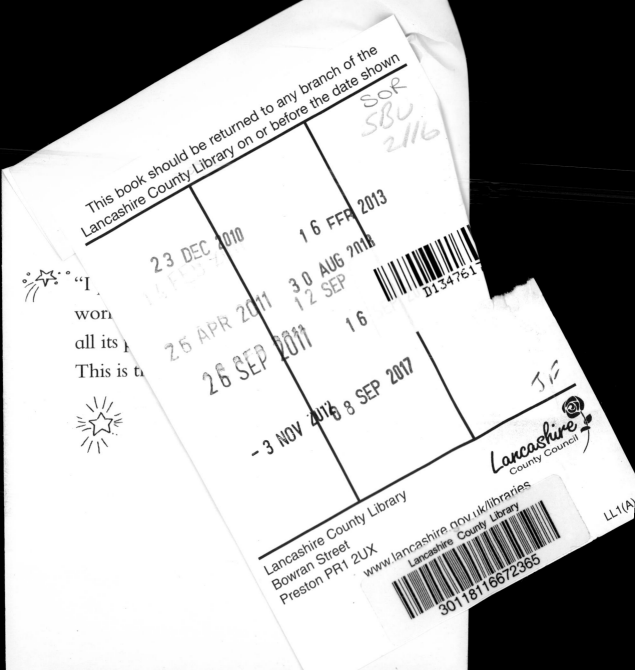

"I
wor
all its
This is t

Sunny

Blossom

Sparkle

Primrose

Misty

Lulu

Poppy

Visit the secret world of the Fairy Bears and
explore the magical Crystal Caves . . .

www.fairybearsworld.com

Fairy Bears

Sunny

Julie Sykes

Illustrated by Samantha Chaffey

MACMILLAN CHILDREN'S BOOKS

First published 2010 by Macmillan Children's Books
a division of Macmillan Publishers Limited
20 New Wharf Road, London N1 9RR
Basingstoke and Oxford
Associated companies throughout the world
www.panmacmillan.com

ISBN 978-0-330-51202-2

1 3 5 7 9 8 6 4 2

A CIP catalogue record for this book is available from
the British Library.

Printed and bound in the UK by CPI Mackays, Chatham ME5 8TD

For Tim

Prologue

At the bottom of Firefly Meadow, not far from the stream, stands a tall sycamore tree. The tree is old with a thick grey trunk and spreading branches. Hidden amongst the branches is a forgotten squirrel hole. If you could fly through the squirrel hole and down the inside of the tree's massive trunk, you would find a secret door that leads to a special place. Open the door and step inside the magical Crystal Caves, home of the Fairy Bears.

The Fairy Bears are always busy. They work hard caring for nature and children everywhere. You'll have to be quick to see them, and you'll have to believe in magic.

Fairy Bears

Do you believe in Fairy Bear magic?
Can you keep a secret? Then come on
in – the Fairy Bears would love to meet
you.

Chapter 1

The school bell was ringing when Sunny the Fairy Bear and her best friend, Dizzy, fluttered into the school playground.

"Honey mites!" exclaimed Dizzy. "There isn't time to show you that backwards-forwards somersault I learned last night."

"Never mind," said Sunny cheerfully. "You can show me at playtime."

"If you're here," said Dizzy. "Miss Alaska is sending someone out on their first task today. It might be you."

"Bouncing bears!" squeaked Sunny. "I hope it is."

Sunny gripped her wand as she entered the class cave. She had reached the last class in juniors and now it was time to go outside into the world to do tasks. Each task involved helping a person or an animal of some kind. The tasks were really important. You had to pass them all to be able to move up to the seniors. Failing meant spending another year with Miss Alaska.

Folding her yellow wings behind her back, Sunny wove past her chattering classmates towards her stone desk. Dizzy slid into her own seat and began talking to Blossom, but Sunny carried on until she reached the magic mirror that hung on the cave's sloping wall.

"Hello, mirror."

Sunny stared into the rectangular glass,

edged with tiny crystals. The mirror was
like a window. Looking at it, you never
knew what you would see. It might be your
reflection or it could be something very
special.

At first Sunny saw her own face reflected
there – a happy-looking Fairy Bear whose
rich honey-coloured fur had pretty yellow
touches. She pulled a funny face and her
reflection pulled one back. Sunny
giggled and pulled another face but
her reflection
disappeared
and the mirror
showed a
different picture –
of a young girl
whose dark
hair was
worn in

a short bob. The girl's expression was so sad it made Sunny gasp. What could be making her so unhappy?

Suddenly Sunny's fur tingled with excitement. Was the mirror telling Sunny something? Maybe she would get to do her first task today. She stared at the girl, hoping the mirror might show her more, but in a glittering swirl of silver sparkles the picture of the unhappy girl faded away.

"Good morning, class. Sunny, hurry up and sit down."

Sunny hadn't heard Miss Alaska come into the class cave. She quickly went to her seat. Miss Alaska's yellow-and-pink wings fluttered impatiently as she held up a sycamore leaf. The watching class fell silent and Sunny trembled with excitement. Whose task was written on that leaf?

"As you know, the time has come to take

your first tasks. The tasks
are very important. If you
fail, you'll have to spend
another term with me."
Miss Alaska smiled as
a groan rippled round
the cave. "I have in my
hand the name of the next
Fairy Bear, and the task he
or she must complete. But before I tell you
who it is let's say the Fairy Bear Promise."

Stone scraped on the floor as the class
stood up and linked paws. Sunny held paws
with Dizzy and Blossom, then closed her
eyes and chanted with everyone else, "I
promise to do my best. I promise to work
hard to care for the world and all its plants,
animals and children. This is the Fairy Bear
Promise."

Miss Alaska held up the sycamore leaf.

"This next task is for . . ." she paused dramatically, her eyes sweeping the room. "Sunny."

"Hooray!" squeaked Sunny excitedly. "I knew it."

Dizzy and Blossom gave her a hug.

"Good luck," they said.

Sunny couldn't wait to hear about her task. She twiddled her wand, impatient to learn how she could help the sad-looking girl in the mirror. Miss Alaska passed her the sycamore leaf. Sunny read it quickly, then stared at Miss Alaska in confusion.

"There's been a mistake," she said. "This isn't my task. It's all about helping a bird and her newly hatched chicks who are in some kind of danger."

"That's right," said Miss Alaska. "There's a map at the bottom to show you where the bird is nesting."

"B-but . . ." stammered Sunny. It didn't make sense. If this was her task, why had the mirror shown her the sad-looking girl?

"What's wrong? Is the task too ordinary for you?" whispered Coral, a pretty white bear with pinky-orange wings and hard blue eyes. "Only *special* bears like me, whose parents work for the king and queen, get *special* tasks."

"We're all special," growled Dizzy, and Blossom timidly nodded in agreement.

Sunny threw back her head and laughed. She never let Coral's unpleasant remarks upset her.

"Sunny," said Miss Alaska sharply, "this is your first task. I hope you're going to be sensible."

"Yes, Miss Alaska," said Sunny, quickly becoming serious.

"When you're ready, you may start," said Miss Alaska. "Good luck. I hope you pass."

Sunny's Surprise

Sunny stroked her gold wand, her paw lingering on the pretty yellow sunstone set in the star at its tip. She waved the wand to test if it was working and a circle of yellow stars burst from from the end, hovering in the air like the rising sun. The class clapped and Sunny curtsied. Her stomach fizzed with excitement as she left the school caves, eager to start her first task!

Chapter Two

Sunny joined a throng of Fairy Bears
heading along the Main Tunnel towards
the Grand Door, the entrance in the trunk
of the sycamore tree that hid the Crystal
Caves from the outside world. Usually she
liked to dawdle, to gaze at the magically
sparkling jewels lighting the tunnel, but
today she hardly noticed them. She couldn't
wait to get going and it seemed to take
ages for her to get to the end of the tunnel.
As she joined the queue for the gnarled root
staircase that led up to the Grand Door, an

excited voice called out her name.

"Sunny!"

Turning, Sunny was surprised to see her mum and her little brother, Treacle, walking up behind her.

"Where are you going?" asked Treacle. "Are you running away from school?"

Proudly Sunny puffed out her chest. "I'm doing my first task," she answered.

"Darling, that's wonderful,' said her mum. "Good luck."

"Can I come with you?"asked Treacle.

"No!" laughed Sunny. "You're far too little."

"Not fair," grumbled Treacle. "Don't want to go with Mum. She's doing boring things. Can I have a go with your wand, then?"

"It's not a toy," said Sunny patiently.

"Please?" begged Treacle, snatching for it.

Sunny held the wand higher, chuckling as Treacle jumped to reach it. The more Treacle struggled, the more Sunny teased him, almost letting him touch the wand then suddenly lifting it higher, until a stream of yellow stars burst from the wand's end, showering her mum.

"That's enough," she growled crossly.

"Treacle, come and hold my paw."

Pulling a face, Treacle went and stood beside her.

"Will you teach me to do somersaults when you get back?" he whispered to Sunny.

"You're too little," she whispered back. "I'll help you practise your flying if you want."

"I'm not too little, I'm . . ."

But Sunny wasn't listening. It was her turn to climb the woody staircase. With a cheery wave she hopped up the stairs and through the Grand Door into the trunk of the sycamore tree. The inside of the tree trunk was as black as tar, but Sunny didn't mind. Like all bears, she loved dark places. Opening her wings, she took off, flying upward towards the squirrel hole near the top of the tree. She flew fast, enjoying the feel of the air rushing past her fur and the humming sound of her wings. Soon the darkness was broken by a pale circle of light shining above her. Sunny slowed and joined the queue of Fairy Bears waiting to fly through the squirrel hole. When it was her turn, she flew outside, blinking happily as her eyes

adjusted to the early-morning sunshine.
What a wonderful day to go flying!
Joyfully Sunny turned a somersault, then,
remembering she was taking her first task,
quickly righted herself. According to the
map on her sycamore leaf, the birds' nest
was in the garden of a house in the nearby
village. It looked easy enough to find.

Sunny rolled the sycamore leaf round
her wand for safe keeping, then flew across
Firefly Meadow, eager to find out why the
birds and their nest were in danger.

A short while later, Sunny flew over the
village's busy high street.

"Not far now," she murmured, dipping
her wings in greeting at a bee travelling in
the opposite direction.

The garden she was looking for was long
and narrow with a few small fruit trees just

in blossom. As she reached a row of old houses, Sunny swooped lower.

There it was! It was very pretty, with lots of hiding places. Sunny hovered for a while, trying to decide where to start looking for the birds' nest. The bottom of the garden looked promising. There was a rickety garden shed with stinging nettles growing against the sides, two apple trees and several overgrown bushes. She immediately discounted the middle of the garden because of the neatly cut grass edged by flowerbeds. The end nearest the house had a stone patio flanked with a sprawling bush and a small plum tree covered in pretty pink blossom.

"Oh!" exclaimed Sunny. Someone was sitting on a rug on the patio.

She hovered in the air, wondering if it was safe to enter the garden. Humans didn't usually notice Fairy Bears, or if they did

they usually imagined they'd seen a furry
bumblebee. The person on the patio was
busy painting a picture. Painting was one
of Sunny's favourite hobbies. Curiously she
flew a little closer. Then suddenly her heart
missed two beats. She recognized that face.
It was the sad-looking girl from the mirror.
Excited, Sunny flew even closer. Was the
girl happy again now?

Sunny knew she should start her task,
but she couldn't help herself. She flew down
and landed on the sprawling bush growing
at the edge of the patio. The girl was too
engrossed in her picture to notice Sunny.
Every now and then she'd glance at the
plum tree from which half a coconut shell
hung. Sunny bounced impatiently on the
twig. Was it safe to fly closer?

A door at the back of the house opened
and a motherly-looking lady came out

carrying a squirming baby. She put him down on the edge of the patio and handed him a brightly coloured toy. The toy was noisy, with parts that rattled and spun.

Startled, the girl turned round then glared at the lady.

"Mum . . ." she began.

"It's only for a second, Ella," her mother answered quickly. "Just while I pop inside to get the washing. Wait there," she added to the baby.

The girl sighed then carried on with her picture, ignoring the baby, who was noisily banging the toy on the ground. Sunny frowned, puzzled at why Ella seemed so annoyed. Sunny's own mother often left Treacle with her while she did jobs.

Growing bored of the rattling toy, the

baby tossed it aside, pushed himself off his bottom and crawled towards Ella.

"Numpna," he gurgled cheerfully.

Ella dipped her paintbrush into a beaker of water.

"Hello, Jack," she said, frowning.

"Numpna," chuckled the baby.

Before Ella realized what was happening, the baby had crawled straight across her picture, knocking the beaker of water over as he went.

Chapter Three

"Stop!" shouted Ella, snatching up her picture. But it was too late. The water trickled across the painting, running the colours into a muddy mess.

"La!" chortled Jack, picking up the upturned beaker and putting it on his head.

"Ella!" cried her mum, stepping out of the house with a basket of wet washing. "What on earth's going on?"

"An accident," said

Ella tightly. "Jack's knocked the beaker of water all over the painting I was doing for my school bird project."

"Oh dear," said Mum, dumping the washing on the patio. She prised the beaker out of his chubby hands.

"Yuck," she chuckled. "Look at your hair."

"Look at my painting," sighed Ella, her voice catching as she fought back tears. "It's ruined."

"It's not that bad," soothed Mum. "I'll hang it on the line with the washing. I'm sure you can fix it when it's dry."

"But it's a mess," said Ella sadly. "It was almost finished too. I was waiting for a bird to come so I could paint it. Only that's not going to happen now Jack's out here. He's so noisy. It's a wonder there's any wildlife left in our garden at all."

"Now you're being silly," said Mum,

laughing. "Jack doesn't mean any harm. He's only little."

"I know, but he's still a nuisance sometimes. I think I'll go inside." Ella sighed as she headed for the back door.

"Ella," called Mum.

Ella hesitated, then stopped walking and turned round.

"Yes?" she said expectantly.

"Be a dear and clear up the mess first."

Ella's face fell and she clenched her fists by her sides.

Sunny held her breath. Ella's expression reminded her of one Treacle made when he was about to cry, but after a few seconds Ella managed a tight smile. Wordlessly she gathered up the paints, beaker, paintbrushes, rug and ruined picture and carried everything indoors.

Impulsively Sunny flew after her. What

a horrible thing to happen. No wonder Ella had looked so sad when she'd seen her in the mirror. Sunny guessed that baby Jack was giving her a hard time.

Sunny's Surprise

As Sunny entered Ella's house she gave a startled growl. She was amazed at how big human houses were. There was a huge wooden table with six giant-sized chairs and a sink large enough to row a Fairy Bear boat in. Ella hung the damp rug on the back of a chair. She threw her ruined painting on the table and put the painting things into the sink. She turned on the tap and Sunny stared at the running water in wonder. It reminded her of the underground waterfall in the Crystal Caves.

Ella washed the equipment quickly and stacked everything on the draining board. Suddenly a long-haired tortoiseshell cat appeared. It made straight for Ella and rubbed its body against her bare legs.

"Hello, Sasha," said Ella, drying her hands on a towel before scratching the cat on her head. Purring ecstatically, the

cat butted Ella's hand for more.
Ella stroked Sasha for a while,
then spying her painting on
the kitchen table she sadly
screwed it up and went to
put it in the bin.

"No!" cried Sunny, and
without thinking she swooped
down to rescue the picture. Sasha gave a
startled hiss and bolted under the table. Ella
froze, her hand poised over the bin as she
stared at Sunny. Nervously Sunny hovered
in the air. What had she done? She hadn't
meant to give herself away. Then Ella softly
whispered, "Hello. Are you a fairy?"

"Sort of," said Sunny delightedly. "I'm a
Fairy Bear."

"Are you like a real fairy? Can you do
magic? What's your name?"

Sunny laughed at Ella's questions.

"My name's Sunny. Fairy Bears can do magic, but we mostly use it to help look after the world and all the creatures and plants living here."

Sunny shyly fluttered her wings as she asked a question of her own. "Why did you screw your picture up?"

"Because it's ruined," said Ella sadly.

"Why don't you fix it?"

Ella laughed. "You're funny. How can I fix it? I don't have a magic wand like you do."

She looked so different when she smiled.

"I'll mend it for you," said Sunny, wanting to keep her happy.

She fluttered closer and, tapping the crumpled paper with her wand, she murmured:

> *"Colours don't run,*
> *let there be sun."*

Tiny yellow stars
fell from Sunny's
wand, covering
the picture
in a swirl
of glitter.
When the
glitter faded,
the painting
was perfect again.
Ella stared in
amazement, then burst out laughing.

"You've added a sun," she chuckled.

Sunny blushed. "I can take it out if you don't like it."

"I love it," said Ella, her face shining with excitement. "I just need the robin to come back so I can add her too. It's for my bird project. We made bird feeders at school from empty coconut shells. We filled them

with melted suet and birdseed. I added extra
sunflowers in mine because I've seen a robin
in the garden and Miss Jenkins, my teacher,
said robins especially love sunflower seeds."
Ella stopped talking and the sad expression
returned.

Sunny couldn't bear to see her so
unhappy. She flew closer and landed on
Ella's hand.

"What's wrong?" she asked.

"It's Jack," sighed Ella. "Mum and Dad
are always busy doing things for him. Mum
said it wouldn't always be like that. She
said as Jack got older he wouldn't need so
much help. But she was wrong. Since Jack
learned to crawl he takes up even more
time! Mum's always chasing after him. He's
so naughty. He keeps breaking things."

"My little brother, Treacle, used to be
like that," said Sunny. "But he's not so bad

now. Babies don't mean to damage things. They're just a bit clumsy."

"Well, I wish Jack would hurry up and stop being clumsy," said Ella forcefully.

The back door opened and her mum came in carrying Jack. Ella jumped and Sunny quickly flew up to the ceiling where she hoped no one would see her.

"Oh good," said Mum brightly. "We were just coming to find you. Jack didn't mean to spoil your painting, darling. Can you forgive him?"

At first a scowl clouded Ella's face, but she forced it away.

"I'll try," she said with a small smile. "I'll put this in my room, where Jack can't get it."

Ella picked up her painting and disappeared further into the house.

Mum went to shut the back door.

Sunny's Surprise

Help! thought Sunny. She mustn't get trapped inside. She zipped through the closing door with only seconds to spare as the door slammed behind her.

Sunny flew straight to the plum tree with the coconut bird feeder and hid behind a clump of blossom. Her heart was beating like a Fairy Bear drum and it took a while for it to calm down.

Once she was over her scare, Sunny realized she was thirsty. The plum blossom smelt delicious. Sticking out her pink tongue, she lapped up some of its nectar, daintily wiping her mouth with her paw when she'd drunk enough. Sunny unrolled

Fairy Bears

the sycamore leaf from her wand and read
her task again. It was strange that the task
was about helping a bird when the magic
mirror had shown her a picture of Ella.
With a baffled shake of her head, Sunny set
off to look for the birds' nest.

She flew round the garden three times,
but didn't even see a bird, let alone a nest.
Sunny rechecked the trees and the wild
area at the end of the
garden. Nothing!
She looked in the
plum tree again
and the bushes
around the patio.
Knowing
how birds
sometimes
nested in
unusual

places, Sunny even checked inside an old pair of wellington boots outside the back door. But apart from a dead spider they were empty too. At last Sunny was sure she'd searched everywhere. She rested in the plum tree while she thought about what to do next. Then it hit her. There must have been a mistake. It wasn't a bird who needed Sunny's help. It was Ella.

Chapter Four

Convinced she was right, Sunny decided to fly back to the Crystal Caves and ask Miss Alaska to check her task. In no time at all she'd reached Firefly Meadow, and without stopping she hurtled down the inside of the sycamore tree. At the bottom she took the gnarled root staircase two steps at a time. Pausing only to close her wings, Sunny ran along the tunnels to the school cave and across the deserted playground, arriving in her class cave hot, sticky and out of breath.

The classroom was empty. Sunny gave

a growl of disappointment. Where had everyone gone?

Sunny's yellow wings fluttered impatiently as she waited for her class to return. Ella needed her. Sunny was anxious to get on with the task of making her happy again.

"Hello, Sunny." Mr Griz the head bear poked his head round the door. He stared at her in surprise over his half-moon glasses. "What are you doing here? Have you finished your task already?"

"I came back to check something," said Sunny. "Do you know where Miss Alaska is?"

"She's taken the class on a field trip, to practise gathering nectar," said

Mr Griz. "What do you need to check?"

"It's about my task." Sunny knew she was talking too fast, but she couldn't stop herself. "I'm sure there's been a mistake — you see, there's—"

With a friendly smile, Mr Griz raised a large brown paw.

"Sorry, but I can't help you. Miss Alaska sets the tasks. I'm afraid you'll have to wait for her to return." He glanced at the moon clock on the classroom wall. "It's nearly lunchtime. Come and have something to eat."

Sunny didn't want to eat, but Mr Griz escorted her to the dining cave, his green-and-gold wings fluttering in delight as they drew closer.

"Ahh!" he said, his nose twitching. "Fruit salad, honey cake and nectar surprise. My favourite!"

Nectar surprise was Sunny's favourite dish too, but she was so anxious that she hardly tasted it. Gloomily she sat on a stone overlooking the playground where she could watch for her class to return. But they didn't come back for lunch. Then one of the dinner bears told Sunny that Cook had provided them with a picnic. Sunny spent the afternoon impatiently tidying the class cave until, just before home time, she heard a noise in the corridor. The Fairy Bears spilled back into the cave, laughing and chattering together.

"Sunny!" exclaimed Miss Alaska with a smile. "Have you completed your task?"

"No," said Sunny hastily. "I need to check something with you."

"Just give me a minute," said Miss Alaska. Growling for silence, the teacher told the Fairy Bears what to do with the nectar they'd collected.

"Right, Sunny," she said at last. "What did you want to check?"

Out of the corner of her eye Sunny saw Dizzy anxiously looking her way. She wiggled a wing reassuringly as she explained to Miss Alaska how she'd been given the wrong task. But, to her utter surprise, when she'd finished, Miss Alaska shook her head.

"There's no mistake. Your task is to help a nesting bird whose family is in danger. If it's too difficult for you, I could give it to someone else?"

"No . . . thank you," added Sunny hastily. Not only would that mean a fail, but she wouldn't get to see Ella again.

"Sorry to have bothered you. I'd better get going."

"It's too late to go back out now," said Miss Alaska. "You can try again tomorrow."

"But . . ." said Sunny.

Miss Alaska gently patted Sunny on the arm with a wing.

"Don't worry!" she said, misunderstanding her concern. "Lots of Fairy Bears take longer than a day to complete their first task. Tomorrow you must use your eyes more. You don't always see things properly."

Sunny blushed. What did Miss Alaska mean by that?

"Go home and think about it," said Miss Alaska kindly, seeing her confusion.

Sunny hurried from the classroom, anxious to get away before Miss Alaska dismissed the class. Sunny knew she was being mean, but she couldn't face talking to anyone right then, not even her best friend, Dizzy. She would go and see Dizzy later when she'd got over her disappointment.

On the way home, Sunny stopped off at the Ruby Grotto. The sparkling red cavern

was her favourite place in the whole of the
Crystal Caves. It was peaceful there and
a good place to think. Sunny stared at the
dazzling columns of crystals that rose up
from the floor and twirled down from the
roof like giant sticks of candy. But even
the wonderful Ruby Grotto couldn't cheer
Sunny up.

She'd been thrilled when Miss Alaska had
picked her to take her first task. But now
it had all gone wrong. Sunny hadn't found
the bird she was supposed to help, so it was
still in danger. And what about Ella? Why
couldn't she help her too?

"Hello, Sunny."

Mum and Treacle came into the grotto,
startling Sunny.

"I thought I saw you come in here," said
Mum. "How did you get on?"

"It was hard. I haven't finished yet," said

Sunny, reluctant to talk about it.

"Never mind." Mum flew closer and gave Sunny a hug. "I'm sure you'll get there soon. Can I leave Treacle with you while I pop along to the nectar cave for some honey?"

The Fairy Bears collected nectar from flowers, and what they didn't need they swapped for honey with the bees. The nectar cave was a popular swapping place. It was near the surface of the ground and had a hole in the roof so the bees could fly in and out when they wanted to, without waiting to be let through the Grand Door.

"Of course," said Sunny, immediately brightening. She didn't mind looking after her little brother. His childish antics made her laugh. As soon as Mum had gone, Treacle begged Sunny to teach him to somersault.

"You're far too little to learn

somersaults," said
Sunny, tickling
Treacle and making
him squeal. "I'll help
you to practise flying
instead."

"I'm good at flying
already," Treacle
insisted. "I'm starting school soon.
Mum and Dad are getting me a wand!"

"You're too young to go to school,"
laughed Sunny. She ruffled Treacle's dark-
brown fur affectionately.

"I'm not too young," said Treacle crossly.
"Watch this. I can nearly do a somersault."

Treacle flew up and hovered in the air.
He screwed up his eyes in concentration,
then suddenly launched himself forward.
Halfway through the somersault, his
wings missed a beat. Treacle flapped them

frantically as he tried to keep himself in the air, but he was falling too fast. He landed on his bottom.

"Ouch!" he grunted.

Sunny helped him up.

"Are you all right?" she asked, gently brushing dust off his wings.

"I nearly did it," said Treacle. "I just need some help."

Sunny smiled. "You don't give up, do you? I'll teach you to somersault when you're bigger. Let's concentrate on flying first. Fly round the grotto six times without stopping. If you manage that, you can try flying in and out of the ruby columns."

"That's easy," said Treacle, pouting. "Can I borrow your wand to make it harder? I need to learn how to hold one when I'm flying."

"Sorry, Treacle, that's a no," said Sunny.

49

It was so sweet the way Treacle wanted to do all the things his big sister did. Sunny chuckled, not noticing the fed-up look on her brother's face.

"Hurry up now. Mum will be back soon and then we'll have to go home."

Chapter Five

The following morning, Sunny woke up
determined to find the bird family who
needed her help. Over a hurried breakfast
of nectar and freshly baked honey biscuits
she reread her task. But there were no
clues as to where in the garden the bird
had built her nest. Disappointed, Sunny set
off for the Grand Door, joining the early-
morning queue to climb the gnarled root
staircase. When it was her turn, she ran up
the stairs and overtook four Fairy Bears as
she flew up the inside of the sycamore tree

and zoomed through the squirrel hole. It
was another glorious day. Sunny flew fast,
skilfully avoiding the other traffic in the air.
Flies were the worst; they had no manners,
cutting across her path and making her
swerve. Soon Ella's garden came into view.
Sunny flew closer, her wings tingling with
pleasure when she saw Ella sitting out on
the patio again, writing in a notebook.
Sunny hovered in the sky above her. She
wanted to say hello, but there wasn't time.
First she must complete her task.

"Honey mites!"

Seeing Ella's
notebook had
reminded Sunny
that she'd left the
sycamore leaf, with
her task written on
it, at home.

Sunny's Surprise

But it didn't matter. Sunny had read the
task so many times she knew it off by heart.
A thrush was feeding from Ella's homemade
bird feeder. Sunny's heart beat a little faster.
Was this the bird that needed help? She
flew over, meaning to follow it when it had
finished eating, but before she was close
enough the back door of the house opened
and the startled bird flew away. Ella's mum
strode into the garden, carrying Jack. She
set him down and handed him a sturdy toy
car to play with.

Suddenly a ringing could be heard,
coming from inside the house.

"Be good," she said to
Jack, before going back
indoors to answer the phone.

Jack banged the car on
the ground. He moved
it back and forth, then

with an extra-hard shove he let go, sending it speeding towards Ella.

"La!" exclaimed Jack, crawling after it.

"Hello, Jack," said Ella absentmindedly, without looking up.

Jack shoved the car again and it rolled past Ella's feet, then veered towards the sprawling bush growing at the edge of the patio.

"Numpna!" exclaimed Jack excitedly. His face grew animated as he crawled over Ella, chasing after the car.

"Jack!" shrieked Ella. "Stop jogging me. You're spoiling my work."

"La!" Jack chuckled, snatching at Ella's notebook with a chubby hand.

"No, Jack! Mum, help me!" called out Ella. "Jack's going to ruin my bird diary."

Jack's face crumpled. Mum rushed outside and scooped him up in the air.

"Really, Ella," she said crossly. "There was no need to shout like that. He's only little and you knew I was on the telephone."

"But . . ." said Ella. "But I didn't mean to shout. Look what Jack did to my homework."

Close to tears Ella held up the crumpled diary for her mum to see.

"If it's homework, then why aren't you working at the table indoors?" asked her mum unsympathetically.

"It's a bird project!" Ella exclaimed. "I can't watch birds indoors."

"Oh! Well, I'm sorry, Ella, but Jack didn't mean any harm. He only wants to play. I'll take him back indoors. We'll give you an hour on your own. How does that sound?"

Ella grunted her thanks as she tried to flatten the creased pages of her diary.

Sunny couldn't bear to see Ella so unhappy. Impulsively she flew down and landed on her hand.

"You came back!" gasped Ella. Suddenly her brown eyes widened.

"Are you *my* Fairy Bear?" she asked shyly. "Do you come and rescue me when I need help?"

Sunny shook her head. "I'm here to help a bird. It's a test I have to pass so that I can move up to the next class. But I can fix your book if you like."

"It's not too bad," Ella admitted. "I've managed to smooth out the pages and —"

She broke off suddenly as a small brown Fairy Bear with gold wings and gold markings landed on her hand next to Sunny.

"Who's this?" she breathed.

"Treacle!" exclaimed Sunny, clapping her yellow wings together in shock. "What are you doing here?"

"I came to give you this. You left it behind." Treacle handed his sister a rolled-up sycamore leaf, adding, "I didn't want you to fail your task."

"But . . ." Sunny stared at Treacle, her mouth wide in disbelief. "Did you fly here all on your own?"

Proudly Treacle flapped a wing.

"I told you I was good at flying. You've never really watched me."

Sunny was amazed and embarrassed. She remembered that Miss Alaska had said something about her not using her eyes properly. Maybe her teacher was right!

"Treacle, you are the best brother ever," she said, hugging him tightly. "I can't

believe Mum let you come out alone."

Treacle hung his head.

"She didn't," he mumbled. "She thinks I'm playing with Zac at his cave."

"Treacle!" groaned Sunny. "She'll be so worried if she discovers you're missing! I'm taking you home, right now!"

"You can't," said Treacle. "You've got to complete your task." His face brightened. "I'll help. What have you got to do?"

"How can you help? You're too little," said Sunny, thinking it was a good thing Treacle hadn't learned to read yet. What if he'd tried to complete the task for her? Then she definitely would have failed.

"Treacle can wait here with me," said Ella. "I wish my little brother was more like him. That would be great fun."

Treacle fluttered off Ella's hand and landed on the sprawling bush, where he bounced up and down on a leaf.

"I bet your brother is fun. Little brothers are the best," he said cheekily.

Chapter Six

Sunny made Treacle stop bouncing so he'd have enough energy to fly home. She left him sitting on the leaf chatting with Ella as she drew a picture in her bird diary. Sunny flew around the garden searching for the birds' nest. It reminded her of a game called Hunt the Honey Pot. She was good at that, but no matter how hard she used her eyes she couldn't see a nest anywhere.

A cold feeling crept over Sunny, making her fur stand on end. Why hadn't she found the nest? Was she too late to help the bird and her chicks?

At the other end of the garden, Ella started laughing. Unable to help herself, Sunny stopped for a moment to listen. Laughter was her favourite sound and she was pleased that Ella was happy. But there wasn't time to dawdle. This task was far more complicated than she'd imagined. Not only was she struggling to complete it, but now there was Treacle to worry about too. If Sunny didn't find the nesting bird soon, she would be forced to abandon the task and take Treacle home. Mum would be distraught if she realized he was missing.

Slowly Sunny scanned the garden. Where was the birds' nest? It had to be here somewhere. Her eyes rested on the rickety old shed. There was a hole near the back big enough for a bird. Maybe the nest was in there. Sunny's heart quickened as she flew inside. The shed smelt musty and was covered in cobwebs, but it was tidy. Immediately Sunny saw there was no birds' nest here – only neatly stacked flower pots, a box of gardening tools and a coil of chicken wire. Disappointed, she flew outside, sneezing dust from her nose. She'd just decided to search the apple trees again when a sharp cry made her jump. Ella was shouting.

Jack! thought Sunny, hovering in the air. What had he done now? Swiftly she flew up the garden. On the patio, Ella was struggling with something. Sunny stared in surprise. Her wings turned to ice as she realized Ella was wrestling with a long-haired tortoiseshell cat.

"Sasha, no!" squeaked Ella, pulling at the cat to stop her from diving into the bush.

"Treacle!" exclaimed Sunny, alarmed.

She'd left him sitting just where Sasha
and Ella were struggling together. It was
like watching a tug of war. Sasha was
determined to get under the bush. Ella was
determined to stop her. Each time the cat
wriggled forward Ella hauled her back
again.

With a pounding heart, Sunny flew to
help. She had to stop Sasha before she hurt
Treacle. She grabbed at
Sasha's fur and
pulled. But
Sunny was too
little to have any
effect. Wriggling
furiously, Sasha
managed to get her
nose under the bush.

Ella and Sunny tugged her back,
but Sasha was gaining ground and slowly

inched forward. Then Sunny had an idea. Letting go of Sasha, she pointed the wand at the cat's bottom and chanted:

"Cat away,
run and play."

The wand grew warmer, the star and its sunstone shone brightly, then a stream of yellow stars burst out, showering Sasha and making her bottom sparkle. A second later Sasha stopped struggling. She rolled on to her back and waved her paws playfully, as if she was batting at an imaginary piece of string. It would have been funny if Sunny and Ella hadn't been so worried about Treacle.

"Naughty puss," Ella scolded her as she scooped Sasha into her arms. "I'm taking you indoors."

Sunny stared at the bush in horror.

65

Broken leaves and twigs lay scattered across
the patio, but there was no sign of Treacle.
She didn't understand why Sasha had
pursued Treacle with such determination.
Cats mostly ignored Fairy Bears.

"Treacle!" called Sunny.

Silence. Was Treacle lying injured
somewhere? Sunny took a deep, calming
breath. She wouldn't think the worst. She

would carry on looking until she'd found
her little brother. Folding her wings tightly
together, Sunny crawled into the bush.
It was very peaceful, like being inside a
green cave. Sunny hopped from leaf to
leaf, calling out Treacle's name. At last a
high-pitched squawk answered her. Sunny
winced. What was that?

Quickly she headed towards the noise.
It was coming from lower down. Pushing
aside a leaf, Sunny stopped in surprise.
There, hidden underneath the bush, was a
large plastic toy with
a birds' nest built
inside.

"Oh!"
gasped Sunny.

At last she'd
found the
family of birds

that needed her help. So that's what Sasha
had been after!

Sunny stared curiously at the nest. It
was the first one she'd seen close up and it
made her feel fizzy with excitement. There
were four newly hatched chicks crammed
together inside. They were very ugly with
wrinkled bald bodies and tightly shut eyes.
Their huge yellow beaks were wide open,
pointing skyward as they waited for food.

Sunny chuckled. What would her parents
say if she and Treacle sat like that, waiting
to be fed!

"Treacle!" she exclaimed, remembering.

Sunny might have solved the mystery of
the hidden birds' nest, but now she'd lost her
little brother. Frantically she darted from
leaf to leaf as she searched for him. Then
someone softly called her name.

"Sunny, I'm up here."

Sunny's Surprise

Sunny stared up and saw Treacle sitting a few branches above her.

"Treacle!" she gasped. "Where have you been? I was so worried about you."

"Watching you," giggled Treacle. "You passed me once before you found the birds' nest and twice afterwards."

For a moment Sunny was furious. Naughty Treacle, scaring her like that! Why hadn't he called out earlier? Then Sunny's anger slipped away, leaving her feeling ashamed. Miss Alaska was right.

She really must use her eyes. It had taken
her ages to find Treacle, but it had taken
her even longer to notice that he wasn't
a baby any more. Fluttering her yellow
wings, Sunny landed next to her little
brother and hugged him tightly.

"Geroff!" grunted Treacle, squirming
away.

Sunny laughed and let him go.

"You might be more grown-up than I
realized,' she said, her wings quivering with
relief. "But you're never too big for a hug."

Chapter Seven

Sunny had finally worked out that her
task was to protect the birds' nest from the
cat. Determined to learn from her earlier
mistakes, she knew that to help she must
study the nest first. She hopped closer,
using the leaves like stepping stones, until
a loud rustling made her stop. The bush
was shaking and Sunny grabbed hold of a
twiggy branch to stop herself from falling
over. Had Sasha got loose again? But the
rustling was caused by the mother bird
returning. Clamped in the robin's beak

was a chunk of suet and seed mixture from Ella's bird feeder. Sunny stood perfectly still and watched as the robin, with her bright red chest, dropped the food inside the chicks' mouths then flew away for more. The chicks sat helplessly waiting for her to return. Sunny had to do a good job to protect them. An idea was forming in her head when she heard Ella's voice anxiously calling, "Sunny, Treacle, where are you?"

Quickly Sunny flew back to Treacle. They had to get Ella away from the bush before the robin saw her, or the bird might take fright and abandon her nest.

"This way," said Treacle. "It's how I got in."

It felt funny to follow Treacle when normally Sunny was the one in charge. But Treacle was full of surprises – seconds later he led Sunny out of the bush.

Ella's face lit up in relief when she saw him.

"Treacle, you're safe! When Sasha pounced, I thought she'd hurt your wing."

"I'm fine," said Treacle, waggling his gold wings and making Ella laugh. "It wasn't me the cat was after. Tell her, Sunny."

Sunny looked around the garden. The robin had flown away. If she was quick, there was time to show Ella the nest.

"Come and see," she whispered, pointing to the bottom of the bush.

Silently Ella fell to her knees and peered through the gap in the branches. She looked for ages and when she stood up she was smiling.

"That's so exciting. I'm going to write about it for my bird project." Ella's eyes sparkled and suddenly she began to laugh.

"You'll never guess what they're nesting in!
It's Jack's toy dumper truck. It went missing
ages ago. I bet Jack knew his toy was under
there, but couldn't tell us because he's too
little to talk. Every time Mum put him
down, he was trying to reach his dumper
truck, not to wreck my work! He's cleverer

than I thought." Ella looked at Treacle
with a grin. "Little brothers are the best. I
can't wait for mine to get older like you.
We're going to have so much fun together."

Sunny was fizzing with excitement. So
the mirror had been right after all! She did
have to help Ella even though it wasn't part
of her first task. It was wonderful to see her
look so happy.

"There's some chicken wire in the shed,"
Ella said. "I'll go and get it and we'll put
it round the bush to protect the nest from
Sasha and Jack. I'm going to play with Jack
too. It'll keep his mind off his dumper truck
until the robins have finished with it."

"Thank you," said Sunny. "The chicken
wire will be a big help, but I can't let you
do all the work or I'll fail my task and have
to stay in Miss Alaska's class for another
year."

She flitted closer to the bush, then waving her wand she softly chanted:

> *"Leaves and branches weave a mat,*
> *keep the birds safe from cats."*

The wand grew warmer in Sunny's paw and the sunstone glittered brightly. There was a sudden hiss as yellow stars burst from the end, showering the bush and making it sparkle. The bush creaked and groaned like a tree in the wind, then swiftly the branches began weaving themselves together.
Before long the birds' nest was protected with a woody fence.

"That was magic!" exclaimed Ella as the last yellow star fizzled away. "We don't need the chicken wire any more."

"Let's use it anyway," said Sunny. "It'll keep the birds extra safe."

Sunny was tired after using such strong magic to protect the birds' nest. She and Treacle hitched a ride on Ella's hand to the garden shed. Ella pulled the chicken wire out. It was heavy and awkward to carry.

"Try rolling it," Sunny suggested.

Ella turned the wire on its side and gave it a push.

"That's better," she said.

She pushed the wire up the garden with Sunny and Treacle hovering alongside her. The chicken wire made a good barrier around the bush.

"That'll definitely keep Sasha and Jack out," said Ella happily.

"Hooray!" cheered Treacle, suddenly clapping his wings together. "You've passed your first task, Sunny."

Ella cheered too, but then she looked sad.

"Does that mean I won't see you again?" she asked.

"I don't know," said Sunny honestly. "But I promise I'll always remember you."

Impulsively she waved her wand in a wide circle, chanting:

> "*From me to you,*
> *A star that's true!*"

The wand trembled and with a loud pop a single yellow star burst from its tip. Sunny needed both paws to lift it as she handed the star to Ella.

"For you," she said shyly. "It's a lucky friendship star to remember me by."

Ella took the star and carefully held it in her hand.

"It's perfect," she sighed. "Of course I'll remember you, Sunny. Thank you for my special star."

"Home time," said Sunny, grabbing

hold of Treacle's paw. "We've got to get you back before Mum finds out that you're missing."

"Wait!" said Treacle. "Jack needs a special star too. It's only fair."

"Grrr!" growled Sunny, pretending to be cross. "Little brothers!"

She waved her wand again and a smaller yellow star plopped out of its tip for Jack.

"Thank you," said Ella. "I'll keep it safe for him until he's big enough to share the secret of the Fairy Bears. Bye, Treacle – thanks for showing me what fun baby brothers can be. Bye, Sunny. I promise I'll never forget you."

Tightly clutching her stars, Ella waved with her free hand as Sunny and Treacle fluttered high into the sky.

"Look, Treacle, there's the robin," cried Sunny.

She slowed to watch as the robin flew towards Ella's garden. Suddenly Sunny felt tingly with happiness. She'd helped the robin and her chicks and passed her first task. Yellow wings flashing in the sunlight, she somersaulted for joy.

"That's so cool," sighed Treacle. "Please will you teach me how to do it?"

"Of course," said Sunny, thinking that would be exciting too.

"Hooray!" cheered Treacle. "When?"

Sunny laughed. "When we get home."

"Race you back," said Treacle, smiling.

"You're on," said Sunny. "But only if I get a head start!"

Sunny

1. Favourite colour - *yellow*

2. Favourite gemstone - *yellow sunstone*

3. Best flower - *sunflower*

4. Cutest animal – *golden-retriever puppy*

5. Birthday month - *August*

6. Yummiest food – *nectar surprise*

7. Favourite place – *Ruby Grotto*

8. Hobbies – *painting*

9. Best ever season – *summer*

10. Worst thing – *rain*

Sunny's Wordsearch

Look closely and try to find all the hidden words below. They can be up, down, backwards, forwards or even diagonal!

CRYSTAL CAVES   SUNNY   MAGIC

FAIRY BEAR   ELLA   WAND   ROBIN

SYCAMORE   MEADOW   SUNSTONE

M	U	D	N	A	W	Y	C
A	E	F	I	N	P	R	R
G	S	A	S	U	N	N	Y
I	Y	I	D	A	B	W	S
C	C	R	G	O	H	J	T
M	A	Y	E	U	W	O	A
H	M	B	I	E	A	C	L
J	O	E	N	L	N	M	C
V	R	A	W	L	I	P	A
B	E	R	I	A	B	Z	V
S	U	N	S	T	O	N	E
A	D	W	I	U	R	N	S

Fairy Bears
Dizzy

Dizzy Dives In!

Dizzy is in a spin! She has
two problems to solve, but only
enough magic for one.
Will she make the right decision?

Fairy Bears

Blossom

Blossom the Brave

Bashful Blossom is determined
to cure Chloe of her stage fright.
But Blossom's magic won't work
unless she believes in herself first.

Fairy Bears

Sparkle

Sparkle Saves the Day

Sassy Sparkle loves pretty things. Her
task is to help a colony of beautiful
butterflies – but lonely Isabel needs a
sprinkling of Fairy Bear magic too . . .

Fairy Bears
Primrose

A Puzzle for Primrose

Brainy Primrose is stuck! Her task is
to help a sad little dog, but she keeps
seeing Lucy in the magic mirror.
Will she solve the puzzle in time?

Misty

Misty Makes Friends

Caring Misty must help Jessica and
her stepsister Becky to become friends.
But first Misty must realize that being
confident isn't easy for everyone . . .

Collect tokens from each Fairy Bears book to WIN!

What prizes can you get?

3 tokens get a Fairy Bears colour poster for your wall!

5 tokens get a sheet of super-cute Fairy Bears stickers!

8 tokens get a set of postcards to send to your friends, plus a certificate signed by the Fairy Bears creator, Julie Sykes!

Send them in as soon as you get them or wait and collect more for a bigger and better prize!

Send in the correct number of tokens, along with your name, address and parent/guardian's signature (you must get your parent/guardian's signature to take part in this offer) to: Fairy Bears Collection, Marketing Dept, Macmillan Children's Books, 20 New Wharf Road, London N1 9RR.

Fairy Bears Token Offer

1 Token

Prizes available while stocks last. See www.fairybearsworld.com for more details

Fairy Bears Token Offer

1 Token

Prizes available while stocks last. See www.fairybearsworld.com for more details

By Julie Sykes

Discover more friendly Fairy Bears!

Dizzy	978-0-330-51201-5	£3.99
Sunny	978-0-330-51202-2	£3.99
Blossom	978-0-330-51203-9	£3.99
Sparkle	978-0-330-51204-6	£3.99
Primrose	978-0-330-51205-3	£3.99
Misty	978-0-330-51206-0	£3.99
Lulu	978-0-330-51207-7	£3.99
Poppy	978-0-330-51208-4	£3.99

The prices shown above are correct at the time of going to press. However, Macmillan Publishers reserves the right to show new retail prices on covers, which may differ from those previously advertised.

All Pan Macmillan titles can be ordered from our website, www.panmacmillan.com, or from your local bookshop and are also available by post from:

Bookpost, PO Box 29, Douglas, Isle of Man IM99 1BQ

Credit cards accepted. For details:
Telephone: 01624 677237
Fax: 01624 670923
Email: bookshop@enterprise.net
www.bookpost.co.uk

Free postage and packing in the United Kingdom